IMAGINING ARAB WOMANHOOD

IMAGINING ARAB WOMANHOOD

THE CULTURAL MYTHOLOGY OF VEILS, HAREMS, AND BELLY DANCERS IN THE U.S.

Amira Jarmakani

CONTENTS

LIST OF FIGURES

ACKNOWLEDGMENTS

It is an honor to have this opportunity to express gratitude to the individuals and institutions that have supported this book from its inception. The Graduate Institute of the Liberal Arts at Emory University provided a fruitful space of incubation as it was there that I first hatched and fleshed out the idea for this book. In particular, I would like to thank Angelika Bammer and Kristen Brustad for their engaged and supportive readings of very early drafts of the book. Without their generous guidance in helping me to craft and frame this project I surely would not have found a way to call it by that coveted four letter word: book.

I have benefited, also, from the institutional support of the Women's Studies Institute at Georgia State University (GSU), specifically in the form of a summer research and writing grant in the summer of 2006. Less tangibly, but perhaps more importantly, I am grateful for the intellectual vigor and wonderful encouragement both from my mentors—Susan Talburt and Meg Harper—and from my colleagues—Juliana Kubala, Layli Phillips, Megan Sinnott, and Charlene Ball—in women's studies at GSU. Their brilliance, humor, and passion have no doubt lightened my load as a junior faculty member. I appreciate also the support of the students in the WSI, in particular Jonelle Shields; my graduate research assistants Elena Weiss, Chanel Craft, and Katie Diebold; and the students in my Cultural Studies of Gender, Globalization and Gender, and Arab and Islamic Feminisms classes, whose thoughtful engagement with me and with my research have invigorated and sustained me.

My analysis has been strengthened in conversation with audience members at Emory University, Otterbein College, GSU, and the University of California—Irvine, where I presented parts of chapters 3 and 4. My deepest gratitude goes to those friends and colleagues who have been generous enough to read drafts of the manuscript, sometimes in a pinch. Many thanks and accolades go to Evelyn Alsultany; Margaret Koehler; Mimi Kirk; Suzanne Ashworth; Terry Hermsen; Joanna Kadi; Kim Segna; Juliana Kubala; and my writing group at

GSU, Lauren Ristvet, Michele Reid, Cassandra White, and Erin Ruel for taking on that task. Though it is sometimes awkward to single people out, I want to specifically acknowledge the support of Nadine Naber, whose commitment to reading and reviewing my manuscript has, in many ways, renewed my own engagement with the book. Any moments of clarity and coherence in my argument are surely indebted to all of the aforementioned readers.

Throughout the various stages of writing this book, I have been nourished by the energy and dedication of my friends and colleagues on the core organizing collective of AMWAJ (Arab Movement of Women Arising for Justice): Katherine Acey, Suzanne Adely, Yasmin Ahmed, Janaan Attia, Lara Deeb, Eman Desouky, Noura Erakat, Huda Jadallah, Nadine Naber, and Heba Nimr. I thank them for keeping me grounded in the ethical commitment that guides and frames this book. In particular, Lara Deeb and Heba Nimr offered both practical and sage advice that helped reenergize me at critical moments during this process.

In addition to the support I received from all those already mentioned, I am grateful for the presence of friends who, in their various ways, have also sustained me along the way: Michelle Roos, Leigh Miller Sangster, Suzy Goldsmith, Mary Gage Davidson, Nader K. Uthman, Katherine Skinner, Patricia Thomas, Kris Segna, and Bobbi Patterson. In particular, I would like to thank Mimi Kirk for believing in me and in my work, and for consistently helping me to believe in my own ability to write this book.

I owe a particular debt of gratitude to my family, whose loving support has strengthened and encouraged my dedication to the issues I take up in this book. I am inspired by the wisdom and strength of my father, Jay Moazza Jarmakani, who has communicated the richness of his history and culture to me in so many silences, gestures, and words. From my mother, Brenda Hopkins Jarmakani, I have learned both the strength of silence and the importance of clear, critical, and pointed speech. I admire my brother, Jeffrey Jamal Jarmakani, for his ability to see things for what they are and for his resolve to maintain his clarity of vision, no matter how painful. I am also grateful for his constant encouragement to, in the words of KRS-One, think very deeply. On both a practical and a profound level, my work has been nurtured and enabled by my partner Kim Segna. Her greatest gift to me—the ability to honor and believe in my story, even when I could not find a way to tell it—reverberates throughout the entire book.

PREFACE

Growing up in Malibu, California with the name "Amira" was an importantly unique and mystifying experience. As a child, I lived in dread of the seemingly innocuous and well-meaning comment: "What a pretty name! What does it mean?" It was the latter part of the comment, of course, that gave me trouble. As a young girl who did not conform to the dominant beauty ideals of the Southern California scene, I never quite figured out how to negotiate that inevitably fraught moment of lifting my head to the questioner and replying, quietly, "It means princess." In a town that was located just an hour (by car) from Disneyland and just minutes from Hollywood, it seemed clear to me that "princess" was a category reserved for communicating the confluence of impossibly magical qualities that cohered in Disney characters—those animated figures of idealized white femininity. (This was before Disney's foray into the wonderful world of multiculturalism with films like *Pocahontas*, *Aladdin*, and *Mulan*, which nevertheless, I would argue, also uphold the aesthetics of white femininity.)

From an early age, then, I knew something about the limits of translatability for cultural categories. Though I knew then that the translation of my name into English did not quite work—that it called up a damaging and, in many ways, toxic caricature rather than the generous, hopeful, modest, and respectful meanings my parents intended when they gave me the name, I did not quite know why. As I grew older, though, I began to link my experience to larger problems of translation when it came to popular U.S. representations of the Arab world. I noticed the way in which imprecise and broad categories took up the space where lives had been and the way in which cartoonish caricatures eclipsed the possibility of considering or representing the realities facing Arabs, Arab Americans, and anyone lumped into the category of Arab or Muslim other in the United States. This realization was the prick that would eventually lead to the book you are now reading.

As I became increasingly interested in the problem of representation, it grew clear to me that the trickiest aspect of confronting images of Arab womanhood is the fact that they present themselves as accurate and authentic portrayals. They contribute to the prevalence of misinformation about Arab and Muslim cultures in the United States while stubbornly obscuring the dearth of contextualized, grounded knowledge in popular understanding of the Middle East within mainstream U.S. contexts. It seemed clear, then, that the response to this particular problem of representation must be twofold—one must work simultaneously to raise awareness about the complex conditions that impact Arab and Arab American women's lives and to reveal the inadequacies and blasphemies of popular representations. Ultimately, both projects—creating representations that speak to the multiple realities of Arab and Muslim women's lives and deconstructing stereotypical images of Arab and Muslim womanhood—must clear space for one another. I began this project with an interest in the former. However, while exploring the realm of literary representation among Arab American feminist writers and Arab women writers who were located outside of the Middle East, I found that it was difficult for Arab and Arab American women to tell their stories without simultaneously responding to the orientalist caricatures that circumscribed their realities. These writers expressed a consistent need to dispel dominant perceptions of Arab women as the quintessential "veiled Woman or exotic whore," as Joanna Kadi says in her introduction to her 1994 anthology *Food for Our Grandmothers: Writings by Arab-Canadian and Arab-American Women* (xvi)[1]—a need that consistently detracted from their own creative process as it kept them focused on other's stories about them, rather than on their own narratives about themselves.

Given the collective impact of popular misrepresentations of Arab womanhood on Arab and Arab American writers, I felt compelled to investigate these caricatures further. Following my initial interest, I began with the conviction that popular (mis)representations of Arab womanhood in U.S. popular culture, though not grounded in the actualities of Arab and Muslim women's lives, nevertheless have real and significant negative consequences for the women they are meant to represent. Pursuing this conviction, however, I eventually became much more interested in asking why—and how—representations of veils, harems, and belly dancers had remained so intriguing and salient to U.S. audiences since at least the turn of the twentieth century. Answering this last question has kept me focused on a close and, I hope, a complex and rich reading of mainstream U.S. narratives—a focus that is, I think, more appropriate to a critical reading of veils, harems, and belly dancers as cultural mythologies. The Arab and

Arab American women's lives they potentially eclipse, though, have remained a critical impetus for my inquiry.

In many ways, academic conventions demand that I refrain from revealing my very personal engagement with the subject matter I analyze in this book. It could compromise the integrity of my argument, the logic goes, to acknowledge that I have a personal, vested interest in deconstructing stereotypical images of Arab womanhood in U.S. popular culture. While a number of scholars in fields like women's and gender studies, ethnic studies, and cultural studies, as well as feminists working in traditional disciplines like Anthropology have worked to debunk the presumption of objectivity in scholarly work, the idea that situating oneself in relation to her work will lead to biased and political scholarship is still, I think, very prevalent. I take this very personal risk, then, in order to clarify the ethical considerations that drive my analysis. I believe, as I have been saying, that orientalist images of Arab womanhood limit the full human potential of the women they purport to represent. However, I believe also that they limit the full human potential of all consumers of the images insofar as they function to obscure many layers of understanding— about the Arab and Muslim worlds, yes, but also about the vague American dreams and imaginings that have sought expression in the shorthand of caricatures rather than in the longhand of thoughtful reflection and introspection. This book, then, is dedicated to honoring the lives of those obscured, maimed, and even killed in the long shadow of orientalist representations.

EXCAVATING ORIENTALIST IMAGES
OF ARAB WOMANHOOD

*There is no document of civilization which is not at the same time
a document of barbarism.*

Walter Benjamin

In the January 2001 issue of *Maxim* magazine, one can find a
short, presumably lighthearted column entitled "How to Start a
Harem: When It's Time to Sheik Your Booty and Chase Some Veil."[1]
Predictably, the images and text in this trite "how to" guide employ
stock orientalist and sexist tropes, sometimes combining them in
crude and seemingly unrelated ways, as in the caption underneath an
image of a man riding a camel that reads: "The worst case of camel
toe we've ever seen." What is perhaps most striking about the column,
however, is its ability to incorporate such a wide range of orientalist
caricatures in just a few brief paragraphs. It invokes the categories of
the harem, the sheik, and the veil while simultaneously deploying
the image of the Middle East as a space of erotic, sexualized fantasy.
Further, it reaffirms the grossest misperceptions of the harem as a
space of pure sexual fantasy, where a man can have "a few dozen ladies
on the side" and a space of absolute male power, where the master
of the harem surrounds himself with eunuchs so he'll "never have
to worry about [other men] dipping their pens in company ink." As
scholars such as Leila Ahmed and Ella Shohat have already analyzed
this type of imaginary harem as a Eurocentric fantasy,[2] to unpack the
orientalist and misogynist aspects of the "How to Start a Harem"
column would be to state the obvious almost to the point of banality.

Considering the source of the offending text and image, a feminist critique is practically a given.

Beyond providing an example of an orientalist and sexist representation of Arab womanhood, the *Maxim* column exemplifies some of the key features of such images. First, they are persistent and pervasive enough to serve as an immediately recognizable shorthand for larger themes of orientalist exoticism, licentious sexuality, and heteromasculinist fantasies about owning and possessing women. As the "How to Start a Harem" column itself indicates, these images lead to others. The category of the harem often implies that of the veil, even though the harem is a space in which women typically do not don the veil, because the harem is often imagined to be occupied by voluptuous women wearing ballooning harem pants, a halter-top, and a transparent veil (as in the cartoon that accompanies the *Maxim* column). This costume, famously worn by the character Jeannie in the popular 1960s and 1970s sitcom *I Dream of Jeannie*, also invokes orientalist images of the belly dancer, as the costume was popularized in colonial cabarets featuring belly-dance performances. Indeed, the *Maxim* column is hardly unique; rather, it gestures to the profusion of orientalist images in U.S. popular culture, from representations of veiled women in recent Reebok and Benetton advertisements, to belly dancers on popular sitcoms such as *The Simpsons* and *Sex and the City*, and to the invocation of the harem on a movie poster advertising the 1977 James Bond film *The Spy Who Loved Me* and in the *Maxim* column.

The publication of the harem column in *Maxim* in January 2001 gestures to the popularity of such orientalist representations of Arab womanhood well before that mythical origin story of U.S. engagement with the Middle East—"9/11." Though the events of September 11, 2001 certainly stimulated an upsurge of images of veiled women in U.S. news media and popular culture, U.S. audiences have been imagining Arab womanhood for far longer. In fact, the categories of the veil, the harem, and the belly dancer have circulated in U.S. popular culture for over a century as interpretive schemata through which U.S. consumers of the images could engage with the themes of erotic fantasy, patriarchal domination, and tradition and timelessness, to name a few. Again, as the *Maxim* column demonstrates, the salience and power of such images can be at least partially attributed to their claim to historical accuracy. In a classic orientalist move, the author, Michael Dojc utilizes Alev Lytle Croutier's book *Harem: The World Behind the Veil*[3] as his factual source to reveal the "truth" about harems (so that *Maxim* readers' "fantasies will be historically accurate"), despite the fact that Croutier herself relies on a range of orientalist representations (including French orientalist paintings) to describe the harem. Even if unwittingly, he replicates a main feature of orientalism according to Edward Said's definition;[4] he uses evidence from within orientalist discourse to validate his own contribution to the field of orientalism, thereby maintaining internal coherence.

More importantly, though, the vast array of orientalist representations of Arab womanhood in U.S. popular culture demonstrate another key feature of orientalist discourse: it is voluminously productive. Just when it seems that the tired stereotypes of the submissive, veiled woman, the voluptuous (and, now, empowered) belly dancer, and the erotic and endlessly available harem slave have lost their luster, another outrageous "How to Start a Harem" column, another overwrought image of a woman "trapped" or "hidden" behind the veil, or another exoticized representation of belly dancing shimmies its way into mainstream popular culture. The sheer popularity of such images implies their salience for the various historical contexts in which they circulate in the United States. The brilliant "conjuring trick," as Roland Barthes might say,[5] of such representations is the way they utilize the conceit of historical accuracy to produce orientalist knowledge about Arab and Muslim womanhood, all the while concealing the function they hold for mainstream U.S. consumers of the image. In the "How to Start a Harem" column, for example, the category of the harem is the imaginative space through which to project masculinist and heteronormative fantasies of erotic desire and male power, as organized around male access to and possession of women. It functions, then, as a representation of absolute male power, through which consumers of the image may grapple imaginatively with the notion of a patriarchal system so complete that women are subject to every whim of male desire and fantasy. As I will argue, though, the impact of such images goes even further. As a resurrection of the stereotype of the oriental despot from the Ottoman Empire, the harem image also engages masculinist constructions of political and national power. In his book *The Sultan's Court*, Alain Grosrichard argues that the notion of Ottoman despotism served as the constitutive other for Enlightenment-based forms of political power in seventeenth- and eighteenth-century France. In this formulation, the construction of the other actually serves as a vantage point from which to observe the self. He writes:

And when I attempt to go and look behind what I believe to be the point from which, over there in that other world, it looks at me, it is myself and our world that I find in the end.[6]

Indeed, following this logic, I analyze representations of Arab and Muslim womanhood in U.S. popular culture, then, to reveal the particularly Euro-U.S.-centric worlds in which they are created.

For over a century, images of harems, veils, and belly dancers have operated as cultural mythologies through which mainstream U.S. audiences grapple with sometimes disorienting social processes, such as consumerism, expansionism, and globalization. As with myths from all cultural and historical traditions, these visual mythologies have a purpose; they serve as texts through which to make sense of unarticulated or inexplicable forces. By learning more about the way these cultural mythologies have operated in several U.S. cultural and historical contexts, one can understand something about the set of national and cultural interests that have animated a mainstream U.S. fascination with veils, harems, and belly dancers for so long. Beyond mere figments of erotic fantasy, they have served as nostalgic emblems for the "lost" past effaced by the progress narrative and as signifiers that function to rationalize militarism and imperialism.

AN ANATOMY OF CULTURAL MYTHOLOGIES

As with many stereotypes of ethnic others, the predominant images of Arab women in U.S. popular culture lie at two opposite poles: Arab women are either represented as erotic, romanticized, magical, and sexualized, as with most images of belly dancers or harem girls, or they are portrayed as helpless, silent, and utterly dominated by an excessive Arab patriarchy, as in representations of the veiled woman or the harem slave. It benefits the creation and propagation of these images to make them appear to be as different, and, indeed, as opposite as possible, since variation implies accuracy or, at the very least, diversity beyond stereotypes. Herein lies a key productive paradox in the cultural mythology of veils, harems, and belly dancers in the United States: the idea that they are historically accurate and authentic representations of Arab womanhood is the lie that makes their fabrication possible. Perhaps this is why, despite multiple correctives to name the misperceptions and inaccuracies in these stereotypes,[7] they maintain cultural authority in the United States as compelling descriptions of Arab and Muslim women's realities. Because I am arguing that images of veils, harems, and belly dancers in the United States function as myths, and not representations of reality, I want to take a moment to explain what I mean by the term cultural mythology and to sketch out the general anatomy of such mythologies. Building on Roland Barthes's formulation in "Myth Today,"

I understand the mythologies of veils, harems, and belly dancers to operate as second order sign systems, which have been unmoored from the particular conditions in which they might traditionally be embedded and retooled as signifiers of dominant ideologies in the U.S. cultural context in which they are created. To apply this theory to the "How to Start a Harem" column, the concept of a harem operates as a mythology insofar as it is dislodged from historically and culturally grounded meanings of the harem as the women's section of a middle- or upper-class household and appropriated as a metaphor for absolute male power and sexual fantasy. In the translation of the concept of the harem from a culturally specific meaning to the mythology of a dominant ideology, the concept itself is transformed, as Barthes says, from history into nature. In other words, any historical specificity drains from the concepts of veils, harems, and belly dancers in various contexts; they lose their contingency in any particular cultural or historical setting and they are re-presented as innocent and natural forms. Cultural mythologies function, then, as emptied forms, which have been appropriated and refilled with the dominant ideologies of the culture in which they are created.

It is important to note, though, that while the categories of the veil, the harem, and the belly dancer may operate as emptied forms in the realm of U.S. cultural mythology, the anatomy of mythology is such that the historical meaning of each of these concepts is never completely obliterated. Rather, it remains, in Barthes's words, as an "instantaneous reserve of history"[8] that the form will endlessly be able to draw upon for sustenance. In other words, the meanings of veils, harems, and belly dancers as embedded in particular histories offer a richness that cultural mythologies can access, and draw upon, despite the fact that these meanings lose their contingencies and are emptied into forms in the instant that mythology reaches, and then transforms, them. In the "How to Start a Harem" article, for instance, the harem could help to politically and historically contextualize the Ottoman Empire, offering gendered insights about power dynamics therein;[9] instead, Dojc transforms it into an emptied symbol of contemporary male fantasy. Recognizing the Janus-faced construction of cultural mythologies, then, crucially enables the project of deconstructing, and demythologizing, problematic representations of veils, harems, and belly dancers, and shifting critical focus back to specificity and contextualized meaning.[10]

Another key feature and, indeed, paradox of cultural mythologies is the fact that they appear to be products of nature. That is, they seem to have no history because they claim to arise from nature itself.

Like the arbitrary relationship between signifier and signified in language systems, in the second order semiological system of cultural mythologies, the relationship between the veil, harem, or belly dancer as emptied form and the dominant narrative that refills it is also arbitrary, even if it is motivated. Though they may present themselves as natural (history transformed into nature), they are actually human-made artifacts. In fact, conceptualizing each iteration of the cultural mythologies of veils, harems, and belly dancers as an artifact will be one of my main strategies as it will enable me to fully explore the cultural context that gives rise to each particular image.

I analyze each image of Arab womanhood as an artifact of the particular historical and cultural context to which it belongs; this enables me to draw a rich description of the contemporaneous forces and processes that help shape the image-as-artifact and its function in the grand narratives of these processes. Because I am analyzing large social processes such as expansionism and globalization, I conceptualize their impact through Raymond Williams's "structures of feeling" framework. The "structures of feeling" formulation allows me to consider large social forces as forming and formative processes, which are rife with complexities, uncertainties, shifts, and unevenness and therefore cannot be reduced to, or contained by, fixed forms.[11] Though I will be considering the dominant narratives of consumerism, expansionism, late capitalism, and imperialism that have circulated in particular U.S. contexts, I do not see them as totalizing and monolithic. Rather, I see them as hegemonic articulations of grand social processes, in the sense of the Gramscian definition of hegemony,[12] as narratives that must constantly be renewed and revised as they adapt to resistant and contradictory narratives. Therefore, I do not argue that representations of Arab womanhood are singularly determined by the grand narratives of social processes. Rather, building on the notion of "structures of feeling," I consider the cultural mythologies of veils, harems, and belly dancers to act as preliminary, in-process articulations of the social experience of these processes "in solution."[13] In other words, in the midst of tumultuous social processes like mass consumerism and late capitalism, the collective social experience of living through such processes—characterized by nostalgia, anxiety, and disorientation—may not have precipitated into a discretely articulated cultural formation. Cultural mythologies, then, are operating within these contexts as diffuse expressions of social experiences that may still lie "at the edge of semantic availability."[14] In this respect, the cultural mythologies of veils, harems, and belly dancers have an intricate and complex relationship to the particular dynamics of the U.S. cultural context in which they are embedded.

The Axes of Power and Progress

As indicated even by the brief examples I have already given, representations of Arab womanhood in U.S. popular culture are quite varied, complex, and even contradictory. In the contemporary context, for example, images of exoticized and hypercommodified belly dancers coexist with representations of the veil as a cloak of submission and oppression. It follows, then, that images of Arab womanhood do not remain static over time; however, I argue that they do maintain certain structural similarities as cultural mythologies. In the late nineteenth century, for instance, imaginative projections of the Holy Land determined much orientalist imagery in the United States; gendered orientalist imagery included landscape paintings of feminized land. At the turn of the twentieth century, however, the figure of the belly dancer had become a wildly popular representation of the Arab world. While these images seem quite different from one another—chaste, virginal, and holy on the one hand and lascivious, exotic, and sensual on the other—the structural similarity between them lies in the way both function as visual vocabulary for structures of feeling rooted in the notions of power and progress. Any continuity among images of Arab womanhood, then, cannot be attributed to similar appearances, but rather to similar functions as nostalgic foils for U.S. progress and as imaginative figures through which to grapple with shifting power relations between the United States and the Middle East.[15] Therefore, I will be analyzing each image as it articulates with two bisecting planes—one determined by the dimension of power and the other by the dimension of progress.

The images I analyze hail from three contexts: the 1893 Chicago World's Fair, early-twentieth-century advertising, and contemporary ads and images. Therefore the constellation of forces I examine are expansionism and industrialization at the end of the nineteenth century, mass consumerism and proto-imperialism in the early twentieth century, and imperialism and multinational capitalism in the contemporary context. In each of these contexts, I am interested in exploring how expansionist and imperialist goals, combined with shifting power relations between the U.S. and the Middle East have helped determine the cultural mythologies of veils, harems, and belly dancers in the United States. Complementarily, I will explore the various iterations of the progress narrative—as a defining aspect of the 1893 Fair, as a motivating ideology of consumerism and expansionism, and as an antecedent to contemporary narratives of globalization—in order to demonstrate its impact on representations of Arab womanhood. It is largely within these social processes (e.g., consumerism, expansionism, and globalization), as they intersect with the dimensions of power and progress, that complex structures of feeling emerge about the social experience of living through such processes. Cultural mythologies of veils, harems, and belly dancers, I argue, serve as visual reflections or echoes of these structures of feeling still suspended in the solution of collective experience.

As I develop my claim about the way representations of Arab womanhood function in U.S. cultural contexts, I will be arguing that hegemonic narratives about the increasing antagonism of the Arab and Muslim worlds toward the U.S. map onto images of Arab womanhood in the form of symbolic barriers, like harem walls and opaque veils. In my discussions of the veil, for example, I note that contemporary representations of veiled women cast them as categorically oppressed, metaphorically implying the brutal patriarchal system under which they supposedly live. Images of transparently veiled women in early-twentieth-century advertisements, on the other hand, often further eroticize the scene as they suggest the figure to be a coquettish, easily available harem girl. Charting these representations on the power axis, I argue that the conceptualization of the veil-as-barrier parallels the rise of mainstream U.S. narratives about Arab and Muslim masculinity as a threat to national security. Likewise, I will be arguing that the mythologies of the veil, the harem, and the belly dancer function as constitutive others to the progress narrative, both as representations of backward, primitive others, and as emblems of a timeless and/or traditional past. If the orientation of the progress narrative, in all of its incarnations, is such that the forward thrust of its momentum implies a break with the past, then the "invention of tradition," to use Eric Hobsbawm's phrase,[16] fabricates a sense of organic continuity with the past. Though cultural mythologies of veils, harems, and belly dancers are not exactly invented traditions in the U.S. context, I adapt Hobsbawm's argument here to signal the way they have nevertheless functioned through the framework of tradition as emblematic links to an imagined past. As markers of the pristine and innocent past, coveted by the uneasy subjects of modernization in the United States, and simultaneously as primitive and backward symbols of the past that the forces of progress define themselves against, images of Arab womanhood serve as the cultural mythologies through which to make sense of a profoundly disorienting experience.

As I explore the power and progress axes more fully, I will be particularly concerned with the ways in which the confluence of social processes in each particular context stimulates profound spatiotemporal shifts. The advanced transportation and military technologies that helped engineer the imperialist project of Manifest Destiny; the rise of the printing and advertising industries, which greatly decreased the amount of time and distance between message and receiver; and the latest phase in capitalism, which has transgressed previous notions of national boundaries, are just a few examples of the way in which particular social processes across these discrete contexts have consistently and systematically altered predominant conceptions of distance, both in terms of time and space. Because representations of Arab womanhood are salient markers of distance, both historically and geographically, they function as a visual vocabulary that can speak to the collective experience of profound social change.

Civilizing Gender and Culture

So far, I have laid out the main trajectory of my argument, which is that the cultural mythologies of veils, harems, and belly dancers operate as artifacts created in U.S. cultural contexts to shore up collective concerns about the disorientations of power and progress. If the primary motivating question for the book, then, is to ask what these cultural mythologies can reveal about U.S. national interests, a complementary and compelling area of inquiry is to look at the way in which these American artifacts nevertheless help to determine popular perceptions of, and official U.S. policy toward, the Middle East. In other words, while I have been arguing that representations of veils, harems, and belly dancers play a role in hegemonic U.S. narratives related to power and progress, the (perhaps more sinister) flip side of that question is to ask how these images function vis-à-vis the Arab and Muslim worlds. How do the cultural mythologies of veils, harems, and belly dancers animate U.S. discourses about Arab and Muslim peoples?

Given that cultural mythologies operate as form rather than meaning, it follows that they play a rather pernicious role in shaping popular perceptions about the conglomeration of cultures, ethnicities, and religions they supposedly represent. Because cultural mythologies present ossified, static images to purportedly represent the multifarious culturally and religiously identified peoples in what I have been calling (in a woefully general and imprecise phrase) the Arab and Muslim worlds, they perpetuate the notion that Arabs and Muslims

(and all those people perceived to be Arab and Muslim) are one monolithic mass. The idea that this sort of fabrication of knowledge about
the Middle East in the U.S. produces simplistic categories through
which to discipline the Arab and Muslim worlds is essentially Edward
Said's main argument in *Orientalism*.[17] Building on his central critique, then, I am interested here in looking at the ways in which U.S.
discourses about the Arab and Muslim worlds are shaped through the
central, regulatory, and specifically gendered notion of civilization.

In the contemporary context, one of the primary examples of civilization as a key disciplinary trope is Samuel Huntington's "clash of
civilizations" theory, which is popular in mainstream, contemporary
U.S. discourses about the Arab and Muslim worlds. The main argument of the "clash of civilizations" thesis is that, after the end of the
cold war, a new formation of global conflict emerged, in which political conflict does not fall along ideological or economic "fault lines;"
rather, it takes the form of civilizational clashes.[18] As Huntington
frames it, "the Velvet Curtain of culture has replaced the Iron Curtain
of ideology as the most significant dividing line in Europe."[19] He
then goes on to describe Islam as a major "cultural grouping"—his
description of a civilization—under which Arab, Turkic, and Malay
subcivilizations can be organized.[20] While he defines civilizations as
"cultural groupings," though, Huntington's thesis centers on the idea
that civilizations represent inherent and irreducible categories of people, sedimented out to the lowest common denominator of religious
or cultural identities, rather than cerebral affinities based on intel-
lectually developed, ideological notions about politics or economics.
His premise of the shift from ideological to civilizational groupings,
then, parallels precisely the same shift that occurs when mythology
transforms meaning into form; he posits that sociopolitical affilia-
tions have shifted to groupings based on "fundamental" cultural differences.[21] In short, he mythologizes political discourse about global
conflict by transforming history into nature.

Shortly after the events of September 11, Huntington's "clash of
civilizations" thesis became a primary framework through which
hegemonic U.S. narratives framed acts of terrorism, where terrorism
is specifically related to "Islamic fundamentalism."[22] Perhaps this
is why Said did not publish a critique of the "clash of civilizations"
thesis until October 2001, eight years after Huntington's article
first appeared.[23] Said's critique is well-taken: he problematizes the
simplistic, monolithic notion of civilization as Huntington crafts it.
However, as feminist scholars Therese Saliba and Minoo Moallem have
pointed out, the "clash of civilizations" thesis also relies on gendered

assumptions.[24] As Moallem argues, women have often been cast as flattened signifiers in a "semiotic war"[25] between nationalisms and colonialisms, both of which are rooted in the system of patriarchy, as each of them fight to claim civilization. In this semiotic war, women as signifiers[26] have operated as markers of civilization, whether it is in the sense of demonstrating national progress through modernization (e.g., educating or unveiling women as a symbol of modernization) or in the sense of preserving national civilization (e.g., wearing the veil as a symbol of authentic, indigenous culture).[27] Both of these modalities of civilization—the notion that modernization can civilize nations and peoples away from barbarism and the notion of grand, ancient civilizations as the "cradle" of modern civilization—operate in a gendered register, whether it is through civilization as written on women's bodies, or the notion of women keeping and nurturing (cradling) civilization.

If, as I argued above, these notions of civilization have operated, as in Huntington's "clash of civilizations" thesis, as a kind of cultural mythology, a primary strategy for demythologizing the trope of civilization is to return it to history. Civilization is not merely a "cultural grouping," as Huntington argues; it is a value-laden term, which was coined in the late eighteenth century during the French Enlightenment.[28] As such, it is embedded in the philosophical framework of the Enlightenment, according to which civilized societies, in strict opposition to societies labeled as barbaric, are dedicated to the notion of progress as rooted in scientific-rational forms of knowledge, to the rights of individuals, to the valorization of private property, and to the ideals of achievement and order.[29] By historicizing this term, I aim to highlight its embeddedness in a particularly Eurocentric metanarrative of modernity,[30] in which the notion of civilization serves as a gendered, culturally constructed trope through which to define western European and U.S. cultural superiority either in opposition to purportedly barbaric, primitive others or as the teleological manifestation of once-grand civilizations. Examples of these kinds of constructions in U.S. popular imagination abound. The Middle East is at times characterized as a backward, primitive region full of squabbling peoples and tribes, at times heralded as the cradle of (western) civilization, or the geographical home of the Christian Holy Land, and at times remembered for its mysterious and fantastical tales filled with genies, concubines, and despotic intrigue, as recounted in *Arabian Nights* (the title made popular by the French translation of *One Thousand and One Nights* or *Alf Layla wa Layla*). In all of these characterizations, which can occur simultaneously in a single representation, the Middle East is presented as frozen in time, as existing outside of history, or to have been left behind by the forward march of progress. Regrettably, these kinds of cultural mythologies along the progress axis have, at times, played a role in determining U.S. foreign policies vis-à-vis the power axis.

One example, again in the contemporary context, of the way in which cultural mythologies animate official U.S. discourse and policy about the Middle East is in the Bush administration's rhetoric in the lead-up to the U.S. invasion of Afghanistan, which rationalized military action, in part, by deploying gendered (and, in this case, appropriating feminist) logic. In the first weekly presidential radio address ever given entirely by a First Lady, on November 17, 2001, Laura Bush laid the rhetorical foundations for deploying the gendered trope of civilization in the service of the U.S. declared war on terror. Several feminist scholars have explored the way in which Laura Bush's comments support popular U.S. discourses that link the (presumed) oppression of Arab and Muslim women to terrorist violence, and, in so doing, craft a rationalization for U.S. Military intervention to "save" the purportedly monolithically oppressed women.[31] Building on these analyses, I am interested here in looking more closely at the First Lady Laura Bush's rhetorical strategy in order to demonstrate how it represents both a replication of and a new turn in the use of the gendered notion of civilization as a key disciplinary trope.

Though Mrs. Bush essentially casts the invasion of Afghanistan as a "civilizing mission," paralleling the undergirding logic of most colonialist movements in the nineteenth century, she also reconfigures the structure of such a mission since the major players are no longer strictly patriarchal nation-states, but instead diffuse, transnational forces. In his famous phrase, "You are either with us or you are with the terrorists,"[32] President George W. Bush locates the current "war on terror" in the same binary framework of colonialist modernity,[33] a point that is made even clearer in a subsequent radio address to the nation, in which he exhorts every nation to "stand with the civilized world, or stand with the terrorists."[34] Mrs. Bush's comments, however, demonstrate how the actors on each side of the binary have somewhat shifted in a contemporary context. She opposes "civilized people throughout the world" to "the al-Qaida terrorist network," "the Taliban," and "the terrorists,"[35] thereby reconstructing the civilized/barbaric framework through a fluid and transnational paradigm.

Nevertheless, what remains consistent in her framing of U.S. involvement in Afghanistan as a civilizing mission is the way in which she discusses the status of women as the basic measurement of barbarism. "Afghan women know," she says, "what the rest of the world is discovering: The brutal oppression of women is the central goal of the terrorists."[36] Rhetorically, this statement achieves two goals simultaneously: it establishes the oppression of women as the defining characteristic of backward, primitive groups, and it deploys the slippery category of "the terrorists" as the quintessential contemporary barbarians, in a context in which mainstream U.S. discourse consistently conflates terrorism with Islam and Muslims.[37] I am not disputing the fact that women in Afghanistan, living under the rule of the Taliban, did (and do) indeed experience extreme patriarchal oppression. However, I do consider it crucial to unpack the assertion that gender liberation, as a civilizing mission, is a primary concern driving U.S. involvement. According to Mrs. Bush's logic, if the "central" goal of "the terrorists" is to oppress women, it follows that the main purpose of U.S. Military intervention is to protect and liberate women. Indeed, she boasts that "because of our recent military gains in much of Afghanistan, women are no longer imprisoned in their homes," implying, again, that women's liberation serves as the impetus for U.S. Military action. Yet much evidence points to the contrary, the most direct of which is the fact that U.S. policy in Afghanistan prior to September 11, 2001 supported the same "barbaric" regimes Mrs. Bush describes as brutal and oppressive in her November 17, 2001 address.[38] Instead of demonstrating a genuine commitment to gender liberation, then, the rhetoric of the Bush administration illustrates the way in which cultural mythologies of Arab and Muslim womanhood[39] (in this case deployed through the metaphor of the burqa as symbol of oppression) function as strategic tools in the U.S. imperialist civilizing mission as configured through the "war on terror." The story of civilization, as told by the representations of Arab and Muslim womanhood I analyze in this book, depends upon an oppositional notion of barbarism and backwardness, which is built into the cultural mythologies of veils, harems, and belly dancers that are crafted in the United States. In this way, they serve as "documents of civilization," to reference the Walter Benjamin quote with which I began this introduction, "that are at the same time documents of barbarism."[40] Beyond merely demonstrating that the notions of civilization and barbarism are constitutive of one another, then they illustrate that the Eurocentric notion of civilization creates, and therefore presages, the conditions for barbarity.

CIVILIZING IRAQ THROUGH
CULTURAL MYTHOLOGIES

On April 10, 2003, just a few weeks after the initial U.S. Military attacks on Iraq and just one day after the ground invasion of Baghdad in what was to be coined "Operation Iraqi Freedom," the national Iraqi museum in Baghdad lost thousands[41] of invaluable antiquities to raids on the museum during the highly unstable early days of U.S. occupation. As news of the stolen antiquities spread, media sources emitted a mournful cry, seemingly in unison, lamenting the irrevocable loss of shared human history; it was a cry made all the more piercing by its juxtaposition with the stifling silence and dearth of images of human casualties from these same sources. Part of what enabled this type of response to the tragic loss of thousands of irreplaceable antiquities is the conceptualization of Iraq, and the Iraq museum in particular, as the site of an ancient civilization that belongs not only to Iraq or the modern Middle East, but also to all of humanity. Such a notion of Iraq as the site of a shared ancient civilization, however, is simultaneously coupled with characterizations of contemporary Iraq as a primitive shadow of the great civilization it once was. In fact, this dualistic perception of Iraq is the necessary fiction upon which the logic of military intervention rests, at least in part. If Iraq is considered to house the evidence—and the remnants—of the majestic beauty and grandeur of ancient civilizations, it is also characterized as needing civilizing (U.S. and British) forces to save it from a state of barbarity and chaos.

What has been rather simplistically referred to as a "clash of civilizations" by Huntington is here revealed as a violent and destructive collision of two distinct conceptual modalities of civilization, or patterns of conceptualizing and representing civilization, both of which are tied to Enlightenment-based narratives of progress and linear advancement. One is the idea of the United States as a civilizing/liberating force, with its connotations of high culture and cultivation, and the other is the invocation of Iraq as the static, universal, ancient origins of contemporary civilized societies. These two modalities of civilization are clearly at play in the rhetoric surrounding the looting[42] of the Iraq museum in April 2003, in which Iraq is described as the archaeological site of the universalized ancient civilization that gave rise to modern civilizations.

The looted Iraq National Museum might seem quite distinct, both geographically and conceptually, from the focus of this book, which is a consideration of images of Arab womanhood in U.S. popular culture. Yet, as I have been arguing, images of Arab womanhood in U.S. popular imagination are implicitly connected to the notions of civilization that undergird the narrative of the ransacked museum. For example, contemporary representations of the veil in U.S. popular culture have been deployed to emphasize the civilized superiority of U.S. culture in relation to supposedly barbaric practices of female oppression. In fact, shifting U.S. interpretations of and engagements with the notion of civilization have largely determined the popularity of varied representations of Arab womanhood in particular historical moments. Moreover, the construction of stereotypical images of Arab womanhood in U.S. popular culture is intimately tied to international politics and especially to relations between the United States and the Middle East. In short, the example of the pillaged Iraq museum foregrounds the complex narratives of progress and power that inform the U.S. fascination with veiled women, belly dancers, and harem girls at the same time that it highlights the urgency that drives this study to demonstrate that U.S. constructed cultural mythologies, and not Arab and Muslim people's realities, have informed official U.S. foreign policy. Furthermore, I am particularly interested in exploring the ways in which the example of U.S. Military occupation of Iraq as a liberating mission bears Benjamin's assertion out. The modern notion of civilization, particularly when deployed as a mission to convert its own "others," is bordered and defined by the notion of barbarism. Indeed, in the instance of Iraq, the U.S. civilizing/liberating mission has given rise to unbearable atrocities that are both quotidian (e.g., daily car bombings) and singularly horrifying (e.g., the Abu Ghraib prison tortures[43]). Perhaps because of the double-edged nature of the notion of civilization, however, official U.S. narratives about the "progress" in Iraq continue to cast U.S. occupation as a project of liberation, failing to acknowledge the fact that the chaotic and violent realities of contemporary Iraq are the flip side of the coin of U.S. presence. The liberating mission promises civilization in its future, while disavowing the backwardness it installs in its wake. Consider, for example, the fact that U.S. Forces utilized the city of Babylon as a military base in April 2003. Though the official justification for occupying Babylon was to protect it from looters, the fact is that U.S. Military presence, including the construction of a helipad in the middle of ancient ruins, caused the destruction of irreplaceable artifacts and ancient ruins in a city sometimes heralded as the very cradle of civilization.[44] Noting that all of the modalities of civilization are at play in the narratives surrounding this example— the United States as the pinnacle of western civilization, Babylon as the ancient origins of that civilization, and the Iraqi looters as barbaric/primitive others to the civilizing force—I would also highlight the way in which such examples reveal the paradoxes inherent in the metanarrative of modernity.[45] Fulfillment of the progress narrative, as it is now constructed, will result in the effacement of the living sites of ancient origins, yet these origin myths are the very foundation on which the Eurocentric notions of modernity and civilization are built. Media accounts demonstrate the centrality of such origin stories by asserting, over and over again, that the ruins represent the shared ancient heritage of civilized humankind. In a January 15, 2005 article about the careless destruction of Babylon, *The Guardian* reports that "these are world sites. Not only is what the American forces are doing damaging the archaeology of Iraq, it's actually damaging the cultural heritage of the world."[46] Put in the framework of the "cultural heritage of the world," one can see why the destruction of Babylonian antiquities received worldwide attention. However, if the unthinking destruction of such rich archaeological sites in the name of protecting them from looters was not tragic enough, the deafening silence and seeming indifference to human Iraqi casualties is staggering.

I do not dispute the devastating effect of the complete and irrevocable loss of rich cultural artifacts. Yet there is something more to be learned from this particularly woeful aspect of the U.S. led war in Iraq. It demonstrates how the modern idea of civilization has operated in disciplinary and destructive ways. In the case of Babylon, the notion of civilization continues to twist and turn in heartbreaking, yet predictable, ways. According to an April 21, 2006 article in the *International Herald Tribune*, the ancient site of Babylon is to be saved by turning it into a cultural center and "Iraqi theme park."[47] Here, civilization, revised and updated in a neoliberal framework, will mean privatizing antiquities. As the mayor of nearby town Hilla reportedly proclaims, "I want restaurants, gift shops, and long parking lots...maybe even a Holiday Inn."[48] In the meantime, the description of the irretrievable loss of antiquities as a "loss for all of humanity"[49] and the stories about the U.S. occupation of "the ancient city of Babylon"[50] are more than just a tragic story; they are enduring and important metaphors that illustrate the insidious ways in which the gendered notion of civilization has been deployed in tragically uncivilized ways. In the modern Middle East, it has often enabled colonialist and imperialist forces, such as France, Britain, and the United States, to justify occupation of Middle East territories as the benevolent responsibility (what Rudyard Kipling famously called the "white man's burden") of civilized countries to bring Enlightenment to primitive nations.[51] In contemporary Iraq, as interpreted through the simultaneous dualistic modalities of ancient civilization and backward civilization, this metaphor has justified preemptive strikes and military occupation. Such a metaphor relies on gendered notions of the occupier as aggressive, valiant savior, and the occupied as a passive, penetrated, and rescued nation.[52] The very notion of bringing liberation to a people and a nation depends on such gendered constructions of victim and savior, and, as my work demonstrates, these narratives are often expressed in common representations of Arab womanhood in U.S. popular culture.

Indeed, this powerful socially constructed notion of civilization and its deployment as an interpretive category through which to understand Iraq permeates popular perception. Both of the full-length books written in the United States about the raid on the Iraq museum employ similarly anachronistic characterizations to describe the event and its impact. In *Thieves of Baghdad*, an apologia about U.S. culpability for the loss of artifacts during the raid, U.S. Marine Matthew Bogdanos writes that "the entire country of Iraq is an archaeological site."[53] Milbry Polk and Angela M. H. Schuster, editors of *The Looting of the Iraq Museum, Baghdad*, describe the museum as "one of the world's great repositories of Western civilization" which contained "not just Iraqi history, but human history, our history."[54] Here, Iraq (through the national museum) is not only described as a frozen and timeless receptacle, it is placed within an implied teleological narrative of an ancient civilization that is the legacy and ancestor of modern "Western civilization."

At the same time, descriptions of Iraqi people are filtered through a perception of contemporary Iraq as uncultivated and primitive. In the introduction to *The Looting of the Iraq Museum*, Milbry Polk counters the regal, timeless image he employs in descriptions of Iraq as an ancient civilization with an explanation of the raid as "gangs of looters [who] swarmed into the museum."[55] In one of his few descriptions of Iraqi people, then, he hints at a barbaric undercurrent to the contemporary inhabitants of this "ancient" land. Likewise, Bogdanos refers to the people he encounters as disorganized and uncivil; he complains that "the entire museum did not possess a single conference table, because no one ever talked to anyone else in a structured way."[56] He further invokes the implication of barbarism by describing Iraq as a "guest culture that had changed little since Hammurabi[57] was making lists of rules."[58] This last suggestion that Arab culture is both antiquated and brutal often permeates popular perception of Arab and Muslim cultures, and Arab men, as dictators of oppressive gender norms.

Indeed, the perception of Arab women as oppressed and silent subjects is so recognizable for a contemporary U.S. audience that it is the trope with which Bogdanos begins his nonfiction thriller, *Thieves of Baghdad*. Readers are introduced to the tale of the stolen antiquities through a dramatic scene in which Bogdanos and Dr. Nawala al-Mutwali, the (then current) director of the Iraq museum, explore the most protected holdings of the museum to see if they, too, had been looted. The scene comes to a climax when al-Mutwali, whose Muslim identity and headscarf had been made much of by Bogdanos, faints due to stress, heat, and low air circulation. Bogdanos attributes this to the fact that "she was covered from head to toe, including the *khimar*[59] that swathed her head,"[60] and worries what the Muslim patriarchs will think of her being compromised with no head covering in front of a non-Muslim man. Even so, he reports that "while one of the women unbuttoned Nawala's jacket, it fell to me to remove her *khimar*. For whatever damage it would do U.S.–Iraq relations, I also held her hand."[61] In this subtle paternalistic turn, Bogdanos deftly reifies the stereotypes about Middle Eastern (patriarchal) culture as brutal, oppressive, and utterly unfeeling toward women in particular. He also conveniently elides the more obvious and pressing reason for the potential "damage" to "U.S.–Iraq relations," which is the U.S. invasion and occupation of Iraq and the failure of the U.S. Military to protect the irreplaceable artifacts that were held in the Iraq museum—not a moment of hand-holding between a U.S. Marine and a professional Iraqi woman.

This compelling scene, drawn all the more vividly by Bogdanos's ghost writer, illustrates the precarious position of women as appropriated symbolic figures in the rhetoric of civilization.[62] More particularly, the Bogdanos example demonstrates how the notion of Iraq as hyper-patriarchal and overly oppressive to women serves as an implicit justification, building on the official rhetoric regarding the invasion of Afghanistan, for U.S. Military intervention.[63] Despite the fact that Iraq has had a vibrant women's rights movement since at least the early 1900s, shown by the existence of feminist journals and publications and the relatively large number of women in leadership positions (all of which has been in decline since Desert Storm in 1991), Bogdanos's account and popular perception both insist that women in Iraq have never had rights or freedoms. Moreover, the popular story of oppressed Kuwaiti women (whose prohibitions were extended to female U.S. soldiers during the 1991 Gulf War, coupled with the less than subtle connections made between the Taliban, al-Qaida, and Iraq immediately following the events of September 11, 2001, have had the effect of mapping the images of veiled, oppressed Kuwaiti women and of Afghan women wearing the burqa onto the perceived realities of Iraqi women. Such sweeping, sloppy conflations demonstrate two important points. The first is the way in which women from varied regions of the Middle East and Central Asia[64] are perceived as a monolithic mass, and the second is the irresistibility of the veil as metaphor. It is so powerful that Bogdanos seems to see the totalizing shroud he expects al-Mutwali to wear, rather than the understated headscarf she actually does wear, according to the photographs he includes in the book.

In his seemingly innocuous anecdote, Bogdanos actually demonstrates the intricate ways in which the strands of my argument interweave. First, Bogdanos's use of the cultural mythology of the veil to begin his book about the looting of the Iraq museum demonstrates its salience, even in seemingly unrelated circumstances. Second, it reveals the anatomy of cultural mythologies, where the meaning of the veil for Dr. al-Mutwali quickly disappears from Bogdanos's narrative and in its place one finds the flattened symbol of the veil refilled with mainstream U.S. constructed ideas about the oppression of Arab and Muslim women. Third, Bogdanos deploys this myth in order to buttress his overall argument about the noble intentions of the U.S. Military's civilizing/liberating mission, thereby demonstrating the function of such representations of Arab and Muslim womanhood in dominant U.S. discourse. Fourth, his invocation of the cultural mythology of the veil clearly serves as a shorthand reference to dominant narratives about power and progress, where his metaphoric unveiling of al-Mutwali demonstrates power relations between Iraq and the United States and where the idea of the veil as antiquated custom serves as primitive other to the U.S. progress narrative. Finally, as I have been arguing, it demonstrates the nefarious impact these cultural mythologies have on Arab and Muslim cultures, where the gendered notion of civilization serves as a disciplinary and destructive force.

EXCAVATING THE IMAGES

Elaborating on the motivating metaphor of the looted Iraq museum, I propose that it is not sufficient to simply call for a return of the lost artifacts, or to lament their irrevocable destruction. To achieve some redemption out of the ruins, one must understand the factors and forces that have determined their value and that have enabled their theft. Because I insist that representations of Arab womanhood be understood as cultural artifacts of the particular cultural and historical context in which they are found, I therefore situate my inquiry at the intersection of the fields of cultural studies and transnational feminisms. My mode of analysis is theoretically indebted to the work of scholars like Donna Haraway, Marnia Lazreg, Anne McClintock, Chandra Talpade Mohanty, Uma Narayan, Aihwa Ong, Therese Saliba and Ella Shohat,[65] who have offered critiques of the way in which "third world" women, or women who claim roots and/ or ancestry in the global South, have been othered in mainstream U.S. feminist discourse and conceptualized as a monolithic mass. Building on the strengths and insights of these feminist scholars, I ground my work in a transnational feminist framework particularly because its focus on relationality, rather than a homogenizing unity, is a useful strategy for approaching difference.[66] Rather than making a universalizing move and organizing around one broad, generalizing category of oppression (i.e., gender), transnational feminisms take what Zillah Eisenstein has called a polyversal approach.[67] In this framework, feminists ground themselves in particular contexts, noting the complex intersections of oppression therein, in order to then strategically form alliances and build solidarity transnationally. Contrary to a blanketing paradigm, this approach creates an interrelated web of critical analysis, with each point grounded in an appreciation for, and understanding of, its own unique realities. Precisely because the cultural mythologies of veils, harems, and belly dancers in the United States operate by evacuating history and context from the forms they inhabit, I locate my critique in a transnational feminist framework, with its careful focus on attending to the richness of historical and cultural layers.

As evidenced by my use of the theoretical frameworks offered by Roland Barthes and Raymond Williams, I also ground my work in the field of cultural studies because it is a field that has sought to understand cultural formations as they are defined by and as they determine hegemonic narratives. Because cultural studies has focused on deconstructing the effects of power inherent in those cultural forms as a political project, it has historically utilized a multidisciplinary set of methods. While these methods have ranged from what Stuart Hall has called the "encoding" aspect of the production of cultural artifacts to the "decoding" moment of audience interaction with the cultural artifact,[68] this book focuses on textual analysis to produce a close reading of the images as culturally and historically situated texts. I bring semiotic tools of analysis to bear on them, in order to demonstrate the similar ways in which they have been emptied of their historical contingency, and refilled with the concerns of the U.S. cultural context that has created them.

I have invoked the scene of the ransacked Iraq museum in the immediate aftermath of the U.S. invasion not only because of the way it exemplifies the gendered modalities of civilization that determine popular perceptions of Iraq, but also to draw on the rich metaphor of archaeology. I am interested in shifting attention away from the notion of the archaeological site simply as the ruins of ancient civilizations, as the stories about the looting of the museum have done, since such notions reify the narrative of a grand, progressive and linear teleology that animate both the primitive and ancient modalities of civilization. In order to find a way out of the anachronistic frameworks that have determined representations of the Middle East, I utilize the archaeological metaphor, in Foucauldian terms, as a site in which to come to terms with the living evidence of rupture and discontinuity, or as a framework for making sense of a set of artifacts that can give insight into the layers of contexts in which they are embedded. In other words, I look at representations of Arab womanhood as artifacts that have been created in a particular historical and cultural context, and which have been shaped by the confluence of social, political, and economic exigencies of the specific historical and cultural layer in which they are found. I am therefore building on Edward Said's suggestion that the field of orientalism produces what Michel Foucault calls a "discursive formation" to analyze representations of Arab womanhood in U.S. popular culture as a set of statements governed by the rules of the larger field of orientalism. This should enable me to draw on the productive discoveries of Said's much utilized and criticized work, while steering clear of its generalizing pitfalls.[69]

While Foucault's *The Archaeology of Knowledge* is primarily concerned with problematizing the history of the sciences, I take his suggestion that the archaeological metaphor he employs may have a much wider application,[70] and I apply it in the analysis of U.S. orientalism as a particular "way of speaking" that is invested, to paraphrase Foucault, in a system of power and nostalgia.[71] Images of Arab womanhood have remained salient to U.S. audiences for over a century because of their persistent ability to refract concerns about power and progress in varied historical contexts. The archaeological project, in Foucauldian terms, is explicitly not focused on finding the "innermost secret of origin;"[72] rather, it is invested in describing and defining the "discourse-object" in terms of the system of rules and relationships that give it meaning in a particular context. As such, it must guard against the linear narrative that wants to understand discourses or artifacts as necessarily emerging from, or giving way to, those that came before or those that come after. The archaeological metaphor provides a framework for identifying the parallels between images of Arab womanhood in different historical contexts in the United States without necessarily positing an evolutionary relationship among them. More importantly, it offers a paradigm of excavation capable of exposing the multiple layers of orientalist representations in the United States while enabling the excavation of a set of cultural artifacts, each of which holds powerful meaning within the sociohistorical context of its own layer.[73]

In addition to avoiding the trap of the search for origins inherent in the linear narrative, the excavation metaphor positions images of Arab womanhood as a set of artifacts constructed, produced, and ultimately determined, by the contextual layer in which they occur. The excavation metaphor is therefore quite purposefully subversive, in that it offers a means of reversing the anachronistic schemata through which Arab womanhood has been imagined and reflecting them back as the worn mythologies of the U.S. cultural context. In other words, this metaphor flips the associative function of the atavistic claim, opening up the possibility of asking questions about what it means for these particular images to have come into existence and to have provided meaning for U.S. audiences in particular historical moments.[74] Because excavation treats each image as an artifact, it understands the images to be products of U.S. culture, and, as each cultural and historical layer is unearthed, it demands a careful consideration of the way in which U.S. nationhood has been constructed in relation to the modalities of civilization invoked by the cultural mythologies of veils, harems, and belly dancers.

LAYERS OF REPRESENTATION— ORGANIZATION OF CHAPTERS

Though I am interested in exploring the enduring function that such images have held for over a century in the United States, I do so by focusing my analysis on three specific contextual strata: the 1893 Chicago World's Fair, U.S. tobacco advertisements featuring orientalist imagery in the 1910s, and contemporary (1970s–present) advertisements and images of veiled women, belly dancers, and harem girls. I ground my inquiry in the 1893 Chicago World's Fair because it provides a unique space from which to trace the flow of orientalist images from classical French painting to twentieth-century U.S. tobacco advertisements, and, ultimately, to the contemporary context.

The 1893 Fair is a particularly rich site for exploring a U.S. engagement with the notion of civilization, as it was an opportunity for the developing nation to demonstrate its achievements, both technologi-cal and political, to the rest of the world. As one of the most impor-tant articulations of a reunified and technologically advanced United States at the turn of the century, the Chicago World's Fair serves as an important site through which to understand the way the turn-of-the-century United States defined itself in relation to other European colonial powers, such as France and Britain. In fact, it serves as an ideal context in which to explore the impact of U.S. concerns with power and progress on the creation and dissemination of orientalist images of Arab womanhood.

In the first chapter, "Traveling Orientalism: U.S. Echoes of a French Tradition," I use the 1893 Fair as a vantage point from which to identify elements and patterns of representation in the French colonial context that prefigure U.S. interpretations of orientalism. Although the French influence on the Fair is evident in the borrowed architectural style of the "White City," the main presentation of U.S. prowess, and in the ethnographic displays that mimicked previous French Expositions, I focus on the Fine Arts display. The impact of French orientalist painting on popular perceptions of Arab woman-hood is well-documented;[75] therefore, I analyze the American orien-talist pieces in the Fine Arts exhibit in comparison with the French orientalist tradition in order to demonstrate the translation of French orientalist structures to a U.S. context. Both sets of paintings exem-plify the way in which the confluence of tumultuous social processes such as colonialism and modernization created a social context that both romanticized and eroticized what it understood to be the primi-tive nature of harem slaves and exotic bathers. If representations of Arab womanhood in U.S. popular culture can be understood as a set of statements within the discourse of orientalism, an analysis of French orientalist paintings will serve to familiarize readers with the rules of this particular discourse.

In terms of the Fair itself, it is the site of entry for a particularly U.S. based understanding of belly dancing. Chicago's Midway Plaisance, as a virtual cornucopia of exoticized foreign cultures, hosted an eth-nographic display that included the "Street of Cairo." The main attraction (and arguably the most lucrative concession on Midway) was the performance of "Little Egypt," a woman imported from Syria to enact what was known as "the belly dance." Little Egypt may have been one of the first, but she is certainly not the last, representation of Arab female sexuality to make a lasting impression on the American psyche. As the precursor to subsequent representations, from *I Dream of Jeannie*, to James Bond and his harem (in *The Spy Who Loved Me*), to the 2001 ad scheme of Camel cigarettes (the seven pleasures of the exotic), Little Egypt's presence at the Columbian Exposition deserves careful consideration. Because her presence at the Chicago World's Fair was an imitation of belly dance (*danse du ventre*) displays that were presented in France at previous world's fairs, Little Egypt provides an exemplary link between European and American orientalisms. Little Egypt signifies a uniquely American deployment of orientalism, though, at the turn of the century as one signifier through which the United States sought to assert its status as a burgeoning capitalist nation in opposition to a primitive and exotic (oriental) other. The second chapter, "Dancing the Hootchy Kootchy: The Rhythms and Contortions of American Orientalism," provides an analysis of the photographic representations of belly dancers at the Chicago World's Fair in order to lay the groundwork for analyzing subsequent popular representations of Arab womanhood.

In addition to providing the location from which to trace the influence of European-produced orientalist stereotypes on U.S. created orientalist categories, the 1893 world's exhibition in Chicago also provides a site from which to project a forward glance toward the role that the advertising industry would play in appropriating and capitalizing on the stereotypes created and consumed at the Fair. As is evident in tobacco advertisements for cigarette brands such as *Omar* and *Fatima* in the early twentieth century, advertisers relied on the power of exoticized orientalist imagery to market their products to an increasingly consumerist American audience. Chapter 3, "Selling Little Egypt: The Commodification of Arab Womanhood," considers yet another orientation of American orientalism insofar as consumerism joined expansionism as the defining indicators of progress.

With the main trajectory of my argument established in the first three chapters, in chapter 4, "Veiled Intentions: The Cultural Mythology of Veils, Harems, and Belly Dancers in the Service of Empire, Security, and Globalization," I turn to the contemporary context to demonstrate that recent images of Arab womanhood in U.S. popular culture are the extension of a century-old legacy of U.S. orientalist representations of Arab womanhood. Contemporary images do not reflect a new fascination with Arab womanhood; rather, they represent a continued concern with temporal and spatial transformations, now stimulated by globalization, even as they reflect shifting power relations between the Middle East and the United States.

Because the archaeological metaphor can lend itself to a linear bias, I want to emphasize that this book does not provide a genealogy of images, nor does it assume that chronology implies causation. Rather than conceiving of the 1893 Chicago World's Fair as the origin of orientalist representations of Arab womanhood in U.S. popular culture, I treat it as a particularly rich layer of representation. I provide careful contextualization of each artifact found in this layer to analyze the representations as a set of statements within the discourse of orientalism. My hesitancy to name an origin is not simply a matter of convenience or rhetorical strategy, but also a deep philosophical predilection, which is bound up in the fraught legacy of the images themselves. A focus on origins or beginnings would further cement representations of Arab womanhood within a linear (rather than cyclical) framework, which is precisely what has determined images of harems, veils, and belly dancers as anachronistic categories of interpretation. Images of the exotic and/or backward Arab woman consistently reference her seemingly inherent or natural connection with primitive origins and, by extension, the primordial past. The cultural context in which these images are consumed, in turn, is intently focused on preserving those emblems of anachronism in the midst of dynamic social forces that seem to efface a presumably simpler past. In this way, figures of Arab womanhood become sealed within a sort of backward glance or nostalgic yearning for a lost past that never actually existed.

As an idea that is not rooted in any particular time or place, the concept of the primordial past has no history; its appeal lies in the fact that it appears to be an abstract signifier of ancient and timeless truths. Because of the way in which representations of Arab womanhood have consistently been associated with timelessness, they have also been cast into a frozen stance as markers of a pure and irrecoverable origin. For this reason, I do not find it useful to name a moment of creation or conception for the legacy of representation that I analyze. As Edward Said asserts in his book *Beginnings*, "We should understand [such a] fixation as the desire to hold the object of study in the moment of its emergence, as if to uncover the pure thing...were finally to grasp its essence."[76] Not only do representations of Arab women often become trapped within the confines of this type of logic, as they are often lauded for their apparent authenticity, but, as I demonstrate, the notion of their essence or authenticity is itself a construction. Whether it is tobacco advertisements or turn-of-the-century U.S. photographs, cultural mythologies manipulate and frame images of Arab womanhood as accurate portrayals of the Arab and Muslim worlds; they are therefore valued for their ability to re-present, and deliver over, an idealized image of an ancient, receding past.

As evidenced by their long life in U.S. popular culture, representations of Arab women have served a crucial function in U.S. society;

they have particularly been invoked during times of intense change and flux to assuage U.S. based fears and concerns about progress and power. The fact that representations of Arab womanhood have persisted as visual vocabulary in each historical context I analyze suggests that there is something urgent and unexamined about their status as cultural artifacts, and that their excavation can project these urgent questions and concerns back onto the U.S. cultural context in which they are created, rather than keeping them frozen and static within the images themselves. The goal of this book is ultimately to deflate the power of the cultural mythologies of veils, harems, and belly dancers by revealing the complex role they play in various U.S. cultural contexts. Such a revelation will ideally stimulate an engaged kind of imagination—one that is focused on creating new possibilities for critical thinking and social justice, rather than on rehearsing worn categories of representation.

CHAPTER 1

TRAVELING ORIENTALISM: U.S.
ECHOES OF A FRENCH TRADITION

The genie of the lamp, that flashed into creation before the astonished eyes of Aladdin, a palace more gorgeous than all the wealth of a mighty Sultan was able to duplicate, has long ceased to roam the world, the subject of talismans, ravishing the earth of its jewels, the sky of its gems, and the ocean of its treasures; but there are magicians still, who rival the proudest conceptions of imaginary demons with realities as splendid as ever oriental fancy painted. This is not an age of miracles, but it is one of works, in which the powers of human genius transcend the beauty and opulence of Arabic dreams...

James Buel, *The Magic City* (1894)

The dizzying grandeur and sheer magnitude of the 1893 World's Fair in Chicago only hints at the amount of time and resources spent on its construction. Even so, it is not the physical structure but rather the ideological scaffolding behind the fair design that proves the most intricate, particularly in terms of the way it both reflected and helped shape mainstream U.S. attitudes at the turn of the twentieth century. The Columbian Exposition (another title for the Chicago World's Fair), a meticulously planned and painstakingly conceived articulation of U.S. progress, aimed to mark the development of the burgeoning "western" power since the arrival of Christopher Columbus on American soil 400 years earlier. However, as the remarks of James Buel indicate, fair organizers positioned that version of progress in relation to a constructed binary of advanced (colonial) powers and primitive (colonized) peoples, the latter to serve as a benchmark against which progress would be measured. The overwhelming message of progress, packaged and presented by fair designers, seemed a benign and straightforward one meant to mark the U.S. path toward technological advancement. As evidenced by the built-in reference to Columbus, the rhetoric of progress also cloaked expansionist and imperialist goals of the United States as an empire-building nation. Buel's introduction to *The Magic City*, a photographic catalogue of the World's Fair, reveals this very conceit in that he speaks of the notion of progress displayed at the Fair by actually describing its supposed opposite. He begins with the story of Aladdin, or "the genie of the lamp" (which most of his readers would have identified with *Arabian Nights*, the French and English translation of *One Thousand and One Nights*), to let readers know that the World's Fair—and, by extension, the United States—had moved beyond the achievements of ancient civilizations and into an era in which power could be measured not by miracles or magic but by technology.

From this brief sketch, one gets a sense of how world's fairs operated as what Robert Rydell has called "symbolic universes"[1] because of the clear ideological underpinning of such grand nationalistic and imperialist projects. The 1893 Fair can indeed be understood as a "galaxy of symbols,"[2] which functions as a rich site through which to explore U.S. manifestations of orientalist logic, and from which to trace French influences on the articulation of U.S. orientalism. In this respect, it offers a concrete structure through which to develop some of the animating themes of this book. As an obvious structure concretizing several orientalist themes, it houses layers of artifacts, including the influence of French orientalist paintings, American paintings of the Holy Land, and belly dancing exhibits featuring dancers from Algeria and Syria. In this chapter, I undertake a comparative analysis of the former two, saving the latter for the following chapter.

The ideological scaffolding of the Chicago World's Fair rests on the twin pillars of progress and imperialism, with capitalism motivating each. It is therefore structurally parallel to representations of Arab womanhood, insofar as these images have functioned ideologically as placeholders for a U.S. engagement with power and progress. Though the world expositions operated as sites through which nations could demonstrate their own progress, it might be more useful to reframe the notion of progress as a modality of civilization. The organizers of the Chicago World's Fair, for example, were interested in constructing an image of the United States as a distinctly civilized nation. They enacted this image in myriad ways, for instance, by modeling the White City (the name for the centralized U.S. exhibits) on neo-classical architecture, by demonstrating U.S. excellence in technology and Fine Arts, and by situating the White City at the pinnacle of a racialized evolutionary scale. Such a notion of civilization, based in opposition to the concurrent construction of others as backward and primitive, was modeled on the cultural standards of western Europe. These standards, tied to notions of technological and scientific advancement, were clearly embedded in an Enlightenment-based set of ideals and were therefore linked to the modalities of civilization deployed by France and the United Kingdom in the colonial period. To develop my analysis of how this modality of civilization operates in an expansionist U.S. context vis-à-vis representations of Arab womanhood, I look here at American orientalist paintings, housed at the 1893 Chicago World's Fair, in comparison to the French orientalist paintings embedded in the context of colonialist France.

Lest my comparison of French and American orientalisms imply that I understand orientalism as a totalizing process that constructs monolithic notions of the "West" and the "East," or the Occident and the Orient, I will delineate the analytical tools Said's theory of orientalism offers to frame my own deployment of these tools. Said has perhaps been most famously criticized[3] for his privileging of the Orient/Occident binary and the way this binary both institutes a reifying structure of the Occident's dominance and obscures the heterologic nature of each category. One of the most problematic aspects of such a construction, Lisa Lowe argues, is the implicit assumption that the region referenced by the term "Orient" is uniform and dominated unequivocally by the Occident with no possible forms of resistance. Such a static and rigid conceptualization of hegemony is clearly not consonant with Said's goal of intervening in the types of power relations suggested by orientalism. It is also antithetical to the Foucauldian notion of discourse, which informs Said's understanding of orientalism as the production of knowledge about the region denoted by such categories as the Orient and the Middle, Far, and Near East (Indeed, even these terms demonstrate the production of categories through which these regions are then framed and understood). Even so, the primacy of the Orient/Occident binary in Said's analysis does potentially obscure his more subtle and complex assertion that orientalism functions as a discursive formation that operates by producing a set of representations that create and propagate the notion that Orient and Occident are oppositional. In other words, I agree with the spirit of Lowe's proposal to intervene in orientalism by demonstrating its heterogeneity and exploding the undergirding binary of difference. However, because orientalism functions by creating a set of representations that reify the binary as a structure of domination, deconstructing orientalism as a discursive process is still a critical strategy of intervention. Because I am interested in understanding why certain elements in images of Arab womanhood remain constant across widely divergent contexts, I must account for the ability of orientalism, in all its variations, to present itself as stable and static, and to shore itself up with the conceit of simple oppositions.

Combining the uses of Said's construction of orientalism with the utility of its critiques, then, I follow Lowe's suggestion that "orientalism may well be an apparatus through which a variety of concerns with difference is figured."[4] Understanding orientalism as an apparatus enables a range of critical and theoretical possibilities, including the ability to conceptualize it as simultaneously rigid and fluid. Though the apparatus functions by systematically installing stable binaries, it also enjoys mobility insofar as it functions in a variety of different contexts and deployments. In this chapter, using the 1893 Chicago World's Fair as a grounding example, I look at how the apparatus of orientalism traveled from the French colonial context to the U.S. expansionist context.

The differences in the two sets of representations (French orientalist paintings and American paintings of the Holy Land) demonstrate the ability of the orientalist apparatus to adapt to the different pressures of each context, while the similarities between these representations magnify some of orientalism's structural machinery. In addition to the reliance on a binary framework, the orientalist apparatus operates both by producing knowledge about its subject and by referencing, or building on, knowledge already produced in other contexts. As for images of Arab womanhood, the representations both participate in creating a set of interpretive categories (i.e., harems, veils, and belly dancers) through which a U.S. understanding of Arab womanhood is filtered as well as shoring up these categories by citing French and British predecessors. Alain Grosrichard sums this process up when he suggests that "if those who live in the seraglio and what takes place in it could, for an entire century, be so closely transposed to tragic drama and furnish material for fiction, it is because they were already representations."[5] In other words, representations of Arab womanhood both create a set of "common sense" notions about the Arab and Muslim worlds and participate in a system of knowledge through which these worlds are regulated and disciplined.

Representations are particularly potent aspects of knowledge systems because they hold privileged positions in relationship to truth.

Though they are clearly constructed, they present themselves as unmediated (re-presented) iterations of reality. Moreover, they accumulate credibility through the practice of citationality; representations do not seem quite as true unless they corroborate the system of representations already established, as demonstrated by Sarah Graham-Brown in an example of a British newspaper that refused to publish a photograph of a harem because it did not seem "real," that is, it did not fit British perceptions of the harem as a lascivious and erotic space.[6] Clearly, the practice of citationality creates a closed system of representation in which, as Said asserts, "the Orient is less a place than a *topos*, a set of references, a congeries of characteristics, that seems to have its origin in a quotation, or a fragment of text."[7]

One of the primary ways the apparatus of orientalism imposes a kind of rigidity on the Arab and Muslim world is by framing it in a system of representation. Said uses the metaphor of the stage,[8] thereby enabling critical reflection about those who create and consume the staged figures and representations. Why are these figures worth watching? What meaning might they hold for the French, British, German, and U.S. audiences that have flocked to them? Perhaps the most compelling aspect of the stage metaphor, however, is the implication that these orientalist representations are fabricated for the purposes of entertainment. These figures on the stage, here images of Arab womanhood, have an audience; they are scripted, directed, and produced for that audience, and they reference a set of performances staged in other orientalist contexts. These performances, of course, do not reveal, as W.J.T. Mitchell puts it, "any sort of naked reality but a world already clothed in our systems of representation."[9] Therefore, they offer a unique opportunity to explore those systems of representation and how the orientalist apparatus functions in the U.S. context. Following both Alan Trachtenberg's and John Berger's[10] suggestions that representations have the capacity to mystify as well as clarify, I am interested in complicating the seemingly straightforward facade of images of Arab and Muslim women in order to explore that which representation mystifies: the particular set of sociohistorical circumstances elided by constructed categories.

FOUR HUNDRED YEARS OF TOURISM: THE COLUMBIAN EXPOSITION

Though one could choose any number of sites from which to launch an exegesis of American orientalism, I have chosen the 1893 Chicago World's Fair, in part, because it provides a clear structural link between U.S. and French orientalisms. These are, of course, not the only iterations of orientalism, but because they are linked in literal and figurative ways through the framework of world expositions, the comparison enables a demonstration of citationality as a fundamental tool of orientalism. Applying and extending Said's assertion that "the Orient seems to have its origin in a quotation, or a fragment of a text,"[11] I will demonstrate that, in the U.S. context, it also seems to have its origin in the reclining pose of an odalisque (such as Jean-Auguste-Dominique Ingres's *The Grand Odalisque*—a French translation of the Turkish word connoting harem [sex] slave), in the tantalizing gyrations of the *danse du ventre* (performed at the 1889 Paris Exposition), and in the imaginative representation of harem life (e.g., in Eugène Delacroix's *Women of Algiers*). World expositions provide salient locations for comparison because they are rigorously structured and organized institutions, and, perhaps more importantly, because their structure belies ideological biases as well. Zeynep Çelik describes the "theme of expositions as a neat ordering of the world according to classes, types, and hierarchies—a system inherited from the Enlightenment."[12] In other words, the highly ordered and hierarchized designs of the Fairs—from architectural design to the positioning of different countries' displays—reflected a modality of civilization rooted in Enlightenment-based valorizations of progress, rationality, and linear development. Both the 1889 Exposition Universelles in Paris and the 1893 Chicago World's Fair manifested these biases in ethnographic exhibits organized according to an evolutionary scale that was determined by the principles of scientific racism. In superficial similarities between the two Fairs, such as ethnographic displays, a deeper ideological parallel informs the way that each envisioned the "Orient."

The notion of progress—and the modality of civilization it invokes—encourages a counterposing construction of the Middle East as primitive and backward with the United States defined in contradistinction to it. According to James Buel's famous description of the 1893 Chicago World's Fair, with which I began this chapter, the United States could demonstrate its burgeoning status and power alongside European countries such as France and Britain by assuring its citizens of the "powers of human genius" that distinguished the scientifically and technologically advanced United States from opulent "Arabic" others, who still believed in the power of magic. Moreover, Buel's assertion that the United States relied on the power of mechanical and technological "works," rather than the untrustworthy whims of "miracles," paralleled the nation's message and promise of economic stability and sociopolitical unity, which came at a crucial time for a country that was both struggling to recover from the Civil War and grappling with a sudden influx of immigrants. In fact, the orientalist apparatus functioned in both the French and the U.S. contexts as the machinery through which chaotic processes, such as imperialism, industrialization, and capitalism, could be ordered and regulated.

World's fairs often served as an opportunity for the country to reify dominant nationalist narratives while simultaneously establishing a new narrative of coherence, harmony, and stability in the midst of tumultuous social changes. The 1889 French Exposition, for instance, celebrated the centennial of the French Revolution, and its ethnographic exhibits also constructed the narrative of a continued revolution through the civilizing project of colonialism. The confluence of disorienting social processes, such as colonialism and modernization, produced an unarticulated structure of feeling that coalesced, in part, in orientalist representations of Arab womanhood. As a key point of comparison for U.S. orientalist representations, I flesh this claim out more fully in relation to French orientalist paintings in the "Imagining the Harem" section which follows.

Similarly, the 1893 Chicago World's Fair (though it was a year late) reiterated the Christopher Columbus origin myth by providing a rhetoric of unity and social harmony to which American citizens could cling. As a celebration of the four-hundredth anniversary of Columbus's landing on American shores, the Columbian Exposition sought to reconfigure and reinscribe a sense of national pride that could gloss over the socioeconomic and racial tensions being played out in the urban labor movement's violent clashes, as a result of industrialization and increased immigration. In fact, the organizers of the Fair sought to inculcate a "nationalizing synthesis"[13] by organizing unifying, ritualistic events, such as the public recitation of the Pledge of Allegiance by schoolchildren all over the country. Francis J. Bellamy, a member of the Fair planning committee, wrote the Pledge of Allegiance and planned its simultaneous recitation to coincide with the opening of the Fair in order to orchestrate a sense of harmonious nationalism. Rydell argues that Bellamy "was deeply worried by widening fissures of ethnic tension and industrial violence in American society," and therefore decided that Americans needed a "grand dramatic ritual that would involve children across the land reaffirming their loyalty to their nation—an 'affirmation' of allegiance."[14]

Fair organizers, then, essentially encouraged U.S. citizens and their children to affirm the expansionist and imperialist goals of their burgeoning nation-state. These goals ostensibly affirmed progress, alluding to the technological advances of an industrializing and modernizing nation. In actuality, however, the notion of progress operated as a euphemism for an Enlightenment-based epistemology that also depended on the logic of scientific racism to buttress its claim of superiority. As the notion of progress depended on the demonstrable existence of a preliminary state from which it had evolved, dominant narratives about progress often expressed racist notions about the backwardness of nonwhite, "primitive" peoples and cultures in relation to "evolved" and "civilized" white westerners. In the U.S. expansionist context, as in the French colonial context, the confluence of turbulent social processes, such as industrialization and expansionism, created an unarticulated structure of feeling in which images of Arab womanhood played a symbolic role. To more fully flesh out this role, I analyze American landscape paintings of the Holy Land in the "Painting Progress" section (see page 51).

IMAGINING THE HAREM

The European image of the harem as a prison-like enclosure in which women are stockpiled for the lascivious desires of the sultan master provides a salient construct through which to understand a burgeoning French colonial power. Although it might be tempting to speak of the "fall" or the "decline" of the Ottoman Empire, the transition between Ottoman and European world powers occurred in concert with the rise of modernity in western Europe. It is thus more useful to recognize a more complicated power dialectic that exerted considerable influence over subsequent French conceptualization and representation of Ottoman structures. In this respect, the image of the harem serves two roles: it provides a metaphor of boundaries (vis-à-vis the harem walls, or the notion of harem-as-prison) and it reifies the stereotype of the Ottoman patriarch as "absolutely despotic."[15] The harem metaphor therefore operationalizes a binary framework through which French nationalism and colonialism gain definition in opposition to an imagined other. The stereotype of the "Terrible Turk,"[16] then, furnished an image of brutal, despotic rule against which a colonial France could cast its own project of domination, which was cloaked as a civilizing mission.

Representations of Arab womanhood, filtered through the interpretive category of the harem, function in this context as an articulation of the confluence of nationalism, colonialism, and modernization in the nineteenth-century French landscape. Hence, it is not surprising

that the image of the harem became a particularly salient and meaningful one for a young French power developing its own style of rule
in opposition to its perception of the Eastern other. Ironically, as the
actual power of the Ottoman Empire waned, symbolic representations
of the remnants of its power proliferated in western Europe in the
works of novelists such as Victor Hugo (*Les Orientales,* 1829), Gérard
de Nerval (*Voyage en Orient,* 1856), and Gustave Flaubert (*Carnets de
Voyage,* 1858), and in the works of artists such as Eugène Delacroix,
Jean-Auguste-Dominique Ingres, and Jean-Léon Gérôme.[17] Such an
outpouring of orientalist material, beginning in the eighteenth century and swelling in the nineteenth century, demonstrates the shift
between Ottoman imperial and European colonial powers as Europe
created more and more representations of the other. Linda Nochlin
argues this point in relation to French orientalist paintings:

> Only on the brink of destruction, in the course of incipient modifica-
> tion and cultural dilution, are customs, costumes and religious ritu-
> als of the dominated finally *seen* as picturesque. Reinterpreted as the
> precious remnants of disappearing ways of life, worth hunting down
> and preserving, they are finally transformed into subjects of esthetic
> delectation in an imagery in which exotic human beings are integrated
> within a presumably defining and overtly limiting décor.[18]

The dialectical relationship between the "rise" and "fall" of world
powers manifests here, Nochlin suggests, in the reinterpretation of
a previously perceived threat to a quaint culture "worth preserving."
From the perspective of colonialist France, the formerly threatening
images of Ottoman rule (such as the brutal despot and his harem)
shifted, engendering a shift in representational boundaries of power.
Contrary to imperial expansion, which incorporated conquered territories into the purview of the Empire, the project of colonialism
functioned according to a clearer demarcation between colonizing
nation-state and conquered colony. Given this shift, it is not surprising that the harem emerged as a salient metaphor for colonialist relations of power.

The very notion of the harem as an inaccessible, mysterious space
for the colonial power gave rise to hegemonic misconceptions, based
on the European preoccupation with the "imagined plurality"[19]
of the harem as an excessive space of sexual indulgence. Indeed,
French representations of the harem reveal a concern not only with
the idea of the unlimited power of the sultan master (as opposed to
the notion of the nation-state as limited and sovereign[20]), but also,
more significantly, with colonialists' imaginative projections of what

might be going on inside, as outsiders were denied access. In fact, the English definition of the word harem primarily understands it in terms of the prohibition that the Eastern patriarch delivers to outside or foreign men. The *Oxford English Dictionary* defines it as "prohibited or unlawful, that which a man defends and fights for, as his family, a sacred place, sanctuary, enclosure; the women's part of the house."[21] The closest definition to that of the Arabic word, *hariim*—the women's part of the house—comes at the very end of the English definition, as if an afterthought. In the minds of the colonizers, the harem emerged as a symbolic representation of the contest for power between Ottoman and European forces. As such, the French attributed great meaning to the walls of the harem, confronting them as the tangible representative barriers to outside access. The term seraglio, specifically coined to refer to a Turkish harem, exhibits such a concern with boundaries. On the basis of both the Italian word *serare*, meaning to lock up or close, and the Turkish word *serai*, meaning lodging or place, seraglio focuses specifically on the confinement of harem women. The primarily western definition of a harem, then, is a space of enclosure "in which the women are secluded." A subsequent definition even metaphorically relates it to a prison, calling the inhabitants "inmates."[22]

The structure of the harem therefore articulates something about the development and deployment of French colonial power and possession; it symbolically reiterates the oppositional relationship between French colonial and Ottoman imperial powers and, in doing so, establishes a construct by which France gains self-definition through the image of an atavistic other. The European concept and subsequent representations of harems can thus be seen as "nodal points around which groups within colonizing and colonized cultures can formulate different and related hegemonic relations."[23] In relation to French orientalist paintings, representations of harems serve as highly determined nodal points for French expression of the power of penetration. In many ways, the French orientalist infatuation with representing scenes from the interior of the harem belies an underlying desire to render the absolute barrier of the harem wall penetrable and thereby demonstrate French ability to render Arab womanhood conquerable.

The actual conditions of the harem in both the Turkish and the larger Middle Eastern (Arab) contexts are more closely approximated by the definition of the Arabic word *hariim*, which denotes a sacred or forbidden space and stems from the same etymological root as the word for respect, *ihtiraam*. It refers to the inviolable part of the house reserved solely for women and to which men must gain permission prior to entering. Rather than functioning as the holding grounds for the absolute patriarch's licentious passions and power games, the harem more closely resembles, as Leila Ahmed argues,

> a system whereby the female relatives of a man—wives, sisters, mother, aunts, daughters—share much of their time and their living space, and further, which enables women to have frequent and easy access to other women in their community.[24]

The harem therefore serves as both a site for communication and exchange reserved solely for women and a space from which they can critically analyze the world of men.[25] However, French orientalist representations wholly ignore this definition because of their particular interest in rendering the "imagined plurality" of Turkish harems and baths visible and accessible to French eyes.

The scenes of decadence and revelry represented (just by virtue of the sheer number of women pictured) in such works as Ingres's *The Turkish Bath* and Gérôme's *The Great Bath at Bursa* could only have existed for an extremely small, elite, and wealthy segment of the population, namely the Ottoman sultan himself. Moreover, even in cases where the sultan did take a number of wives and concubines, the space of the harem was not a place of isolation and exclusion for women as if it were a private prison or brothel (as the bath scenes would seem to suggest). Because the power dimension in Ottoman society was more horizontal than vertical, Leslie Peirce suggests that the innermost portion of the Ottoman Empire (i.e., the sultan's harem) is the site of greatest leverage, since "instead of moving *up*, one moves *in* toward greater authority."[26] Therefore, even in the extremely rare cases in which one man had many wives, women in the harem were not ineffectual harem slaves but rather influential members of the community. Indeed, Peirce argues that "the matriarchal elders had considerable authority not only over other women but also over younger males in the family" and that "visiting rituals provided women with information and sources of power useful to their male relatives."[27]

Given these details, it is curious that women in orientalist paintings are overwhelmingly pictured in passive positions, are frequently nude, and seem to have little purpose other than as subjects of the observer's gaze. Clearly, these French representations are only concerned with the "reality" of Middle Eastern or Ottoman life to the extent it can provide an imaginative and projected backdrop on which to map French concerns. "The Orientalist artist tries to conceal his art, insisting on a plethora of details which authenticate the total visual field as a simple, artless reflection of a supposed Oriental reality."[28] The French orientalist obsession with authenticity, then, stands in for and elides an ethical commitment to understanding and presenting the complex historical realities and conditions of the East. The apparent interest in accurately representing the Orient and its people actually reflects a French desire to obscure the very real conditions of colonialism that allowed France the luxury of creating and disseminating such images of the East in the first place.

PAINTING THE HAREM
(DELACROIX, INGRES, AND GÉRÔME)

Representations of harems appeared abundantly in both Britain and France during the eighteenth and nineteenth centuries. They were so dominant, Edward Said claims, that they produced their own internal set of references, each often predicated on a "quotation" of another.[29] The orientalist genre in nineteenth-century France encompasses at least three distinctive, and sometimes conflicting, schools of art. Even so, three of the most celebrated French orientalist artists, Eugène Delacroix, Jean-Auguste-Dominique Ingres, and Jean-Léon Gérôme, who utilized the styles and techniques of Romanticism, Neoclassicism, and Realism, respectively, found themselves more bound by their similarities of subject matter than divided by their profound artistic differences. Most notably, they repeatedly represent "oriental" women (sometimes Arab as in Delacroix's *Women of Algiers in Their Apartment* and sometimes Turkish as in Ingres's *The Turkish Bath*) in the familiar site of the harem. Although these representations are by no means identical (Delacroix's *Women* are dressed in "authentic" oriental garb while Ingres's women are nude), the painters both utilize figures of Arab womanhood as a common trope or form through which to engage with the epistemological concerns of the time period in which they were painting.

Certainly there are plenty of ways Delacroix, Ingres, and Gérôme can be contrasted due to their conflicting styles: As a Romantic painter, Delacroix displayed intense colors, using them to imaginatively project embellished, re-created memories of the Middle East. Rather than reveling in the complexity of color, as a Neoclassicist, Ingres paid uncommon attention to line, producing a fluid linearity. For this reason, he consistently returned to the subject of the female nude, a figure deeply entrenched in a long legacy of artistic tradition. Meanwhile, Gérôme, a documentary Realist, sought to re-create his subjects in perfect likeness so that they were "scientific in their exactitude."[30] Although Gérôme is somewhat similar to Ingres in terms of his reverence for the classical form (he also concentrated quite extensively on the nude figure), he differs from both Ingres and Delacroix in his unwavering quest to produce, or rather reproduce, his subject in an objective and detached manner. However, despite these distinctions between the three artists, their manipulations of the orientalist genre are quite similar. For all of them, aspects of the Orient, and figures of Arab womanhood in particular, serve as pictorial foils through which to explore their own concerns with tradition and timelessness.

The "Forbidden Glimpse"

Eugène Delacroix's investment in the Orient as the backdrop for his Romantic masterpieces implies that he saw the region and its inhabitants as a "project of the imagination"[31] rather than an independent culture deeply entrenched in its own philosophical traditions and historical realities.[32] The French occupation of Algeria in 1830 deeply influenced his understanding of the region. The colonial project not only enabled him to visit the exotic and distant lands he had previously experienced through the filter of fantasy but also changed the nature of what he had known as the Ottoman East. Though the decline of the Ottoman Empire began in the late 1600s (according to dominant narratives), the colonization of Middle Eastern territory succeeded in disintegrating the physical and spatial boundaries that had previously precluded ordinary French citizens from having any sort of intimate knowledge about the area. In 1832, Delacroix traveled to Algeria and Morocco for a six-month visit, which presumably offered him the opportunity to gain experiential knowledge of the "real" Middle East.[33] However, even after this visit, his artistic perspective still determined his understanding of the region. Because he traveled with the expectation that he would find artistic inspiration, his "project of the imagination"[34] did not demand a complex understanding of the Orient as a site of dynamic cultures. Instead, it required a set of stable and potent orientalist signifiers, with which he could create his own meaning, as implied by Donald Rosenthal, who explains that "he never felt the need to repeat his brief voyage, for the hold it retained on his imagination did not weaken."[35] Indeed, Delacroix's imagination created the subject matter for his work, while fragmented memories of the Middle East provided the tools with which to explore his passion for representing the beauty and grandeur of nature in a (French) world increasingly engaged with industrial and technological advances.

The Middle East particularly appealed to Delacroix because he perceived it to be untouched by the continuously progressing blade of modernization, which contributed to the effacement of a pristine environment. For him, native Arabs embodied this purity of "Nature." In his journal he writes:

> They are closer to nature in a thousand ways: their dress, the form of their shoes. And so beauty has a share in everything that they make. As for us, in our corsets, our tight shoes, our ridiculous pinching shoes, we are pitiful. The graces exact vengeance for our science.[36]

Delacroix's Romantic disposition, buttressed by the authority of the colonial project, framed his "Enlightened" perception of the Middle East as an innocent space only penetrable by a more knowing gaze.

The ultimate manifestation of this knowing gaze appears in his famous painting *Women of Algiers in Their Apartment* (1834). Though he was not the only orientalist painter to travel to the Middle East (Gérôme made seven visits over a period of twenty-three years), his trip is notable in that it provided "raw" material (recorded in his journal) that would inform his work for the rest of his career. He traveled to North Africa in 1832 and spent six months in Morocco, the only Arab state to have escaped Turkish domination. Despite his long stay in Morocco, it was his brief three-day visit to the newly colonized Algeria that determined one of his most famous representations of a harem, as it was during this time he is said to have convinced a man to let him peek into his harem.[37] The representation that emerged from this "peek," *Women of Algiers*, therefore represents a very particular European vision of a harem, especially considering the complex power dynamics of colonization that facilitated Delacroix's access to the scene. Nevertheless, because Delacroix experienced an "actual" sighting of a harem, *Women of Algiers* is often lauded for its authenticity and ethnic realism. Although this image is admittedly more dedicated than some to an accurate representation of the ethnic and cultural details of the Algerian women pictured in it (they are clothed and sit in a semicircle as if to engage in conversation), it cannot help but fall short of capturing the complexity of the scene. This shortcoming is not surprising in light of the fact that Delacroix created the masterpiece once he was safely settled back in France and therefore relied on both his memory of the "peek" and his Romantic imagination to lend authority to the accuracy of the image.

Not only does *Women of Algiers* present an image of the Orient but it also participates in the creation of a European understanding of the authentic Middle East, evidenced by the following observation on the part of Jean-Auguste Renoir, a later admirer of Delacroix:

> By nature, obviously, I incline to Delacroix...The *Women of Algiers*—it's the most beautiful painting in the world...Its women are really Oriental...the one who has a rose in her hair...And the negress! She really moves like a negress! That painting savours of seraglio incense: when I am in front of it, I imagine I'm in Algiers.[38]

Renoir's claim that Delacroix's women are "really Oriental" and that the black female servant "really moves like a negress" points toward his epistemological bias, shared by Delacroix, that a pictorial image, filtered through the ideological lens of the painter, can present an unmediated picture of "real" Middle Eastern life.

Furthermore, Delacroix himself utilizes re-created fragments of the Orient as prisms through which to engage with his own philosophical predilection toward truth. As he notes in his journal:

> I didn't begin to do anything passable in my trip to Africa until the moment when I had sufficiently forgotten small details, and so remembered the striking and poetic side of things for my pictures; up to that point, I was pursued by the love of exactitude, which the majority of people mistake for truth.[39]

Here, Delacroix reveals his goal is not to produce a documentary-style realist painting of the Middle East (North Africa). His version of truth is not to be found in a conservative replica of an actual scene, but must be realized from within, sparked and catalyzed by the epiphanic impression and recollection of the moment he laid eyes on that scene. Therefore, his purportedly authentic representation of the Algerian women in their harem is instead undeniably self-referential. He owes much of this philosophy to the influence of Michelangelo and Rubens, both of whom he writes about extensively in his journal. From Michelangelo, he adopts the notion that artists utilize aspects of nature (keeping in mind that, for Delacroix, the people of the Orient are representative of nature) by which to reveal their own ideas about truth and beauty. From Rubens, he adopts the theory that, while it is crucial for artists to understand and study their great predecessors, they must not blindly imitate the masters, but rather use them as templates for reinterpretation. Both philosophies guided Delacroix's predilection to reinterpret his subject(s). As demonstrated by the above journal entry, Delacroix could not access his own artistic vision until he let go of the "small details" of the Middle East he visited.

Despite *Women of Algiers*'s claim to authenticity, then, the way it is framed serves to further absent the women it pretends to "see" or represent. The unrepresented details of the painting are the very circumstances by which Delacroix was able to obtain his view of the women. He achieved access first to Algeria by means of the French colonial project and gained entry into the private quarters of an Algerian household by means of the status afforded him as a colonizer. Therefore, the scene he presents is one gained by double penetration. In this way, the most striking absence in the painting is the "presence that is always an absence: the Western colonial or touristic presence."[40] In her article "A Forbidden Glimpse," Algerian novelist Assia Djebar points out that "the painting itself is a stolen glance."[41] In other words, while the painting announces itself to be intently focused on the three women themselves, it can instead more accurately be described as a representation of the new perspective gained by colonial forces. The image is not about Algerian women; rather, it is proof of Delacroix's ability to gain access to them. As Djebar puts it:

> There is no way for us to probe the souls of these dolorous women who seem as though they are drowned in their surroundings. They seem to live at another level, *absent* from themselves, from their bodies, from their sensuality, from their happiness.[42]

These women are "drowned in their surroundings," as Djebar says, because Delacroix is more fixed on the symbolic representation of the harem, of which the women are representative members. His attention to the artistic details of the water pipe, the carefully rendered ethnic clothing of the women, the ornateness of the oriental rugs on which they sit, and the faux Arabic calligraphy on the wall behind them, do not actually provide evidence of the authenticity or accuracy of his painting. Instead, they indicate, again, his engagement in the project of codifying an authentic way of life, one exemplified by the harem women because of his assumption that they are more primitive and therefore closer to nature. The details of their painstakingly represented "enclosure" are further highlighted by the image of the black female servant, whom Delacroix locates toward the outer frame of the painting, rendering her in an exaggerated posture as she squeezes by the women on her way out the door. That the black female servant does not seem to register as one of the "women of Algiers" mentioned in the title of the painting emphasizes the complex racial hierarchies embedded in the painting, where non-white women serve as signifiers through which French white womanhood is defined (more on this below). Here, the discourse of the harem utilizes "female incarceration as a regulative psychobiography"[43] for assuaging French anxieties about gender and domesticity. Not only did the concept of the harem, perceived in the West as a backward Eastern custom, reinforce French notions of colonization as a "civilizing" mission, it also solidified the idea that French women enjoyed more liberties than their Middle Eastern sisters. The trope of the harem as a site of female incarceration buttressed the argument that European women were at least freer than oriental harem slaves, even if that freedom was circumscribed by the boundaries of the bourgeois European home.[44]

Finally, the *Women of Algiers* seem to be "absent from themselves," as Djebar asserts, because they are frozen in the static dimension of Delacroix's original glance. They are ultimately removed from the circumstances in which they were first perceived and relegated to a "world of timeless, atemporal customs and rituals, untouched by the historical processes that were 'afflicting' or 'improving' but, at any rate, drastically altering Western societies at the time."[45] In other words, these representations of Arab womanhood served as emblems and assurances of the stability and perseverance of a timeless ideal in the midst of rapid social change.

Present Only in the Props

Delacroix's contemporaneous rival was Jean-Auguste-Dominique Ingres, a Neoclassical painter famous for his development of the female nude figure. Although Ingres also proved to be extremely influential in the orientalist genre, he never actually visited the Middle East. Nevertheless, he capitalized on stereotypical notions of the region as an exotic locale in which to set his own studies of the female nude. One of his later representations, his masterpiece *The Turkish Bath* (1862), blatantly references the European image of the "imagined plurality" of the harem or bath. The painting is reported to derive its authority from the fact that Ingres read the travel diaries of Lady Mary Wortley Montagu, a British woman married to the ambassador to Constantinople.[46] Because she had access to the inviolable spaces of the harem and bath by virtue of her gender, her accounts of these spaces would have been particularly invaluable to Ingres. However, rather than reflecting her observations, Ingres's painting displays the opposite. While Montagu describes the women's relationships to each other by writing, "there was not the least wanton smile or immodest

gesture among them,"[47] one need not look further than the two
women cradling each other in the lower right-hand corner of Ingres's
painting to witness the type of gesture that would have seemed
"immodest" to a nineteenth-century European audience. Montagu
also writes about the bath as a space of lively activity and exchange
among the community of women "in different postures, some in
conversation, some working, other drinking coffee or sherbet."[48] In
comparison, Ingres paints his women languishing listlessly on pillows
or cushions, seeming to revel in the ecstasy of their own decadent
passivity. In fact, the only part of Montagu's description that Ingres
seems to have valued is her description of the classical beauty of the
women she encountered: "They walked and moved with the same
majestic grace which Milton describes of our general mother. There
were amongst them as exactly proportioned as ever any goddess was
drawn by the pencil of Guido or Titian."[49] Indeed, *The Turkish Bath*
more closely resembles an excruciatingly well-planned homage to the
artistic tradition of the female nude figure in western art. Yet while
Guido and Titian utilized allegorical and mythological themes to justify the eroticism of their scenes, Ingres capitalized on predominant
western European preconceptions about the spaces of the harem and
the bath as bastions of licentiousness in order to frame, and thus justify, his own study of the white European female body.

The Turkish Bath is not meant to serve as the likeness of the Turkish
or Arab custom. Instead, because of the restricted Victorian social
mores of the time, it functions as a socially acceptable means by which
Ingres could display his own creative additions to the tradition of the
female nude. Furthermore, that the painting is framed in circular form
suggests his "construction of the picture as a peephole view onto a
zone forbidden male access."[50] Like Delacroix's *Women of Algiers*,
The Turkish Bath does not represent Turkish or Arab women, but
rather the assurance of western European accessibility to them.

Ingres's first posterior nude, *The Valpinçon Bather* (1808), is vir-
tually the same figure foregrounded in *The Turkish Bath* (first completed in 1830). Almost every element of the central figure is identical
to the *Bather*, including her head-wrap, as if Ingres had been looking
for a place to display her in the twenty-two years that separated the two
representations.[51] The similarity of the two images, coupled with the fact
that Ingres could not have had access to a bath (even if he had visited
the Middle East) suggests that his nudes are not only modeled after
the European nudes that came before, they *are* the same nudes. The
representation of Arab and Turkish womanhood, then, exists only in
the props of the scene—in the setting, the adornments, and the coffee

cups and trays. It is therefore clear that Ingres's Turkish women are, in fact, vessels upon which his reverence for the classical artistic tradition is mapped.

Ingres's *The Grand Odalisque* (1814), perhaps his most well known piece, also demonstrates the French understanding of the Orient as a site of wanton and licentious female sexuality. *The Grand Odalisque* is considered a "rival to the reclining female nudes of Gorgione and Titian, or Goya and Manet." However, Ingres's painting is distinguished from its predecessors in that it "proposes an imagined East, rather than classical myth or modern life, as the preferred *location* for studying the female form."[52] A complex understanding of this famous painting depends not only on the ability to locate the piece within the trajectory of its predecessors and rivals but also on knowledge of the established nude tradition, to which it contributes. The trajectory of the nude tradition in western European art spans at least 500 years; consequently it has utilized different settings and locations for nude representations within varied historical and social contexts. While earlier artists such as Titian and Gorgione used mythological or allegorical tropes to justify the representation and display of the naked female form, the modern artist Manet painted his reclining nude, *Olympia*, as a prostitute because an upper-class European woman could never have been represented nude according to the mores of the time. To be sure, it was shocking that a prostitute be represented to an elite French audience, but her nudity explained her licentious profession. As Sander Gilman notes, "In the nineteenth century, the prostitute is perceived as the essential sexualized female."[53] Ingres's odalisque draws upon an exoticized setting to validate his representation of "the sinuous arabesque line which stamped this figure with extraordinary beauty."[54] Again the woman's body adheres to European aesthetic standards while the props and setting validate the erotic scene. This becomes even clearer upon examining the phases of the image. Ingres first painted the figure itself, a traditional European nude, and then added the props: the fan in her hand, the turban, and the water pipe. These adornments, then, signify the sensuality of the orientalist scene in order to give Ingres erotic license. These markers of Arab womanhood attest to the fact that *The Grand Odalisque* disallows a fullness of Arab female presence. Rather than a presentation of its complexity, the figure of Arab female sexuality is appropriated as a canvas upon which Ingres can make his own indelible mark.

The Grand Odalisque, reminiscent of French Manneristic painting of the sixteenth Century,[55] was heavily influenced by Titian's reclining nude.[56] In fact, Ingres painted a copy of Titian's *Venus of Urbino* in 1822.[57] Given Ingres's consistent efforts to represent sensuality by his attention to linearity in his paintings, it is not surprising that *Venus of Urbino* had such a hold on him as it "reveals the transition from serene contemplation of female beauty to intense sensuousness."[58] It also serves as a model for Ingres's odalisque in that it presents the reclining nude in a bed (rather than in nature) gazing seductively back at the viewer. That Titian's *Venus of Urbino*, painted in 1538, and Ingres's *The Grand Odalisque*, painted in 1814 (and redone many more times), can be considered two different incarnations of the same figure reveals much about the nude tradition. Although the settings and adornments in such paintings change over time, the nude seems to transcend context, emerging as a timeless and ahistorical figure. Ingres's interpretation of the reclining nude extends the stamp of timelessness to its exotic orientalist subject, who is denied presence and historicity, and is instead frozen into the static dimension of timelessness and tradition.

Authenticity Revisited

The representations of Jean-Léon Gérôme, the famous French orientalist whose *Snake Charmer* graces the cover of Edward Said's *Orientalism*, are generally categorized as Realist or "documentary"—an indication of his claim to authenticity. In fact, he visited the Middle East seven times and employed photography as a means of recreating his scenes in apparently accurate detail. Yet for all his attention to minutiae, Gérôme's representations still manage to elide a complicated presentation of the very real circumstances that determined the scenes pictured. As Linda Nochlin claims:

> A "naturalist" or "authenticist" artist like Gérôme tries to make us forget that his art is really art, both by concealing the evidence of his touch, and, at the same time, by insisting on a plethora of authenticating details, especially on what might be called unnecessary ones.[59]

These details are meant to stamp the image with detached objectivity while simultaneously obscuring the reality of Gérôme's orientalist perspective that actually frames the scene.

Gérôme's *The Great Bath at Bursa* (1885), for example, supposedly presents a precise "documentary" portrayal of the ornate architecture and structure inside of a Turkish bath. Like in Ingres's *Turkish Bath*, Gérôme here seeks to represent a "real" view of a bath's interior. Given Gérôme's predilection toward "dispassionate empiricism,"[60] however, one might expect his representation to more closely reflect

Lady Mary Wortley Montagu's suggestion that the bath functions as "the women's coffee-house, where all the news of the town is told"[61] by displaying scenes of women engaged in activity and communication. Instead, the women in the painting much more closely resemble nude female figures from the western art tradition. The white female nudes populating the scene engage in the familiar (imagined) activities of oriental decadence: some smoke the water pipe, some relax on an oriental rug, and others simply repose in seemingly distracted reverie.

In contrast, the scene's black female figures mainly engage in active tasks and seem to serve as either a support to the centralized posterior nude or as caretaker of a small white child. Gérôme's inclusion of the black female servant not only reflects the way in which nineteenth-century painters utilized racial hierarchies to make powerful statements about the predominant aesthetic ideal, but also highlights the social processes (such as colonialism) that helped determine such representations. The black female figure, then, is not presented for the sake of Realist accuracy; rather, it is a means of establishing a symbolic artistic contrast between black and white. A mid-nineteenth-century artistic manual claims: "White is the emblem of harmony; / Black is the emblem of chaos. / White signifies supreme beauty; / Black ugliness. / White signifies perfection; / Black signifies vice. / White is the symbol of innocence, / Black that of guilt, sin, and moral degradation."[62] Such contrasts, imbued with the racist ideological biases of nineteenth-century thought, actually serve as potent markers of an orientalist perspective that understands the harem to be a space of sexual abandon:

> In an established western visual arts tradition, the representation of a black servant served to sexualize the setting. By the mid-nineteenth century, scientific discourse associated the sexual appetite of the black woman with lesbian sexuality. This association was further enhanced by the belief, commonly held by western audiences and fostered by numerous European travel accounts, that lesbian relationships occurred in the women's baths.[63]

The unstated assumption in the above claim is that lesbianism, as a "deviant" form of sexuality, is hypersexualized, and implies the conflation of lesbian sexuality, black female sexuality, and Turkish/Arab sexuality as markers of licentiousness. In this way, Gérôme's *Great Bath at Bursa* is not an accurate and artless re-presentation of an aspect of Middle Eastern life; it is a highly determined orientalist scene fabricated by the painter to provide a space to display his interpretation of artistic tradition in the figure of the female nude.

Another of Gérôme's paintings, *Moorish Bath* (1870), further reveals how the artist employs racial hierarchies to encode his Realist images with orientalist ideology. The painting, also titled *Lady of Cairo Bathing*, immediately establishes an exotic setting for the image, yet even the briefest of glances highlights the extreme juxtaposition of black and white bodies at the foot of the bath. This symbolic contrast points not to the documentary reality of the scene, but to the way the image is infused with political concerns. "If nothing else, the maid indicates the status of her mistress, which is always a notch above her own...and inevitably points to the colonial enterprises of the Second Empire."[64] Although Gérôme's photographs may have reinforced his memory enough for him to re-create the decorative detail of the tile, his representation of the two women is unquestionably drawn from a set of cultural assumptions—reinforced by an established western art tradition—that reads the black female body as a marker that can sexualize the setting. "By the eighteenth century, the sexuality of the black, both male and female, becomes an icon for deviant sexuality in general; as we have seen, the black figure appears almost always paired with a white figure."[65] The fact that the black female servant leans down to bathe the white woman's back serves to further eroticize the scene. As for the white woman, she is not based on a photograph or even a viewing of a "real" Middle Eastern woman, but, according to Roger Benjamin, on a European model. He writes "the white models, who were in fact French, are soft and pliant and representative of a pampered, leisured class."[66] Again, the purportedly represented Arab woman actually serves as a vessel through which Gérôme's racialized interpretation of a classical artistic form may be presented.

What remains consistent across the representations of Ingres, Delacroix, and Gérôme is the presence of orientalist materials and settings to justify the eroticized subject material. Therefore, it seems likely that during the orientalist era, characterized as it was by the social processes of colonialism and modernization, Arab women's bodies—fragmented into orientalist props—emerged as salient canvases upon which a variety of artistic modes and styles could be mapped. The power of these images derives from the very ahistoricism to which they lay claim. Upon close examination of the western art tradition supporting the orientalist genre, it is apparent that the orientalist representations of the Middle East do not strive to accurately portray an area of the world, but instead utilize a specific colonized location, coupled with colonialist racial hierarchies, in order to project western fantasies and concerns onto an exoticized landscape. That each of the three painters presented literally imported figures from other generations of painting and inserted them into the represented culture's context creates a cultural as well as representational timelessness that ultimately robs those represented of their presence in a specific space and time.

On the other hand, they reveal a great deal about the particularities of the culture creating the representations. As Sander Gilman has argued, "images are the product of history and of a culture that perpetuates them. None is random; none is isolated from the historical context."[67] Moreover, no image is isolated from the complicated network of power dynamics that determine the conditions of its creation. The final painting I examine in this section, Gérôme's *Dance of the Almeh*, also called *The Belly-Dancer* (1863), demonstrates how the painter embedded these complex concerns with power into the fabric of even the most "exactly observed"[68] representations.

Despite its title, *Dance of the Almeh* focuses more on the harem and its symbolic import than on the slightly off-center figure of the belly dancer. Although belly dancing increasingly drew the interest of French citizens because of its prominence in French world's fairs in the latter part of the nineteenth century, it was still principally understood as a practice that took place behind the locked doors of the harem, away from a penetrating western male gaze. Therefore, this image, like Delacroix's *Women of Algiers*, is as much a representation of the female performer as it is pictorial evidence of the French colonial power's gained access to the scene.

However, Gérôme's painting reifies one final act of colonial transgression. Not only has the western man gained access to the harem, he does so despite the presence of Middle Eastern men, thereby highlighting their inferiority. Perhaps because westerners perceived belly dancing as one of the secret pleasures of the harem master (rather than a dance that women performed amongst themselves), Gérôme presents it as an activity, oozing with erotic sensuality, performed for an audience of male spectators. The dancer's dress, "harem" pants and a transparent halter-top ensure that her body is sufficiently revealed and that her breasts and nipples are entirely visible. In addition, her head lolls and her eyes roll back in an expression of apparent ecstasy. It seems she derives pleasure from being watched; however, her harem audience looks on with distracted interest. Recalling the English definition of the word harem as that space a man "defends and fights for," the ultimate presence of the colonial gaze here renders the Arab male presence powerless and ineffectual. As Nochlin asserts, "Gérôme's Orientalist painting managed to body forth two ideological assumptions about power: one about men's power over women; the other about white men's superiority to, hence justifiable control over, inferior, darker races."[69] In this case, the figure of Arab womanhood stands in as a complex marker of the highly determined power relations in the colonial context. Moreover, the image of the harem (and the odalisques and belly dancers that go in them) serves as a metaphor through which the apparatus of orientalism functions to shore up French notions of liberty through "civilizing" colonialism.

THE POWER AND PULL OF
INVISIBLE PRESENCE

Despite the consistent elision of Middle Eastern realities in French orientalist painting, the bodies of Arab women and the concomitant ideas about Arab womanhood are not completely effaced. On the contrary, they are undeniably present and full of meaning in that they occupy the space of the colonial project. In other words, the particular histories and contexts to which these figures of Arab womanhood belong—the activities they might undertake in the inviolable space of the harem, or, what Barthes might call their *meaning*—is appropriated by myth and turned into form:

> The meaning is *already* complete, it postulates a kind of knowledge, a past, a memory, a comparative order of facts, ideas, decisions. When it becomes form, the meaning leaves its contingency behind; it empties itself, it becomes impoverished, history evaporates, only the letter remains.[70]

The possible meanings of Arab womanhood rooted in the lives of the women Delacroix purports to represent in his *Women of Algiers*, for example, have not disappeared; rather, they have lost their "contingency" in time and space and have become a disconnected (and therefore empty) form. This form, in turn, is refilled and imbued with the import of a whole new concept: "Through the concept, it is a whole new history which is implanted in the myth."[71] This "new history" that filters into the representations of the harem is none other than the history and narrative of the French colonial culture creating the images in the first place.

Therefore, the concept of Arab womanhood is "empty but present" with regard to form and "absent but full" with regard to meaning.[72] Because it is clearly present as form, it follows that it is visible, at least at the most surface level. However, it is the fullness of a contextualized meaning that is absent, consequently yielding a representation of Arab womanhood that Barthes calls a perceptible absence: "The function of myth is to empty reality: it is, literally, a ceaseless flowing out, a haemorrhage, or perhaps an evaporation, in short a perceptible absence."[73] In other words, the cultural mythology of the harem acts as a placeholder for the constellation of social processes—such as industrialization, colonization, and emerging forms of nationalism—that allow it to be appropriated in the first place. The "new history" that rushes in to permeate depictions of the harem is the history, first, of a colonial project that has achieved a level of domination enabling it to represent others. Second, it is the history of the process of industrialization that has produced technologies allowing the colonizer to access and dominate the region.

Furthermore, these obscured power relations converge upon representations of Arab womanhood, rendering them authentic or "real" and suggesting that they arise out of nature rather than out of history. This concept of authenticity locks images of Arab women into a closed system of representation. Figures of Arab womanhood are thus reduced to a stabilized form, making them ripe for co-optation. Following this figure now to the U.S. context, I am interested in exploring the similar function that such orientalized figures have played in the French colonial and U.S. expansionist contexts. Because citationality is a major feature of the orientalist apparatus, the French colonial context also provides a comparative example for U.S. representations of reclining odalisques and anglicized female figures bearing the marks of ethnicity in orientalized props.

PAINTING PROGRESS

French orientalist images of the secluded harem slave and contemporary U.S. representations of the silent and oppressed veiled woman notwithstanding, images of Arab womanhood in western Europe and the United States have not always been understood through the filter of perceptible absence. Take the case of the belly dancer, an image known in both France and the United States: through this mythology, Arab women have been figured as hyper-visible, potent markers of the exotic other. Indeed, the myriad variations that exist in representations of Arab female sexuality throughout at least two centuries of western European and U.S. images testify to the heterologic nature of orientalism. Yet despite the obvious differences in the cultural mythologies of the veil, the harem, and the belly dancer, the fact that they continuously reappear across a wide array of sociohistorical contexts implies that they function in tandem within a closed system of representation. In this way, the seemingly diverse images of veiled women, reclining odalisques, and belly dancers have actually remained static and stable signifiers of both the exoticism and the invisibility of Arab women, suggesting a similar structural foundation for all three mythologies.

Because it is my ultimate claim that the figures of Arab womanhood in French orientalist painting and the representations of Arab female sexuality in U.S. popular culture are predicated upon similar frameworks, here I discuss the moments of overlap and connection between the two systems of representation. Since the images traversed the time and space that separates turn-of-the-century United States from nineteenth-century France, I utilize Said's "Traveling Theory" as a tool by which to theorize the movement of these types of representations of Arab womanhood. In particular, I expand on his theoretical foundation, applying it to four distinct stages of the transition of orientalist imagery from France to the United States. Said specifies the four stages of traveling theory as a set of initial circumstances (here orientalist France), a distance through which the images have traveled (in this case, from nineteenth-century France to turn-of-the-century United States), the conditions of acceptance and resistance that shaped the representations (in the U.S. context), and the transformation of these images in their new contextual location.

The field of French orientalist painting provides a point of reference for this study; I utilize it as "a point of origin, or what seems like one, a set of initial circumstances in which the idea came to birth or entered discourse."[74] Although I do not suggest that the French colonialist context is the site of the genesis of European images of Arab womanhood, Said's notion is applicable in that it is an arena in which a particularly salient set of factors coalesced to produce an undeniably influential series of representations. French preoccupations with power and possession in an unsettling and chaotic period of colonialism and modernization manifested themselves in highly structured representations of the harem. As I have argued, French orientalist images of the harem were, in some ways, organized around the harem walls that were presumably meant to seal the colonizers out. The very act of making these barriers visible, then, was a potent commentary on the shifting stakes of power between colonialist France and its imperial predecessor, the Ottoman Empire. Furthermore, the representative figures inside the harem functioned as receptacles for French anxieties and fears that had surfaced in response to profound structural changes provoked by the social processes of modernization and colonialism. While the colonial project had drastically altered predominant perceptions of spatial distance by bringing into sharp focus the now not-so-distant colonies, modernization radically shifted the common understanding of time and historicity as people felt themselves bound to the unyielding track of a linear notion of progress fundamentally detached from a familiar notion of the past. The bodies of Arab women, cast as harem slaves, were one location upon which nostalgic yearnings for this lost and distant past were consistently mapped.

In the turn-of-the-century United States, Arab women's bodies continued to function as nostalgic foils for a progress-bound society. Yet the particularities of this orientation toward Arab womanhood had been altered in the "distance transversed" from one spatial and temporal context to another; during its "passage through the pressure of various contexts,"[75] the representations underwent a metamorphosis. Said's metaphor suggests an implied physics to the process: the pressure of moving through different contexts causes a permutation of the image. In this case, the figure of Arab womanhood transforms from one of invisible presence to the hyper-visible and exoticized belly dancer. Because the figure of the belly dancer plays such a large role in the U.S. context, particularly at the site of the Chicago World's Fair, I spend the next chapter focusing on this figure. For the remainder of this chapter, however, I focus on the Fine Arts exhibit at the 1893 Chicago World's Fair to flesh out how U.S. orientalism both borrows and diverges from French orientalism.

Despite the fact that the Fine Arts building housed and displayed seemingly traditional or classical works in comparison to the many novel industrial and technological displays in the transportation and manufacturing buildings, the goal of this structure was aligned with the rest of the Fair—that is, to demonstrate and measure U.S. progress in the world. Because France's Beaux-Arts tradition wielded such power within the art world at the turn of the century—demonstrated by the influence of the Paris Salons—the Chicago World's Fair art exhibit became a self-conscious demonstration of the ways American art had reached and even surpassed the excellence of its French predecessors. Carolyn Kinder Carr documents the politics behind the mapping of the concept of "progress" onto the Fine Arts display:

> It was no coincidence that the American pavilions were next to the French...an important purpose of the exhibit was to demonstrate that American artists were at long last capable of competing head on with this aesthetic rival—and winning the contest.[76]

In fact, the Fine Arts committee came under attack from American artists such as J.G. Brown who claimed that the members of the jury only accepted art that adhered to "French notions" of aestheticism.[77] One jury member's response demonstrates the terms of comparison that no doubt infiltrated the process of selection: "Chase was of the opinion that 'the war [is] not strife between foreign and American ways of painting, but between the good and the bad—and only incidentally between the old and the new.'"[78] This response lends transparency to the very real way these terms of comparison aligned themselves. Despite the fact that the jury supposedly chose works of art that were "good," or artistically superior, many contemporary artists felt the aesthetic guidelines were inextricably tied to "foreign" (mainly French) standards. Furthermore, "old," or classical, styles of painting were categorically held in higher esteem. It is indeed ironic that a Fine Arts display meant to showcase the "progress" of American painting shut out innovative American painters deeply invested in representing the "new" world.

It is no surprise, then, that one of the most discussed artists in the exhibition was the French-trained John Singer Sargent, who had spent most of his life abroad.[79] Although Sargent worked in a variety of styles and genres, he is most well known for his portraits. Of these, he exhibited five at the World's Fair. Because the Fine Arts committee decided to accept no more than three paintings from each individual artist, it is significant that Sargent was allowed six,[80] and it is even more notable that the majority of them were portraits. Portraiture, generally commissioned, can be understood as one means by which American artistry reconciled democratic ideals with elite attitudes toward possession, in that any individual ostensibly had access to elite status as long as s/he had the means to pay for it. In this way, the genre could operate within the myth of meritocracy while simultaneously upholding class, race, and gender-based hierarchies.[81] In the self-proclaimed land of opportunity in the late 1800s, the United States was eager to present an image of social harmony. Despite growing unrest in the labor force, evidenced by increasingly violent strikes (particularly the Haymarket Riot in 1886) and restrictive immigration laws (such as the 1882 Chinese Exclusion Act) to keep "foreign" workers from competing for "American" jobs, the fair planners preoccupied themselves with projecting an image of the status and nobility achieved by some in the new land. The inclusion of Sargent's portraits in the Fine Arts exhibit reified this dominant U.S. narrative, as they "render[ed] unabashed the sheen of what money could buy."[82]

However, it is Sargent's sixth painting in the display, *Study of an Egyptian Girl* (1891), that situates him clearly as an American orientalist painter. Although heralded as "the outstanding portrait painter of his generation,"[83] Sargent was not entirely satisfied as a portraitist. *Egyptian Girl* served as Sargent's entry into the classical art tradition of the female nude form. As such, it represented a distinct departure from portraiture, which revolved around public notions of stature and propriety. In fact, Sargent is quite well known for his transgression of such social mores with his exhibition of *Portrait de Mme ****, which later became known as *Madame X* (1884). Contrary to custom, the subject did not commission *Madame X*; rather, Sargent pursued the American-turned–French socialite Madame Pierre Gautreau for the painting.[84] His interpretation of her classical beauty, however, proved too provocative and risqué for the debut audience at the 1884 Salon in Paris. Not only did he paint her in a revealing dress, but he also represented her right shoulder strap as if it had slipped off her shoulder and was pressing into the upper part of her arm, allowing him to accentuate the contours of her muscle and skin. This bold display of flesh caused such uproar at the Salon that Sargent altered the original painting and restored the shoulder strap to its upright position.

The details of the *Madame X* scandal highlight the unspoken codes and assumptions that allowed Sargent to paint his *Egyptian Girl* completely nude. Contrary to Madame X, the "Egyptian girl" was not the subject of his painting, but rather the object upon which he mapped his interpretation of the classical female nude figure. Although Ingres did not necessarily directly influence Sargent, this particular foray into the orientalist tradition certainly references his legacy.[85] The figure's ethnicity, or the fact that she was Egyptian, was enough to assuage public discomfort at the thought of seeing a nude woman.[86] In other words, the figure was not primarily seen as a naked female body, but as the vessel by which to represent the nude form. Indeed, considering John Berger's claim that "in a lived sexual experience nakedness is a process rather than a state,"[87] one can more clearly understand the distinction between the shocking representation of *Madame X*'s nakedness (as a fluid and raw process) and the palatable artistic rendering of the *Egyptian Girl*'s nudity as a static personification of timelessness. Abstracted from the social and historical conditions of the time period, she represents the durability and stasis of a classical and revered form of painting, just as mythological figures had done in preceding centuries.

In this respect, the way the United States received the concept of Arab womanhood as it was construed in France reveals a considerable amount of overlap between the two. Nevertheless, the "conditions of acceptance or ... resistance which then confront the transplanted theory or idea"[88] also ensure that key elements of the representations had shifted from the French to the U.S. context. These divergences demonstrate the differential "pressures" that colonialism and expansionism exert on the representations, as indeed, they represent differing strategies of imperialism. Rather than dominating discrete and geographically distant colonies, for example, the U.S. garnered resources and raw materials by expanding westward across the American continent toward its "manifest destiny." In this way, the U.S. colonized territory that was cast as "virgin" land; consequently, it did not construct its burgeoning power against a specter of political power in the way France had understood its colonial rule of the Middle East as antithetical to the despotism of the "Terrible Turk." In fact, during the late 1800s in the United States, many Americans imagined the Middle East was the location of the Christian Holy Land rather than an increasingly usurped territory of the once threatening Ottoman Empire. Furthermore, mainstream narratives cast the United States as something of a Puritan "promised land," as the Pilgrims' landing and survival was credited in part to "divine action."[89] This imagined, fantastical correlation to the Holy Land was a point of departure for American orientalism that distinguished it from its French predecessor. In fact, Chauncey M. DePew's opening-day remarks at the 1893 Chicago World's Fair belie an American conceit that the United States was living testament to the evolution of Christian civilization from an ancient biblical past:

> This day belongs not to America, but to the world. The results of the event it commemorates are the heritage of the peoples of every race and clime. We celebrate the emancipation of man.... Ancient history is a dreary record of unstable civilizations.[90]

As the self-proclaimed pinnacle of civilization, the vision of U.S. empire presented at the 1893 Chicago World's Fair was as a stable and powerful heir to ancient (Christian) civilization.

FASHIONING EMPIRE THROUGH LANDSCAPE

The notion of the Holy Land proved both powerful and malleable enough to serve as a motivating metaphor for a burgeoning imperialist

U.S. nation. U.S. identification with the Holy Land enabled a sense of U.S. exceptionalism as a city on a hill,[91] an image that rejected the idea of Britain as the patrilineal "father" of the United States,[92] and promoted the notion of manifest destiny as a divine right.[93] Like in the French colonial context, the apparatus of orientalism functioned as a means of rationalizing empire. However, it operated through a different set of metaphors and images in the U.S. context, such as the notion of the Holy Land and the figure of the belly dancer (as opposed to the harem metaphor utilized in the French colonial context).

The development of U.S. imperialism was distinctly tied to land insofar as the nation grew by conquering western territories and indigenous peoples and acquiring so-called frontier land.[94] It should come as no surprise, then, that landscape paintings were quite popular in the nineteenth century, as demonstrated by the well-received Hudson River school of painters. As Albert Boime argues, landscape paintings belie imperialist U.S. designs on the territories of the Americas in that they represent the "magisterial gaze, the perspective of the American on the heights searching for new worlds to conquer."[95] Landscape paintings could simultaneously straddle twin concerns of U.S. expansionism: first, through the "magisterial gaze," they represented U.S. goals of empire; and second, through representation of the natural world, they depicted the "need to retain the pastoral fantasy to counter the capitalist hegemony [which] lies behind the drive to find new frontiers."[96] As U.S. national identity was articulated through the metaphor of the Holy Land,[97] landscape paintings of that region offer a salient introduction to the specificities of U.S. orientalism.

If Sargent's *Egyptian Girl* demonstrates the crossover of American orientalist and French orientalist themes, Sargent's other contemporaneous work—Holy Land–themed materials—reflect a distinctly U.S. articulation of orientalism. In 1890, Sargent was commissioned to paint ceiling murals for the Boston Public Library, a project with which he engaged for at least twenty-six years. His idea for the project was to "decorate opposite ends of a large hall with imagery symbolic of the Old and New Testaments."[98] In order to gain inspiration, Sargent traveled to Egypt to research Old Testament themes,[99] which is presumably where he received the inspiration for his *Egyptian Girl*. As with his subsequent trip to Syria and Palestine in 1905–6 to do research for New Testament themes, Sargent appears to have viewed the Middle East as a location where he could collect "real" specimens, artifacts, and images of biblical times to lend authority to his work. That he traveled to Egypt and the Levant in the early twentieth century for such research underscores his assumption that the space of the contemporaneous Middle East had not changed since ancient times and was somehow immune to the progression of history.

While Sargent is not primarily a Holy Land painter, his brief foray into the topic (he painted a number of "holy" landscapes during his trip to Syria and Palestine in 1905–1906) reflected the lasting impression the region had made on the nineteenth-century American consciousness.[100] The landscape of the Middle East, imagined as uninhabited and timeless, operated as a parallel fantasy of the divine right of the U.S. to conquer and usurp indigenous American territories, also imagined to be "virgin" and ahistorical.[101] This kind of imaginative parallel, in which the Americas were cast as the new "Promised Land," helped animate the narrative of expansionism as a civilizing mission. In this narrative, two modalities of civilization coalesced: the idea of the Holy Land as the origin of western civilization, combined with the notion that the United States was destined to spread this notion of civilization across the expanse of the Americas.

Though U.S. fascination with the Holy Land peaked in the latter half of the nineteenth century,[102] the notion of the Levant (New Testament) and Egypt (Old Testament) as sites of origin for western (U.S.) civilization remained salient into the nineteenth century, as evidenced by its role in world's fairs, such as the St. Louis Exposition. Indeed, the fair designers' informational pamphlet about the "Street of Cairo" on the Midway Plaisance at the 1893 Fair, offers the following comment on a U.S. understanding of Egypt:

> The all-pervading charm which everywhere surrounds the name of Egypt may be traced back to the days of our childhood, to the time when we first heard the story of Moses and of Pharaoh's daughter, of Joseph and his brethren, and the flight of the Holy Family into Egypt. It is the charm which the teaching of Biblical history has impressed upon our minds when most capable of reception, and the beauty of the impressions have made us loth [sic] to destroy them. Hence, in all that pertains to Egypt, we have more than a passing interest.[103]

This interest in Egypt, clearly mediated by an American fascination with its own religious origins, represents a self-referential interest in the Christian dimension of national American identity. In fact, the imagined Holy Land was so important to U.S. national identity that it became a prominent theme for American landscape painter Frederic Edwin Church.

Church took up an interest in the representation of the Holy Land in the late 1860s, a time when American pilgrimage to Middle Eastern Holy Land sites was at a peak. The 1860s also saw the first "real" replica of the Holy Land, entitled "Lakeside at Chautauqua," constructed on U.S. soil. Though American interest in the Holy Land clearly related to its status as a sacred site, the intense infatuation with the area also had to do with more secular notions of space and time. Because the concept of the Promised Land had immediate relevance for the construction of early American identity, popular U.S. imagination figured the U.S. as divinely connected to the Holy Land. As John Davis argues:

> [T]he Puritan colonists took pleasure in conceiving of themselves as a second "chosen people," a favoured nation selected by God to fulfill the final prophecy of the New Jerusalem, to create a shining "city upon a hill" atop the ruins of the fallen Hebrew empire.[104]

Therefore, the American "errand into the wilderness"[105] was overlaid with the ideological import of American exceptionalism. Because the U.S. landscape, or wilderness, played such a powerful role in how U.S. citizens conceptualized this errand, and because the errand was cast in scriptural and biblical terms, it should come as no surprise that American painter Church would transition seamlessly from American to Holy Land landscape paintings.

Of Church's Holy Land paintings, the most famous is *Jerusalem from the Mount of Olives (with Engraved Key)* of 1870, an apt example of the manifestation of the orientalist apparatus in nineteenth-century U.S. representations. *Jerusalem* was, in part, an extension of Church's work with the American Palestine Exploration Society (an offshoot of the British Palestine Exploration Fund) to establish an "accurate" map of Palestine. The accuracy of this map, of course, depended on British and American excavation and cataloguing of biblical sites of importance.[106] Although Church's *Engraved Key* to *Jerusalem* shows the artist's inclination to map his own interests onto the region, the painting also betrays the ideological import such representations held for the painter and his U.S. audience. Although framed as a representation of the city of Jerusalem, the image is actually a view of the city from the secluded and pristine "Mount." Therefore, the city sits in the background, foregrounded by an expansive landscape dominated by olive trees. Like other American landscape paintings, Church's depiction of the Holy Land affords its viewers what Boime calls a "magisterial gaze": it positions the viewer as surveyor, owner, and overseer of the expansive landscape. Moreover, it encourages identification with the Holy Land as a primarily pastoral and natural space. Indeed, Davis argues that Church himself identified with the olive trees, "these stately, aged behemoths (the largest forms in the entire composition), rather than with the tiny Arab figures who converse among themselves and fail to exhibit the same degree of awareness as their arboreal neighbors."[107] The painting's trees are thus endowed with a greater sense of presence than the people, leaving the impression that the space of the Holy Land is held indefinitely in biblical, natural, or ancient time, remarkably untouched by human progression.

In fact, many American travelers to the region experienced it as a liminal space and time undeniably removed from their own modern world. According to Davis, "they often experienced their Palestinian sojourn as if they were traveling into some distant, biblical past, with the contemporary Ottoman realities remaining unacknowledged and ignored."[108] This highly charged space was thus suspended in time, or rather, out of time, since it was denied the historical specificity of its contemporaneous context. Instead, the image of the Holy Land that Church and others projected onto the landscape was that of the ancient origin of (a Christian and American) western civilization. Indeed, if artists recognized the Arab natives or Turkish rulers at all, they seemed only blemishes to this grand, idealized image:

> The primary perceived defect was the economic destitution felt by the majority of its inhabitants. Notwithstanding spectacular Roman vestiges at Baalbek and Palmyra in particular, and thriving Moslem cities such as Cairo and Damascus, centuries of internecine conflict and impoverishment seemingly had reduced a historically glorious region to shadows on shifting sands.[109]

This notion of the Ottoman East as the antiquated holding grounds of ancient ruins marked a significant shift in orientalist imagery from the French to the U.S. context that would impact the construction of representations of Arab womanhood for decades to come. Not only was the space of the Middle East now understood as a sacred and ancient site, but the apparition of the threatening "Terrible Turk" that had so determined French orientalist representations was now replaced by a weak, lingering Ottoman presence that was an irritating, if ineffectual, obstacle to the sacrosanct site of the origins of western civilization.

While it is clear that an orientalist interpretation of Arab womanhood traveled from colonialist France to an imperialist U.S., it is also evident that it was "accommodated (or incorporated)" and "to some extent transformed by its new uses, its new position in a new time and place."[110] In other words, because of the different interpretations

the U.S. and France had of the Ottoman East, U.S.-based representations of Arab womanhood transformed from secluded harem
slaves into the predominantly visible and erotic signifiers of the
belly dancer (at the Chicago World's Fair and then amusement parks
around the country) and the transparently veiled woman (in tobacco
advertisements in the early 1900s). As I will discuss in further detail
in chapters 2 and 3, the potent markers of the harem walls as indicators of transgressed Ottoman barriers were conspicuously absent from
turn-of-the-century U.S. representations. As U.S. imperial interests
were mediated, in part, through the motivating metaphor of the Holy
Land as justification for American expansion, the Ottoman Empire
did not register as a threat to U.S. power. Such a dismissive attitude
toward Ottoman presence and power manifests itself in the shifting
nature of representations of Arab womanhood: suddenly, in the U.S.
context, belly dancers were liberated from the enclosed prison of the
harem and the sultan himself was reduced to a jovial and somewhat
laughable character.

Through the strategic location of the 1893 Chicago World's Fair,
I have analyzed the construction of orientalist images in both the
French and U.S. contexts to demonstrate that the system of representations of Arab womanhood functioning within the U.S. context
is reminiscent of how images of harems and odalisques operated in
a French orientalist context. Having established the groundwork for
a comparative framework, then, I now turn to a fuller consideration
of the 1893 Chicago World's Fair, through the figure of the belly
dancer (in chapter 2), through images of Arab womanhood in early-
twentieth-century tobacco advertisements (in chapter 3), and finally
through representations of Arab womanhood in the contemporary
U.S. context (in chapter 4). In each case, I argue that figures of Arab
womanhood serve as comforting symbols of timelessness and tradition in the midst of profound social change, demonstrating that what
has actually traveled from context to context is not a particular image
or stereotype about Arab women, but rather the salience of these
representations for U.S. audiences.

Chapter 2

Dancing the Hootchy Kootchy: The Rhythms and Contortions of American Orientalism

The theme of the girl's dance was love, but it was the hot, voluptuous passion of the East, not the cool, chaste sentiment of our land. Every motion of her body was towards the illustration of her drama, the languorous looks, the open lips, the waving hands, the swaying body, all told her passion.... Then, in a perfect paroxysm of undulations, in which hips, stomach and breast protruded and whirled, the girl rises on her toes and crouches in a series of wriggles towards the stage, like one in an epilepsy.

Joseph Smith, *Illustrated American*

The danse du ventre, as the movement is known, and which was executed by girls not only in the Egyptian Theatre, but also in the Persian, Turkish, and, with some modification, in the Moorish Theatres, on the Plaisance, is a suggestively lascivious contorting of the abdominal muscles, which is extremely ungraceful and almost shockingly disgusting. Curiosity prompted many to view the performance, but very few remained more than five minutes before this was fully satisfied.

James Buel, *The Magic City*

If the 1893 Chicago World's Fair serves as an exemplary site through which to trace U.S. engagement with the metanarrative of modernity, the figure of the belly dancer exemplifies the way in which the orientalist apparatus could be deployed as a strategy for negotiating the disorientations of modernity. By using the phrase "metanarrative of modernity," I am referencing the critiques that explore the universalizing, Eurocentric assumptions that are often smuggled into the notion of modernity.[1] In particular, I am interested in exploring the way in which the metanarrative of modernity operates by disavowing the colonialist and imperialist power relations in which it is rooted, and in demonstrating how the sublimated aspects of this powerful metanarrative found expression through the cultural mythology of the belly dancer. In this sense, the figure of the belly dancer serves as a construction of alterity that reinforces the Enlightenment-based presumptions built into the metanarrative of modernity, rather than as an instantiation of alternative or vernacular modernities. In other words, images of belly dancers rendered in photographic albums of the Fair serve as mythological figures through which to trace contemporaneous U.S. engagements with the disorienting processes of modernization and expansionism.

As evidenced by the commentary of Buel and Smith, both of whom wrote widely received descriptions of "that dance" from the 1893 Chicago World's Fair, popular fascination with the dancing girls at the Fair seems to be linked to their sexuality in particular. Smith's and Buel's comments focus on the "hips, stomach, and breast" or the "abdominal muscles" of the dancers rather than on the dancers themselves, demonstrating the excess of attention that U.S. audiences brought (and bring) to that particular region of the female body, which is undeniably linked to notions of female sexuality. Echoing Gayle Rubin's assertion that "disputes over sexual behavior often become the vehicles for displacing social anxieties,"[2] I argue that the sexualized and orientalized figure of the belly dancer operates as a locus through which to trace the particular disorientations of the turn-of-the-century U.S. context. By analyzing the structure of the Fair, and the way dancing girls were situated within that structure, I can flesh out a particular confluence of concerns, focused loosely around the teleological narrative of progress and in shifting notions of time and space, that settled figuratively onto belly dancers' bodies. Though the chapter is organized around my analysis of belly dancing at the Fair, particularly through a critical reading of popular photographs of dancing girls, I will begin by describing the structural logic of the Fair as an undergirding framework for belly dance performances. After setting the scene, I will look more closely at the commodification of belly dancing as an integral mythology of the progress narrative in order to build up to my discussion of popular photographs of dancing girls from the Fair. I end the chapter by looking at oppositional discourses of Arab womanhood at the Fair and by reading against the grain of the hegemonic narrative. Ultimately, I am interested in demonstrating the complexity and the contradictions of the belly dance figure as cultural mythology.

The comments of Smith and Buel also suggest that the popularity of dancing girls at the 1893 Fair centered on their ability to move and contort their bodies, and that fairgoers had deeply ambivalent reactions to these bodily undulations. As a marked contrast to the rigid and contained corseted bodies of the Victorian era, the belly dancers' bodies became known for a fluidity and freedom of movement that was both "passionate" and "disgusting." The figure of the belly dancer, then, emerged as a spectacle that was not only a form of entertainment for its U.S. audience, it was a deeply profound symbol of ambivalence about the rapid social change brought by the forces of modernization and consumerism. While it might not come as a surprise that turn-of-the-century U.S. audiences flocked to the eroticized displays of the belly dancers, the contemporaneous commentaries of Smith and Buel actually indicate that spectators were equally attracted to and repulsed by what they perceived to be the overly sexualized and lascivious movements of the Arab female body. In some small way, then, belly-dancing displays at the Chicago World's Fair seemed to function similarly to minstrel shows in the nineteenth century, which operated as racialized structures of feeling, according to Eric Lott. Rather than understanding minstrel shows solely as racist articulations of white hegemony, Lott is interested in the complex ways in which blackface minstrelsy performances tapped into white "panic, anxiety, terror, and pleasure"[3] regarding antebellum race relations. In exploring the combination of terror and pleasure, and of appropriation and exploitation in blackface minstrelsy, he argues for a more complex reading of it as a multifarious signifier for power relations and racial formation in the nineteenth century. The white working class ambivalence toward blackface minstrelsy that Lott loosely terms "love and theft"[4] is echoed in turn-of-the-century ambivalence toward belly-dancing displays, which simultaneously attracted and repulsed spectators. Although I would not argue that blackface minstrelsy and belly dancing are constructed by identical racial logic, I find the notion of ambivalence[5] to be extremely useful for my analysis of turn-of-the-century belly dancers because it signals the way in which a complex dialectic of attraction and rejection figures into the construction of the belly dancer as racialized and sexualized other. In the grand conceit of the metanarrative of modernity, othered figures such as the orientalized and sexualized belly dancers are, of course, not left out of the narrative but are rather constitutive of it. If modernity can be construed as that which "creates progress through the production and management of alterity,"[6] belly dancers at the 1893 Chicago World's Fair are emblematic of the way in which the social construction of difference undergirded the notion of progress. The women imported to perform this increasingly popular dance were therefore introduced into a context in which they would undergo what Rosemarie Garland Thomson calls the "social process of enfreakment;"[7] they were sensationalized as utterly and absolutely different bodies, to which throngs of spectators flocked against their own better moral judgment.

Even so, the lure of dancing girls at the Fair cannot only be attributed to their deviance from contemporaneous norms and codes of sexuality; indeed, the real surprise of their performances seemed to be in their resemblance to the ordinary. In the caption to one of his photographs, Buel describes three of the dancers as "destitute of animation, formless as badly stuffed animals, as homely as owls, and graceless as stall-fed bovines."[8] The repulsion of the audience members, then, does not seem to be entirely connected to the licentiousness of the dance and the performers, but also to the familiarity of the dancers' bodies, which were supposed to have been freakishly different. As Robert C. Allen notes: "It is the shock of resemblance and similarity in this radical other, and not the freak's total alienness, that is at the heart of the freak's power to enthrall and disgust."[9] Belly dancers, who Smith said moved "like one in an epilepsy," did not seem to be that radically different from their American counterparts at first glance. The westernized belly dancing costume that came out of the colonial cabarets, with low-slung skirt, bare midriff, and a halter-top, had not yet been popularized. If these dancers were considered to be scantily clad, it was because they left their ankles uncovered and their waists uncorseted. Buel's own photographs of the dancers illustrate their relatively conservative dress. If they did wear a halter-top, it was only over a full-length blouse, which covered the midriff and stomach as well. As with the production of freak shows, then, the performers were not radically different from the audience members, but rather they were crafted and groomed to be different. The process of enfreakment, for belly dancers, was structured into the elements of their exhibition. The power and draw of the belly-dancing displays had to do with the ways in which they reflected the conflicting feelings of attraction and repulsion back on the audience members themselves. The dancers were the embodiment of tension between the shock of familiarity and the thrill of absolute and exotic difference. This tension, which was mapped onto the bodies of belly dancers, was not about the exotic sexuality of the performers; rather, it reflected the needs of the turn-of-the-century U.S. audience to gain an assurance of self-definition in relation to the display of titillating otherness.

THE WHITE CITY AND THE MIDWAY PLAISANCE: "TWO SIDES OF THE SAME COIN"

As the venue that popularized the belly dance for turn-of-the-century Americans, the Midway Plaisance at the 1893 Fair set the scene for the way in which the eroticized Arab female body would be appropriated within a U.S. context. The belly dance entered popular U.S. imagination by way of exhibition and it was therefore, at its debut, already imbricated in a preexisting structure of display that presented it as a spectacle to be consumed. Therefore, the belly-dancing exhibits stood at the nexus of burgeoning consumerism and a national interest in demonstrating progress through modernization. In addition to being erotic and sexualized crowd-pleasers, they reified larger societal tensions that bubbled just underneath the surface of a World's Fair that was meant to display U.S. power and progress to the rest of the world.

As evidenced by Buel's and Smith's drastically different observations of the belly dance, the exhibits were "structured around the tension,"[10] to use Allen's phrase, inherent in their spectacular display. They were at once wildly erotic displays of sensuality dripping with the "voluptuous passion of the East"[11] and an offensive set of movements, which were "extremely ungraceful and almost shockingly disgusting."[12] Moreover, one type of reaction to the dance did not preclude the other—they often both existed in the same individual. In fact, just three pages prior to Smith's description of the dance as "hot" and "voluptuous," he describes the dancers as "shockingly unpicturesque, unromantic, and vulgar."[13] Again, this sort of simultaneous attraction and repulsion to the figure of the belly dancer is not only related to these mysterious and romantic figures from the imagined Orient, but it was also built into the framework of the Fair itself, which was also structured around the tension inherent in turn-of-the-century reactions to the progress narrative.

Belly dancing exhibits were located on the Midway Plaisance, which was largely considered to be the entertainment section of the Fair. However, the larger frame of exhibition was the "White City," which housed grand neoclassical buildings that were meant to demonstrate burgeoning U.S. prowess of technological advancement and superior civilization. In fact, Robert Rydell describes the two oppositional spaces of the 1893 Fair, the White City and the Midway Plaisance, as "two sides of the same coin."[14] In other words, while most accounts of the Columbian Exposition, another name for the 1893 Fair, situate the White City and the Midway Plaisance at opposite ends of the spectrum of style and class, Rydell suggests that neither could have existed without the other. Scholars such as John F. Kasson, Holly Edwards, and Robert Rydell stress the fact that the White City was meticulously planned as an example of the pinnacle of American progress. It was designed with the outward goal of displaying American achievement to the international community, but it was also created with the inward goal of establishing and reiterating a refined and unitary vision of U.S. culture. John Kasson puts it this way:

> The fair's designers and wealthy supporters intended the lesson of the Columbian Exposition to endure: an embodiment of public order, cultural unity, and civic virtue, an animating vision of American cultural achievement for an age of disorder, strife, and vulgarity.[15]

The "disorder, strife, and vulgarity" that resulted from a rapidly urbanizing country demanded an equalizing assurance of order and unity; the White City was to project such an assured and stable image. Yet, though Kasson casts the Midway as somewhat of an afterthought, as if it were the sideshow meant to provide recreation away from the "melancholy air"[16] of the White City, it is clear that the Midway's role in the grand scheme of the Fair was much more pronounced. Despite the Midway's seemingly secondary status as the less sophisticated entertainment section of the Fair, it seems that the "ordered and refined" White City and the "chaotic"[17] Midway were mutually dependent upon one another for existence.

Given this background, the conflicting reactions of Buel and Smith to the belly dancing performances clearly replicate a pattern of oppositions that was already built into the structure of the Fair. The belly dancers were repulsive, or "shockingly disgusting," because they so blatantly defied the refined, or "cool and chaste," femininity that would have been acceptable in the White City. At the same time, belly dancers were attractive because they embodied and demonstrated the loosening of the types of restrictions that were characteristic of the Victorian era. As Allen describes, "all that had been suppressed in the White City's representation of the female body as frozen, solemn, and chaste reemerged in the undulations of the cooch dancer."[18]

The belly-dancing displays were not alone in this respect. In fact, all of the ethnic exhibits on the Midway functioned to assuage collective anxiety about the rapidly changing face of U.S. society. This anxiety was related, in part, to changing notions of space. As the United States became more urbanized and industrialized, and as transportation technologies greatly decreased the amount of time it took to traverse long distances, popular conceptions of space and time also drastically changed. In addition, much of the social and political turmoil of the time reflected the rupture between past and future that a new set of labor conditions highlighted. The growing urban centers and regimented work days that characterized industrial capitalism also stimulated a shift in the way that individuals experienced space and time. As E. P. Thompson argues in his essay "Time-Work Discipline," the process of industrialization in Europe stimulated a change in people's relationships to time. Faced with a "time is money" work ethic, workers began to perceive of time as something to be consumed or spent. Given this drastic shift, which compartmentalized time into bounded and discrete units, it is no wonder that the imagined timelessness of the East operated as a foil for the progress narrative. At the same time, historian Frederick Jackson Turner addressed spatial concerns in his "frontier thesis," delivered in conjunction with the opening of the Columbian Exposition, in which he claimed that the frontier had officially been effaced. In essence, his thesis communicated the idea that the results of progress and westward expansion had been so thoroughly effective that the wild and untamable frontier had, for all intents and purposes, been conquered. Embedded in this grand proclamation are the contradictions of the progress narrative. Along with the satisfaction elicited by the notion of the vanquished frontier comes a simultaneous concern about the permanent effacement of innocent, pastoral settings. Though the dominant narrative of the World's Fair celebrates the boons of progress, it is interesting to look at those spaces of the Fair which seem to preserve older values in the face of such furious advancement. Certainly the White City was one articulation of, and homage to, traditional aesthetic values. The architecture in particular was designed in a neoclassical style in order to entrench the new America in the traditions of a grand and distinguished European past. However, the Midway Plaisance functioned, in many ways, as a space of release for the restrictive and contained articulations of White City grandeur. In particular, the "primitive cultures" displayed on the Midway Plaisance operated as a convenient foil upon which a collective nostalgia for an innocent and natural past could be projected. This foundational tension between progress and its receding past was continually highlighted by the forces of modernization. As the United States found itself to be increasingly, and unfailingly, moving forward with the thrust of progress, it became even more dependant on that image of the past it seemed to be leaving behind. The designers of the Cairo exhibit, one of the main displays of Middle Eastern culture, offer this telling suggestion in their descriptive pamphlet:

> Enter the eastern portal, which is low and broad, and you realize your dream of the Orient. You forget the magnitude of the buildings in Jackson Park and the "sky scrapers" of Chicago, and enter into the strange life which is before you. There is nothing to remind you of the 19th century, save the costumes of the visitors who are there, like yourself, and whom you might wish elsewhere, that you might enjoy your dream.[19]

Here, the fair designers reveal their intent to create an anachronistic space of pastoral purity, far removed from the type of urban-industrial development that is evident in the "sky scrapers" of Chicago. Indeed, they describe this seemingly primitive space as a "dream" where "there is nothing to remind you of the 19th century," revealing how orientalist dreams functioned to construct fairgoers' realities.

In this way, then, the Fair functioned as a "symbolic universe," to use Rydell's metaphor, that was stabilized by the mutually reinforcing structures of the White City and the Midway Plaisance. While the symbolic import that these structures maintained was meant to signify social harmony (unity and coherence) on the outside, their more entrenched hegemonic function was as signifiers of a social (and racialized) hierarchy. As with the assumption of universality in the progress narrative, this notion of unity ultimately depended on the maintenance of difference. As Robert Rydell explains:

> [T]he vision of the future and the depiction of the nonwhite world as savage were two sides of the same coin—a coin minted in the tradition of American racism, in which the forbidden desires of whites were projected onto dark-skinned peoples, who consequently had to be degraded so white purity could be maintained.[20]

In other words, the White City, as classic guarantor of white purity, gained definition and clarity against the perceived disorganization and vulgarity of the Midway. The "manifest destiny" of America's progressive and expansive future could only be understood in contrast to the "past" it was leaving behind. Furthermore, because the idea of the past was tied to the pastoral purity of the disappearing landscape, the concept of the lost past encompassed both spatial and temporal dimensions. Through the racialized and orientalized bodies of "savages" and hootchy-kootchy dancers, the receding past was displaced onto a distant, faraway place cast anachronistically in a premodern space.

It is into this complex constellation of meanings that belly dancing exhibits were introduced, and into this preexisting hierarchy that they were slotted. There is considerable academic debate about the intentionality behind the organization of exhibits on Midway. Although some argue that the displays were arranged from what the designers considered to be the most advanced civilizations to what they considered to be the most primitive cultures as a linear extension of the pinnacle of culture and civilization purportedly represented in the White City, others argue that the layout had more to do with foregrounding the most lucrative concessions.[21] In large part, the two aspects of the debate can be understood through the two main designers of the Midway: anthropologist Frederick Ward Putnam and future real-estate developer Sol Bloom.[22] In their stories, the threads of progress and consumerism as defining structural elements of the 1893 Fair weave together. Putnam, along with his chief assistant Franz Boas, were interested in continuing the tradition of ethnological exhibition begun at the Paris Exposition in 1889. They put a tremendous amount of concentrated energy into the task of collecting and organizing data about a number of cultures and peoples toward the goal of creating an edifying set of exhibitions that could accurately and authentically portray the steps of civilized progress in discrete cultural scenes.

Unfortunately, Putnam was to find his energy and work thwarted by the directors of the Fair who left installation of the Midway exhibits in the hands of Bloom. As Curtis Hinsley argues, Putnam's educational project was ultimately subsumed by Bloom's commercial enterprise:

> From the moment of his arrival in Chicago every conceivable obstacle seemed to be placed in Putnam's way by exposition directors; they were far more solicitous of the commercial and industrial exhibits and showed less and less interest in serious anthropology.[23]

The orchestrators of the Fair were much more interested in capitalizing on the potential for income with the Midway displays than they were in fostering an educational ethnological exhibit. So, while the 1889 Exposition in Paris presented both the educational and commercial aspects of the anthropological exhibits, the Chicago Fair

masterminds focused mainly on the economic success of the ethnographic villages in Paris and promptly decreased Putnam's space in
the Anthropological Building by sixty percent.[24]

Bloom, on the other hand, was afforded increased space and
resources for his project. After visiting the Paris Exposition in 1889,
he had arranged to bring representatives from the Algerian Village,
many of them belly dancers, to the United States in order to stage his
own "authentic" exhibit. Serendipitously, plans for the 1893 World's
Fair had recently begun. After Chicago was officially named as the site
of the four-hundredth anniversary Columbian Exposition, Bloom's
incubating idea took form when a friend who had admired his "knack
for making money"[25] asked him to manage all of the amusement
concessions on the Midway. In this way, not only did he take on
responsibility for a much larger space than he had anticipated, but he
also reported to the fair commissioners as his overseers rather than to
Putnam who was originally meant to coordinate the area.

Although belly dancing, also called *danse du ventre* (literally,
"dance of the stomach")[26] was only "officially" performed at three
concessions (The Turkish Village, A Street of Cairo, and the Algerian
Village), its popularity and ability to draw crowds ensured the appearance of imitators. Because fairgoers had grown to associate belly dancing with the Orient, concessions such as The Persian Palace "added
bastard *danse du ventre* to its bill of fare to boost admissions."[27] The
belly dance was beginning its long career in the United States as an
exotic, and appropriated, lucrative enterprise.

CONSUMING THE HOOTCHY KOOTCHY

The Chicago World's Fair was not only meant as a unifying force in
the sociopolitical realm, but also as a jump-start to an economically
depressed economy. A number of prominent cities, including New
York, had competed with Chicago to host the Fair not only for the
prestige, but also because of the revenue that the Fair would inevitably bring. If the fair designers' stated goals were to demonstrate the
technological advancement of the States, the intended outcome of
these achievements was increased production and expansion. In other
words, the Fair was an opportunity to showcase the United States'
ability both to acquire raw materials and to manufacture products.
Umberto Eco describes world's fairs as quintessential capitalist spaces
because they are focused on organizing and cataloguing the many
products of the hosting nation's progress, including new transportation, manufacturing, and communication technologies: "In this sense

of an enormous collection of goods, an exposition could be seen as representing the Missa Solemnis of traditional capitalist society."[28] In his description of a world exposition as a "collection of goods," Eco is expanding on Walter Benjamin's earlier assertion that world's fairs function in such a way as to offer themselves up as a mass display of goods.[29] In this respect, then, the early expositions serve as highly organized historical markers of the way in which industrial capitalism is able to manipulate "raw" materials. In the 1893 Chicago World's Fair, the "display of goods" can easily be located in the official exhibitions of U.S. achievement found in the buildings of the White City such as the transportation and machinery buildings, which featured U.S. inventions and innovations. If the White City boasted superiority on the production side of the capitalist equation, though, the Midway Plaisance reconstructed colonialist logic whereby subjugated peoples, cultures, and regions provided the raw materials for production. Benjamin's critique of world exhibitions highlights the way in which they replicate classic capitalist relations; within this framework, individuals are objectified while commodities are animated.

> The world exhibitions glorify the exchange value of commodities. They create a framework in which commodities' intrinsic value is eclipsed. They open up a phantasmagoria that people enter to be amused. The entertainment industry facilitates this by elevating people to the level of commodities.[30]

The entertainment venue of the Chicago World's Fair was the Midway Plaisance, and it was there that people were elevated to the level of commodities. The displays were organized as contained and isolated representations of cultures from different parts of the world. Yet fairgoers did not pay entry fees merely to see a collection of artifacts; instead they flocked to those exhibits that displayed people who had been imported to embody and perform the cultural activities of their particular region of origin. Because the Midway functioned as a marketplace, exhibition techniques presented people as "raw materials" available for purchase and consumption.[31]

What had begun as a purportedly edifying anthropological project was therefore actualized as an exchange of goods and services. The consumerist dream that was played out on the Midway was intimately related to the positivist rhetoric of progress that so permeated the Fair. Situated in obvious juxtaposition to the assertion of U.S. commercial prosperity projected in the White City, the Midway offered a glimpse of the flip side of "civilization." In fact, the anthropological exhibits on the Midway seem to have been organized according to a view that ordered the cultures of the world on a scale that adhered to an evolutionary hierarchy. As the "Bird's-Eye View" of the Fair illustrates, the grandiose buildings of the White City were displayed prominently along the edge of the lake. Midway, on the other hand, extended backward perpendicularly from the White City; the transition between the two was represented by the Woman's Building, which was the only official site reserved for the display of white American women's accomplishments. This marginalization of white women's achievements proved to be a fitting link to the space of the Midway, where the ethnographic displays appeared to be ordered from most "civilized" (e.g., The Irish Village) to the most "savage" (e.g., Native Americans and the Dahomeyan peoples of West Africa). In this way, a gender and race hierarchy was encoded into the very organization and layout of the Fair itself, which situated white women and western Europeans such as Irish and Swedish peoples closest to the civilized vision of the fair designers and "primitive" indigenous peoples furthest away from American civilization.[32] At the same time, this racial hierarchy was overlaid with a consumerist goal. Again, in the "Bird's-Eye View," the most prominent landmark is the Ferris Wheel, which was located at the center of the Midway to highlight the centrality of the entertainment aspect of the ethnographic displays.

Interestingly enough, the "Street of Cairo" exhibit, one of the main belly dancing venues, was also located in the center of the Midway, a detail that further highlights the situation of belly dancing at the nexus of modernization (progress) narratives and consumerist narratives. Egypt (through the "Street of Cairo" exhibit) presumably fell in the middle of the evolutionary hierarchy because it had failed to progress from its once-grand civilization; its legacy of civilization, it seems, kept it from the bottom of the hierarchy. In terms of the argument that the Midway was organized according to commercial interests, it is no surprise that belly dancing exhibits were situated near the Ferris Wheel. As a symbol of the entertainment value of Midway, the Ferris Wheel would have drawn crowds to the belly-dancing exhibits, and vice versa. Indeed, individual concessionaires were not the only ones to use belly dancing to attract crowds. The planners of the exposition had initially added additional amusement concessions to help offset the enormous costs of the Fair (which is why they hired Bloom). However, according to Donna Carlton, a meeting of the Concessionaires Club at the end of May 1893 revealed disappointing attendance figures for the Fair in general. In order to stimulate interest, they began a discussion "about how the strange Oriental dance could be used for publicity purposes," and orchestrated a scandal around which the belly dance buzz could build. Fair planners convinced a prominent Chicago minister to condemn the dance in his sermon, which quickly created a public furor. As Carlton puts it: "Their efforts attracted attention in the newspapers all over the country, and soon young men were arriving eager to see more than 'steam engines and electric lights' at the exposition."[33] The fair planners fabricated a controversy and stimulated public debates about the morality of the dance in order to attract more visitors to the exhibits. Therefore, Bloom's original scheme depended not only upon fairgoers' desire to see the lascivious dance, but also upon a societal reaction of shock and dismay at the lack of morals displayed by the dance. This moment of shock is the point at which the ambivalence that the exoticized figure of the belly dancer represented for the turn-of-the-century American public becomes apparent. Her ability to both attract and repulse visitors ultimately held her at the center of attention. The belly dancer's body was thus the locus of a public tension, which, I am arguing, reflected broad, collective concerns about the tumultuous processes of consumerism and modernization.

The increasing commercialization of exhibits that had been created under the guise of edification at the Fair was just one more facet of the articulation of progress. The continued advancement of the nation depended on its ability to stimulate consumption and to buttress the ideology of economic development. This ideology, in turn, highlighted the emerging industrial capitalist mode in the United States, in which consumerism would play a major role in shaping how people related to each other and to the world around them. The Midway itself was somewhat of a transitional space for the shift toward consumerism, as Holly Edwards argues. "Much of this display revolved around the dense and opulent array of exotic artifacts, not unlike the extravagances of American department stores."[34] The belly dance was part of the "goods" that were packaged for consumption. Evidence for this lies in the fact that belly dancing was one of the most lucrative concessions on the Midway, and in the fact that it was marketed to increase attendance to the Fair in general. A cartoon in the *World's Fair Puck* gives some indication of its consumerist success. The cartoon satirized the way in which one proprietor changed "his original and financially unsuccessful display intended for good Christians, 'Life in the Holy Lands: Scenes from Biblical Days…A Moral Show,' to 'Life in the Harem. Dreamy Scenes in the Orient. Eastern Dances. The Sultans [*sic*] diversions.' "[35] The latter frame of the cartoon shows hoards of men dashing for the "harem." In addition to its commentary on the construction of belly dancers as sexualized objects offered for the pleasure of men, the image also documents the interplay between orientalist themes. Though the mythologized "Holy Land" was an extremely salient theme for U.S. audiences in the latter half of the nineteenth century and also at the 1904 St. Louis Fair, at the 1893 Chicago World's Fair the orientalized figure of the belly dancer as symbol of female sexuality proved to be most compelling.

Moreover, belly dance concessions belonged to carefully constructed exhibits, which deployed the disciplinary trope of civilization in multiple ways. In the "Street of Cairo" exhibit, for example, which was modeled after the *Rue de Caire* at the 1889 French Exposition,[36] a fairgoer might encounter men tending to camels and donkeys or the sensationalized sight of a veiled woman in addition to the famed belly dancers. Photographs and descriptions of the Cairo exhibit focus either on the primitive, backward, and traditional aspects of Middle Eastern culture or on the fantastical and romanticized elements of the culture. In both cases, the perceived reality of the scene seemed to function as a tangible counterpoint to the progress narrative of the White City. For instance, photographic albums from the 1893 Fair all document fairgoers partaking in an ostensibly authentic Middle Eastern activity: donkey and camel riding. The caption to a photograph entitled "The Camel and His Attendant" proclaims:

> To take a ride on the camel, as if actually in the streets of the famous Egyptian city, but surrounded by hundreds of "guying" Americans was a novel sensation....It was one of the most realistic entertainments of the great Plaisance.[37]

Significantly, the "novel sensation" to which the caption refers comes not from watching the introduction of a new invention, but from observing or participating in the purportedly age-old activity of camel riding. While it was critical for the fair designers to reaffirm and reassert the positive aspects of what they called progress during a sea of radical change, it would prove to be impossible to prevent a nostalgic backward glance that such intense change would foster. The "real" Middle East was perceived as an anachronistic space, hermetically sealed in a pastoral space untouched by industrial development. The new promise of a positivist and progressive future was measured against this looming perception of a distant past, which seemed to have been lost to U.S. citizens.

Similarly, the notion of the Middle East as traditional and antiquated buttressed the U.S. progress narrative by providing a justificatory logic for advancement in the name of imperialism and expansionism.

In light of the fact that the relatively conservatively dressed dancers of the 1893 World's Fair were considered to be shocking and lascivious, it is ironic that the practice of veiling was perceived to be an oppressive custom. Buel's caption to the image of a veiled woman (figure 2.1) from the Cairo exhibit reads:

> In the street of Cairo at the World's Fair there was exhibited the peculiar manners of the Egyptians, and a veiled lady was of course one of the curious objects displayed, though she did not always appear in that unsightly disguise, thus proving that she was not a slave to this requirement of all Mohammedan women.[38]

Despite the fact that turn-of-the-century U.S. women were strapped into rib-breaking corsets, the veiled woman was cast as a "slave" to her oppressive and backward culture. This type of cultural myopia, in which the oppressed Arab woman is positioned as the unfortunate opposite to her liberated western sister (a topic I will revisit in chapter 4), is characteristic of the way in which orientalist notions about the Arab world have typically functioned in the U.S.

The characters of the camel attendant and the veiled "Mohammedan" woman, however, largely served as background figures to the coveted dancing girls who seemed, at once, mysterious and romantic as well as shocking and unsightly. The framing of belly dancers as fantastical, mysterious figures situates them squarely within the citational-orientalist tradition, whereby belly dancers in turn-of-the-century U.S. representations reference harem girls in nineteenth-century French orientalist paintings. One of Buel's photographs of a dancing girl, for example, tags her as "An Odalisque From the *Seraglio*," a title that clearly references French orientalist representations of the harem. Even Smith's description of the Midway in a special issue of *Illustrated American* (1893) characterizes the Cairo exhibit as if it were the replica of a harem scene in a French orientalist painting.

> Walking to the end of the street and looking back to the gateway, a series of latticed windows is seen on the interior of the archway, that seem to suggest the secrecy of the seraglio, an idea that is deepened by a tiny flapping door in one of the casements, that looks like the portal of a dovecote and engenders visions of peeping Circassian beauties and black faced eunuchs.[39]

On the basis of this description, the exhibit seems to have been constructed in such a way as to highlight the "secrecy" and "mystery" of the Orient, which would ultimately invite fairgoers to experience the

Figure 2.1   Egyptian Girl in the Street of Cairo

Source: Photo by James Buel in *The Magic City* (St. Louis: Historical Publishing Co., 1894), courtesy of the Manuscript, Archives, and Rare Book Library, Emory University.

titillating power of purchasing their way into the long-forbidden space of the seraglio, or harem (see chapter 1 for definition and discussion). Indeed, turn-of-the-century U.S. fairgoers were not only afforded the luxury of achieving access to the interior of the harem, they were actually buying the scopic privilege of watching the sultan's own dancing girls. Buel's caption to his photo of the "Odalisque" alludes to the easy transgression of patriarchal Ottoman boundaries afforded to fairgoers who were able to purchase entry into the performance.

> She was heralded by the Algerian Concessionaire as an Odalisque, fresh from the Seraglio, and the Sultan's favorite. This was rhetorical, even if not true, so she was accepted as a beauty and invested with a mystery that made her a very interesting personage.[40]

Notably, the sultan's presence is "rhetorical" in the context of the 1893 Fair. Contrary to the French orientalist context, in which the figure of the sultan, even if absent, rendered the space of the seraglio forbidden to other men, the lascivious sexuality of the dancing girls alone seemed to code the seraglio of the 1893 Fair as a forbidden space, while the sultan was effectively erased from the scene.

The replication of the prototypical harem scene as a secret and forbidden space was a crucial aspect of these belly dancing displays given the sexual mores of the time, since it fabricated a sense of barriers and distance between the fairgoers and the presumed licentiousness of Arab female sexuality. Kasson's argument to explain belly dancing's popularity at the turn of the century is that the genteel cultural order of the Victorian era had given way to a less inhibited mass culture and that belly dancing quite literally symbolized the loosening of societal restrictions. Indeed, the dance did seem to function as the lascivious and outrageous counterpart to a highly restrictive Victorian culture. The basic movements employed by the performers highlighted the free flow of energy to the very part of the female body that society ladies' corsets were meant to restrict. As Holly Edwards remarks: "With its liberation of that core, the hoochy-coochy was the sartorial and corporeal transgression of some very basic notions of propriety."[41] Belly dancing was certainly poised to serve as the exotic other to Victorian ideals of upper-class white femininity.

Yet, at the same time, the body of the belly dancer was a safe vessel through which to experiment with new attitudes toward sexuality since her "power was contained and distanced by her otherness."[42] Though the largely male audience was no doubt attracted to what Smith calls a "perfect paroxysm of undulations," the potential danger introduced by these exotic sexual bodies was mitigated by their absolute difference, by their very enfreakment. "The threat her sexuality might represent was diffused through her construction as exotic, ethnological other."[43] In other words, the belly dancer's body had become a sort of canvas; it was a space upon which a U.S. audience could cast its concerns, questions, and needs about shifting attitudes toward female sexuality. The spectators' fascination with the sensationalized bodies of these exotic dancers, then, had little to do with Arab female sexuality and more to do with the threatening and subversive power of female sexuality. Indeed, the simultaneous attraction and repulsion of fairgoers points to the ambivalent attitude that they had toward this power.

Buel claims that "curiosity prompted many to view the performance, but very few remained more than five minutes before this was fully satisfied." His insistence that fairgoers needed only a few minutes of observation to satisfy their interest suggests the intensity and power of the performance, rather than its ineffectiveness. As Barthes posits about the nature of the striptease performance,[44] it suggests that the belly dance exhibition is a "spectacle based on fear," because it draws attention to the power of female sexuality.[45] Buel's five-minute window of attraction to the belly dance display, then, can be understood as a means for mediating and controlling the potential threat that the dancers' sexuality poses. Barthes suggests that a similar mechanism is employed by the striptease spectator: "A few particles of eroticism, highlighted by the very situation on which the show is based, are in fact absorbed in a reassuring ritual which negates the flesh as surely as the vaccine or the taboo circumscribe and control the illness or the crime."[46] Applying this observation to the belly-dance form, it suggests that the highly structured and contained spectacle of the belly dance serves, in some ways, as an inoculation against the perceived profanity of the unbridled sexuality it presents.

Circling back to my suggestion that the problematic of sexuality is one way in which U.S. fairgoers negotiated the disorientations of modernity, I would highlight the way in which the dimension of power illuminates this discussion. As Foucault argues in the *History of Sexuality*, constructions of sexuality and the discourses surrounding it in the modern era operate as productive loci through which new forms of power emerge and are contested. In other words, as Ann Stoler explains, "For Foucault, sexuality is not opposed to and subversive of power. On the contrary, sexuality is a 'dense transfer point' of power."[47] In the ambivalent reactions toward belly dance, then, one can see modern technologies of power at work. White bourgeois sexuality, the primary unit of productivity in the framework of biopower, is constructed and regulated through its engagement with popular discourses about sexuality. As Ann Stoler argues in her elucidation of and extension on Foucault's work, these technologies of sexuality gain definition through an oppositional relationality with racialized figures, such as the orientalist figure of the belly dancer at the 1893 Chicago World's Fair.[48] Ambivalence toward belly dancing at the turn of the century, then, represents more than an ambivalence about female sexuality; it also seems to be intimately tied to profound disorientations of the modern era, including emerging technologies of power, shifting dimensions of time and space, and the sublimated nostalgia of the progress narrative.

CREATING AND MARKETING LITTLE EGYPT

One of the most pervasive and lasting images of Arab womanhood, the belly dancer, debuted in the U.S. not at the White City but rather through its bizarre other, on the teeming bazaar of the Midway Plaisance. From the outset, then, the belly dance form entered the United States through the avenue of consumerism and became immediately immersed in the logic of the progress narrative. Though belly dancing is often cast in the U.S. as an ancient, primordial dance form, its popularity has actually depended on its construction vis-à-vis the forces of modernization and burgeoning imperialism in the U.S. context. Through a consideration of Little Egypt, the mythologized belly dancer from Midway; Ruth St. Denis, a performance artist and dancer who incorporated orientalist themes into her work; and photographs of dancing girls from the 1893 Fair, I am interested in tracing the threads of consumerism and of progress as they are manifested in these examples of belly dancing. Each of these cases bear out the assertion that the progress narrative depends on the production and management of alterity.[49] The story of belly dancing grows out of mythologized figures like Little Egypt and is therefore rooted in the construction and fabrication of authenticity. The claim of authenticity, in turn, works in the service of the metanarrative of modernity by constructing naturalized, primitive others against which progress can be measured. In this respect, the mythological figure of the belly dancer is anything but authentic; she is a fabricated symbol of authenticity who has subsequently been objectified and commodified in U.S. popular culture. The fairgoers at the Columbian Exposition helped to create the legacy and legend of the mythologized dancing girl, who came to be known as "Little Egypt." As Donna Carlton asserts in her book *Looking for Little Egypt*, many media and even academic sources attribute the increased publicity and attendance of the Fair to one specific dancer named "Little Egypt." Despite her star status, however, "there is no record of Little Egypt at the 1893 exposition or at any off-Midway show."[50] In reality there were a number of "dancing girls," any one of whom could have claimed the moniker of "Little Egypt" in the years following the Fair. That there was no dancer who self-identified as Little Egypt during the time of the Fair is not surprising. What is significant, however, is the way that her legend functions in popular accounts of the dance and its history. The concessions which, it should be remembered, originated out of an idea to provide accurate ethnographic displays of different cultures, had transmogrified into opportunistic "shows" that capitalized on national identification in opposition to a primitive and "natural" East. Ironically, the name "Little Egypt" serves as a residual and persistent link to the "Street of Cairo" exhibit, thereby signifying the imbrication of American belly dancing in the discourses of consumerism and in the logic of scientific racism, whereby ethnographic displays were arranged according to a colonialist/imperialist notion of evolutionary hierarchy.

While there are few specific details available regarding any of the actual dancers at the Fair, Wendy Buonaventura, a British belly dancer, has documented the story of Fahreda Mahzar, a woman brought from Syria,[51] who retrospectively claimed the title of "Little Egypt." Presumably, Mahzar claimed the title because she considered herself to be one of the primary performers on the "Street of Cairo" exhibit. Through her story, it becomes possible to trace out key elements of the construction of authenticity vis-à-vis belly dancing in the United States. Buonaventura, Kasson, and Edwards document the fact that the belly dance performances, especially the ones performed by the "native" and "authentic" dancers who also called themselves Little Egypt, were among the largest attractions on the Midway Plaisance. Due to her popularity, Buonaventura claims, Little Egypt (whom Buonaventura equates with Mahzar) was the most "imitated" act.[52] As the most imitated and also one of the first belly dancers in the United States, Mahzar can provide a frame of reference from which to understand future interpretations of the dance she was imported to perform. While Buonaventura does not give an account of Mahzar's feelings and ideas about her performance on the Midway, she does document the fact that she vehemently protested, and even had a lawsuit pending against, the "lewd" and "outrageous" interpretations of her performance that some subsequent dancers (also calling themselves "Little Egypt") displayed.[53] In fact, in Robert C. Allen's study of burlesque in the United States, he notes that within months of the 1893 Fair "practically every burlesque troupe in American [sic] had added a Fatima, Little Egypt, or Zora to do her version of the famous *danse du ventre.*"[54] Allen and Mahzar would agree that the "cooch" dance, as Allen calls it, became a kind of performative code for licentiousness, which eventually transformed the subversive elements of burlesque, Allen argues, into the objectifying performance style of striptease.[55] However, while Allen takes it as a given that the sexualized elements of the "cooch" dance are inherent to the belly dance form, Mahzar grew incredulous at the bold and outrageous performances of her imitators.[56]

Mahzar's moment of protestation is one in which one can clearly see the construction of the particularly U.S. based concept of belly dancing in the works. The dance Mahzar was contracted to perform (*al-raqs al-baladi*) was a traditional folk dance usually performed in a drastically different context in Egypt. The dance her audience saw was one almost entirely composed of movements originating or culminating in the pelvic region of the body (hence belly dance). In fact, contemporaneous American feminists, such as Julia Ward Howe, "reacted against the dance as being 'simply horrid, no touch of grace about it, only the most deforming movement of the whole abdominal and lumbar region.'"[57] The slippage between these two perspectives on the dance—that of the "native" performer and that of U.S. spectators—is the space from which belly dancing was to be reimagined and reconceptualized.

The spectacle of belly dancing, now developed and defined through the eyes of its American audience, was thus transformed into a lucrative commodity, performed in the name of art. Its characteristic style and form was quickly reduced to the exaggerated display of pelvic thrusts and shimmies, which is probably why Mahzar was soon overshadowed and outdone by the performers who followed her. Immediately following the Fair, imitations of the dance began to crop up—not just on the Midway at the Fair—but also at neighboring amusement displays. In fact, as Kasson's study of Coney Island demonstrates, the belly dance soon became a standard feature of the burgeoning amusement business, and, as demonstrated by Allen's work, it played a major role in the development of burlesque and striptease entertainment forms. Donna Carlton asserts that belly dancing "soon became a staple for the booming amusement industry—the new American carnivals and amusement parks and the continuing tradition of the American circus."[58] From its auspicious beginnings, then, belly dancing in the U.S. has been associated with the carnivalesque; it metaphorically speaks to the undulations of subcultural resistance, while simultaneously being appropriated and exploited for capital gain.

If negative publicity, in part, was what attracted crowds to the Fair exhibitions originally, it was the claim of (exotic) authenticity that kept a consistent flow of customers toward "that dance" in multiple venues in different time periods. Despite the clear indication that the belly dance performance was fabricated for a U.S. context, it was the very guise of authenticity that permitted the exhibition of the dance, by ensuring its absolute difference from a refined, Victorian cultural aesthetic. Therefore, it eventually became clear that entertainment venues shunned more indigenous performances of *al-raqs al-sharqi* in favor of commodified versions of the "cooch" dance. Since the illusion of authenticity enabled the further exoticization of belly dancing as a sensual performance, venue managers did not value accurate representations of the dance. During this time period, then, orientalist notions of the exotic Middle East in combination with market forces shaped the popular image of the belly dancer, which remains common in the contemporary context. The dancing girls at the 1893 Chicago World's Fair who were such a shock to Victorian mores wore costumes that revealed only the dancers' ankles. The costumes largely associated with belly dancing today, which leave the abdomen bare, did not become popularized until the 1920s and 1930s, which coincides with the integration of the striptease into burlesque performances.[59] During this time, also, the cabaret style began to influence belly dance costumes and styles.[60] The elaborately decorated and tasseled brassieres and low-slung harem pants or gauzy skirts began to take their place as the quintessential belly dancing outfit.

Even appropriations of the dance that defy popular notions of it as a sexualized and exotic display for the pleasure of men corroborate the discourse of authenticity that has framed U.S. constructions of the belly dance. After making a debut at the Columbian Exposition, belly dancing has reemerged in a few historical moments in the United States in radically different venues, from the cabarets of the 1920s and 1930s to the U.S. feminist movement in the 1970s (that had developed a mythology of "goddess worship" as a form of spirituality), and finally to the contemporary exercise industry (which celebrates the dance as a tool for helping women to develop a positive body image).

In the 1970s, a liberal white U.S. feminist movement sought to rescue belly dancing from its reputation as a spectacle of lasciviousness and restore it to its "original" use and meaning within the context of ancient matriarchal rituals. In doing so, however, this version of U.S. feminism still appropriated the dance for its perceived spiritual and ritualistic elements, thereby cementing it further in the discourse of authenticity. Performance and dance scholar Donnalee Dox notes that "most writings by [contemporary] western belly dancers prefer to locate the origins of belly dancing in the temple or birth rituals of the 'ancient' East, and in so doing give the dance an aura of universal femininity."[61] She refers here to people like Zarifa Aradoon who traces belly dancing all the way back to 25,000 B.C., at which time the "female body [was] worshipped for childbearing capabilities"[62] and Rosina-Fawzia Al-Rawi who praises belly dancing for its "circling, bouncing, and vibrating motions."[63] Al-Rawi goes on to lament the transition from mostly matriarchal to patriarchal societies, which, she also claims, marks the transition between belly dancing being performed as a ritualistic spiritual dance and belly dancing being performed for the entertainment of men.[64]

Perhaps because these writers focus, as Dox indicates, on the lost feminine powers and energy of the matriarchy, they are invoking a concept of femininity that claims to be universal in nature. In other words, they trace the belly dance far back to an origin that seems to have no cultural specificity and which can therefore speak to the situation of all women everywhere throughout time. As Dox notes, many U.S. based interpretations of the belly dance are actually a "composite of culturally specific dances which, when blended together in the standard (western) five-part set, appear as a single form."[65] These details suggest that some members of the American belly dance movement seek to reclaim those aspects of the tradition of belly dancing that can support an American feminist celebration of the power of female sexuality, and dismiss the part of the dance that derives from historical and cultural specificity, thereby fabricating cultural authenticity in the service of a universalized, hegemonic white feminist narrative. Through the construction of authenticity, then, the mythologized figure of the belly dancer serves as a foil for various discourses of progress (or liberation) even as she is appropriated in the service of consumerism.

A further example of the way belly dance contributed to narratives of authenticity is performer/dancer Ruth St. Denis, precursor to the cabaret style, who developed her style from an array of orientalist markers. Buonaventura claims that most European and American audiences gained their initial understanding of "Oriental dance" through her, which is ironic since St. Denis was an American woman born in New Jersey who was "self-taught" in her interpretation of the belly dance.[66] Like the American belly dancers of the 1970s who would follow her, St. Denis seemed drawn to belly dancing because of her romanticized perception of the dance form as imbued with a spiritual element and because the fluid movements enabled a "celebration of the body."[67] If "oriental" props and settings gave French orientalist painters license to depict female nudity, St. Denis similarly appropriated the props, setting, and movements of the *raqs sharqi*, or belly dance, to give her greater license of movement given the restrictive social mores of the time. Insofar as St. Denis sought to represent the "spiritually mysterious orient"[68] through dance, she exemplifies the orientalist apparatus at work in multiple and various contexts. Though St. Denis was not necessarily interested in accurately representing the cultural dance forms from which she borrowed, she did turn to the "East" as an essentialized and timeless inspiration for notions of spirituality. This may be why Buonaventura, herself drawn to orientalist constructions of the "timeless sensual" and the "timeless feminine" in the East, focuses on St. Denis in *The Serpent of the Nile*.[69] Buonaventura claims that St. Denis's "main inspiration was the East, or her own particular version of it,"[70] which is an eminently fitting description since St. Denis capitalized on orientalist notions of the East as primitive, exotic, and sensual in order to fashion her own unique image.

Notably, St. Denis demonstrates the citational nature of orientalism in that the "research" she conducted on "non-Western" themes seemed to reference traditional orientalist artworks and texts,[71] and her own representations of the East in dance and performance often conflated and mixed Indian and Middle Eastern elements. In fact, St. Denis received creative influence and inspiration from such popular images as an *Egyptian Deities* cigarette advertisement. Suggests Donna Carlton: "She glanced up at a colorful art deco poster for 'Egyptian Deities' cigarettes and the image penetrated her being. Suddenly she saw herself in the picture, a priestess embodying the ancient goddess Isis, seated on a golden throne."[72] While it is impossible to know exactly which particular image St. Denis saw, an analysis of a 1914 advertisement for *Egyptian Deities* cigarettes (figure 2.2) reveals a number of elements from the overall image that could have impressed themselves upon her. The majestic and monumental backdrop sets an ancient yet regal scene for the royally reposed figure on his throne. In front of him are his numerous subjects who look on, with him, to the performance of the belly dancers. The text reads: "You can half see in their smoke the sunlight on the spears of the fighting men, the laughter in the eyes of the dancing girls." St. Denis clearly took the ad's message to heart to "half see" or imagine her own vision of what an "Egyptian Deity" might look like, so that she could incorporate spiritual elements into her performance. Here again, St. Denis's

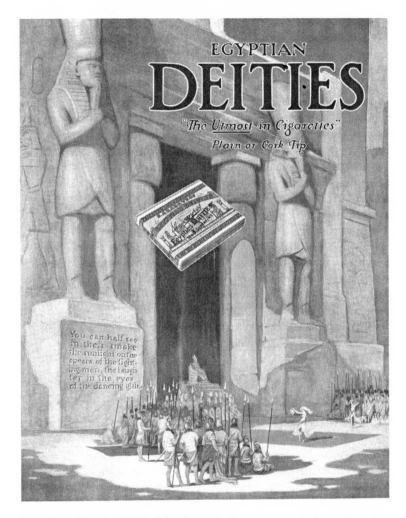

Figure 2.2 Egyptian Deities Advertisement

Source: Warshaw Collection of Business Americana—Tobacco Industry, Archives Center, National Museum of American History, Behring Center, Smithsonian Institution.

fascination with the "deities" of the East serves as a precursor to the goddess spirituality movement in 1960s and 1970s U.S. feminism, which permeated American belly dance movements as well.[73] These examples demonstrate a patronizing reverence for the "deities" and their ancient civilization in that both St. Denis, representative of the cabaret style, and the 1970s goddess spirituality belly-dance movement focus on the way in which belly dancing is associated with the primordial past. Furthermore, for St. Denis at least, the essence of the "Orient" can be gleaned from an image used to sell Turkish blend cigarettes in the United States. The imagined spirituality of belly dancing is, importantly, both fabricated and essentialized, characteristics which render the belly dance ripe for appropriation and incorporation into the progress narrative.

The many versions of the belly dance—from the sideshow spectacle at the World's Fair to the healing ritual of a liberal feminist movement—capitalize on the much-heralded ancient nature of the dance in order to lend a timeless authority to its practitioners. Ironically, this preoccupation with origins actually reveals the western European–based Enlightenment construct of modernity, in which linear notions of temporality equate origins with what is old, ancient, or essential. Indeed, in the case of belly dancing, which is often perceived as originating before recorded history, or as prehistoric, origins seem to be equated with timelessness. Even if fabricated, the notion of the belly dance as essentialized spirituality gains authenticity by virtue of its implied relationship to innocence, nature, and purity. In these senses, then, belly dance is constitutive of the progress narrative insofar as it functions as the essentialized, timeless other to the forward thrust of advancement.

Photographing Little Egypt

The infamy of "that dance" introduced and celebrated at the Chicago World's Fair, the belly dance, survives through the images collected in photographic albums, such as Buel's *The Magic City*. I look here, then, at photographs of the "dancing girls" from the 1893 Fair in order to highlight the way in which popular notions of belly dancers as essentialized others reverberated in, and were compounded by, popular perceptions of the photographic medium as a transparent, unmediated representation of reality. An exploration of the intersections between belly dancing and the photographic medium will enable me to more fully flesh out the way in which the tendency to essentialize functions as a strategy for coping with the disorientations of modernity.

Photography played a significant role at the 1893 Chicago World's Fair, both in terms of showcasing various aspects of advanced U.S. society through photographs as artifacts and in terms of documenting the Fair in the spate of photographic albums that were published in the years following the event. The 1893 Fair represents a moment of transition for the medium of photography, which was shifting from the realm of art into the arena of industry whereby it intersected with the ideological underpinnings of the progress narrative. Photographs could simultaneously demonstrate technological prowess and preserve a frozen representation of the rapidly receding present for a society increasingly oriented toward the future. Further, photographs were increasingly utilized as "tools of investigation and research" in fields like archaeology, anthropology, and psychology in order to lend them the authority of "scientific precision."[74] The photographs of the dancing girls, then, stand at the nexus of the scientific racism of the progress narrative and the commercial interests within burgeoning consumerist industries like advertising.

The perception of photography as a tool for capturing and documenting the essence of its subject situated it as the perfect medium through which to shape reality, or at least popular perceptions of it. The notion of photography as impartial, objective documentation also aided in obscuring the persuasive and creative functions of the medium, which increasingly came to be used as a tool for advertising goods and services.[75] Therefore, photographs often obscured the conditions that enabled them to be presented as objective reality; they obfuscated, for example, the fact that those with enough resources and capital (like James Buel) were literally afforded the ability to construct a particular narrative about the "magic city" at the 1893 Fair. The collection of photographic albums that emerged as official documentation of the Fair all demonstrate the tension between recording and creating reality that is inherent in the medium. These albums, or "catalogues," were often nothing more than a compilation of photographs taken and collected by the author, arranged in whatever manner the collector saw fit, and adorned with captions meant to describe the purportedly objective reality exhibited in the photo. Far from being an objective and sterile representation of the events of the World's Fair, the photographs published are not only framed by the perspective and words of the editors of the volumes, they are also framed by the complex sociohistorical processes that surrounded their production. At the turn of the century, photography itself was determined by industrial capitalist forces, which helped to transform the medium of photography into a tool of consumerism. As Julie K. Brown notes: "By the 1870s in the United States, progress in photography was identified by its commercial product rather than by its science, technology, or art."[76] The albums of the Fair are therefore indicative of the ways in which the claim to capture the objective reality of the Fair nevertheless served the interests of profit more so than the goal of edification.

At the same time, again as demonstrated by Buel's album, photography can serve as a powerful metaphor for power relations insofar as it presupposes the power of the photographer to represent his/her subject. In her study of women and photography in the Middle East from 1860–1950, Sarah Graham-Brown argues that the rise of photography in the mid to late 1800s coincides with the European imperialist project,[77] an observation that can be applied to the late-nineteenth-century U.S. expansionist context. Photography clearly aids an orientalist/colonialist project insofar as it contributes to the production of knowledge about colonized peoples vis-à-vis supposedly objective forms of documentation. In addition to rendering its subjects known, however, photography also highlights the embeddedness of power relations in a spatial dimension insofar as it functions to symbolically collapse the distance between imperialists and their subjects. By capturing colonized and otherwise subjugated peoples in still images, the process of photography at once inscribes and obfuscates the literal and figurative space between the world of the photographer and that of his/her subjects.[78]

I am particularly interested here, therefore, in noting the ways in which the photographic medium is imbricated in social processes (i.e., industrialization, imperialism, consumerism) that unsettle predominant notions of space. As Benjamin warns in both "A Short History of the Photograph" and "The Work of Art in an Age of Mechanical Reproduction," the mechanized and industrialized aspects of photography threaten to efface the spatiotemporal boundaries that separate the object represented from its viewer. In this way, it renders the distance between photographed subject and viewer into an object of manipulation. The "unique manifestation of a distance" that makes up a "peculiar web of space and time"[79] is flattened, generalized, and objectified by the photographic medium, which leaves no trace of the particular or peculiar behind. In short, the history of the photographed subject, its embeddedness in a particular place and time, and the contingencies of its existence are erased by the "desire of contemporary masses to bring things 'closer' spatially and humanly."[80] The ability to collapse distance, then, accompanies the process of colonialism and industrialization. Moreover, the reproducibility of the photos, the "mechanical reproduction" to which Benjamin alludes, belies an underlying relationship between imperialism and consumption. As will become apparent in my discussion of early-twentieth-century tobacco advertisements, photography and its reproducibility enabled the advertising industry to reach mass audiences and, in the case of orientalist tobacco ads, reinforced imperialist attitudes toward the Middle East by commoditizing Arab womanhood.

Therefore, the desire to "bring things close," to use Benjamin's formulation, manifests in the process of technological advancement that gives rise to photography, in the project of imperialism, and in mass consumerism, all of which intersect to form the critical nexus around which a concern with distance is figured. In the midst of social processes that function to erode space by collapsing traditional boundaries of distance, the inclination to bring things close seems to function as a reactionary move to capture and preserve that sense of distance. Ironically, the medium of photography, which participates in eroding spatial boundaries, operates simultaneously as a means of figuratively preserving those very boundaries. In the example of photographed dancing girls at the Chicago World's Fair, these images function as emblems of distance, as incontrovertible proof of the persistence of natural space.

Another irony of the photographic medium, then, is in the way it is perceived as pure documentarian, or recorder of reality, while simultaneously working to shape and produce reality. For instance, in the project of orientalism, as defined by Said, photography certainly aided in the production of knowledge about the "near" or "middle" East by supposedly documenting the reality of life in these regions. However, photographs of "authentic" Arab women served to render these othered women known more so than to maintain accuracy. Indeed, photographic images of Arab womanhood were not only produced at U.S. world's fairs, but also in European studios designed to set the orientalist scene. As Graham-Brown asserts, the photographs produced in western Europe were meant to "transform these imaginative arrangements in the studio into 'proof' of the way people in the Middle East and elsewhere looked and behaved."[81] Photography's perceived partnership with "proof" situated it as a tool with which to accurately document the events of the Fair. In turn, authors such as Buel utilized and exploited this perception of photography as a medium for objective documentation to create a lasting vision of the "magnificence of the Fair" as "preserved by photography."[82] Through this process, subjects of the Fair, like the dancing girls on the "Street of Cairo," were not only made accessible and knowable, they could also be "preserved," to use Buel's phrasing, like specimens in a science experiment.

One of the most widely analyzed photographs of belly dancers at the World's Fair is Buel's "Three Dancing Girls From Egypt" (figure 2.3). The power of this photograph, I would argue, echoing Djebar's analysis of Delacroix's *Women of Algiers in Their Apartment*, lies in its ability to doubly frame the women it represents.

Figure 2.3   Three Dancing Girls From Egypt

Source: Photo by James Buel in *The Magic City*, by James Buel (St. Louis: Historical Publishing Co., 1894), courtesy of the Manuscript, Archives, and Rare Book Library, Emory University.

Not only does photography reveal the dancers to a U.S. audience (in much the same way that Delacroix was afforded a "peek" into the otherwise forbidden zone of the harem), it also captures and enframes them. In this frozen slice of film, the permutations on space begin: the "dancing girls" are simultaneously held distant and drawn near; they are brought close as emblems of distance. First, though, they must be transformed into static objects or symbols and entombed in an anachronistic time and place. The photographic image gives the impression that they are held still in a time and place that may never be regained, but which can nevertheless be preserved. Barthes describes this process as a kind of anesthetization:

> When we define the Photograph as a motionless image, this does not mean only that the figures it represents do not move; it means that they do not *emerge*, do not *leave*: they are anesthetized and fastened down, like butterflies.[83]

Contrary to the idea that these photographs present the realities of the dancing girls' lives to U.S. audiences, Barthes's formulation acknowledges the way in which this framing closes in upon the dancers themselves. This aspect of photography—what Barthes calls the "studium"— provides the objectifying veneer of documentation that blurs the image into a generalized symbol of atavistic Arab womanhood.

Extending Barthes's metaphor of photographed figures as "butter-flies" that are "fastened down," the dancing girls are presented here as objects of study that can be known. These are the grounds, at least, upon which Buel is able to draw his conclusions about them:

> Writers of Oriental stories have created the impression among the unin-formed that houris of the East are sylph-like and beautiful; but close contact reveals them as we behold them here, destitute of animation, formless as badly stuffed animals, as homely as owls, and graceless as stall-fed bovines. But truth compels us to add that the dancing girls in the Midway were not the best types of their race either in form or character, and that their abdominal muscles were the only portions of their anatomy or mind which showed any cultivation.[84]

Buel's tone here is not merely condescending and offensive; it is also downright *familiar*. In claiming that the dancers are "not the best types of their race," he purports not only to know the dancers repre-sented, but to be familiar with the entire race. Combined with the fact that many of the dancers were most likely not from Egypt (the one on the left is thought to be Mahzar from Syria), Buel's brazen com-ments corroborate the fact that the dancers were literally cast (by stage director Bloom) as representative types or specimens of the Orient. Further, Buel's comments about their lack of cultivation (read civiliza-tion) highlight the embeddedness of these dancing girls–as–specimens in the narratives of progress and civilization. They are coveted for their ability to provide fairgoers and fair designers alike with the assurance that the relics of civilization are not completely obliterated in the wake of changes caused by the forward thrust of progress. In this sense they occupy what Anne McClintock calls "anachronistic space;"[85] not only do they represent a faraway region, they also stand in for a distant period in time. Photography further seals them in place. The result is a sort of distant embrace; they are held close as emblems of distance.

Role of the Hootchy Kootchy in the 1893 World's Fair

I have argued that the idea of the Orient was used, in part, as a point of contrast to highlight the immense progress made by the United States. In doing so, I build on the work of scholars such as Rydell; Said; Haraway; Lutz and Collins; and Shohat and Stam,[86] to name a scant few, who have critiqued Eurocentric ways of knowing that marginalize the colonized and previously colonized parts of the world as oppositional others whose purpose is to help constitute the hegemonic center. In particular, I am interested in noting here the ways in which my argument builds on Linda Steet's study *Veils and Daggers: A Century of* National Geographic's *Representation of the Arab World*. Though I discuss *National Geographic* in more detail in chapter 4, I would mention, as does Steet,[87] that the role of *National Geographic* has been similar to that of world's fairs in that both seek to simultaneously edify and entertain the U.S. public while upholding the ideology of progress. Further, *National Geographic* has adhered to a strict principle of "absolute accuracy"[88] and therefore exploited the notion of photography as objective documentation of reality. In the late 1800s, in the period overlapping with the 1893 Chicago World's Fair, Steet demonstrates that the purportedly objective reality presented in *National Geographic* about the Arab world can be summed up by one journalist's comment that "the Arab is an anachronism."[89] Representations of Arabs as atavistic others in fora such as *National Geographic*, the Midway Plaisance at the 1893 World's Fair, and the photographic albums produced after the Fair, demonstrate the way such images came to be indispensable to the very notion of progress. Moreover, the lost past that orientalist images purportedly represent have continued to hold a certain amount of capital for an American audience. One example can be seen in the way that popular performer St. Denis utilized orientalist tropes to develop her "sensual" style of dance, and the way in which she accessed this sensuality by reviving what Buonaventura calls a "golden past"[90] through orientalist notions of the "East." The more the Arab world served as a comparative reference to U.S. progress and as a foil for the accomplishments of technology and modernization, the more securely it became entrenched in the dichotomous opposition by which a White City–identified United States sought to define itself.

As the opposition that helped constitute the centrality of the White City image, the "Orient" (and specifically representative figures of Arab womanhood) participated in the construction of a balance of dualities that undergirded the illusion of social harmony and unity. The much desired and painstakingly orchestrated "nationalizing synthesis," to recall Rydell's, Findling's, and Pelle's term, of the World's Fair depended upon exotic and marginalized sideshows to lend internal coherence to the idea of the White City as pinnacle of civilization. Comparable in form and purpose to freak shows, the belly dance exhibitions at the Fair gained popularity because they had the ability to organize the collective audience in a perceived semblance of unity, and they were therefore able to fashion what Thomson calls the "American cultural self,"[91] the normalized national subject. Despite the racial tensions and economic fissures that lay just under the surface of the U.S. social landscape, fairgoers coalesced as spectators to celebrate the triumph of American progress over unreliable and un-Enlightened "old Arabic dreams" and to therefore publicly witness the snuffing out of the genie's lamp, to recall the metaphor with which Buel opens *The Magic City*.

In the midst of the capitalist and industrialist upheaval characterized by modernity, the figure of the belly dancer emerged in quivering clarity as an identifiably different body on which the mainstream could cast its doubts about the fact of change. Applying Thomson's assertion about the way such unique and different bodies "function as magnets to which culture secures its anxieties, questions, and needs at any given moment,"[92] I argue that the figure of the belly dancer, or the "dancing girl," and the attending photographs of these dancers serve a particular purpose in the turn-of-the-century U.S. cultural landscape. The figure of the belly dancer functioned to provide fairgoers, at least, with a previously unarticulated vocabulary by which to understand and experience the vast changes and felt chaos of their own madly shimmying and wriggling world.

ON COUNTERDISCOURSE: OPPOSING AND RESISTING ORIENTALISM

In her study of Islamic architecture at world's fairs,[93] Zeynep Çelik notes that by the second half of the nineteenth century "Islam had come to mean the binary opposite of Europe."[94] That is, the very construction of belly-dancing concessions and Ottoman, Persian, and Egyptian exhibits at the Fairs belies an orientalist framework whereby the East, or Islam, comes to be seen as the irreducible antithesis of western civilization. If nothing else, such an observation should reveal that the "clash of civilizations" thesis is neither novel not prescient, but that it is a reiteration of orientalist discourse which constructs such oppositions. The reality, as Çelik, Lowe, and others have pointed out, is much more heterogeneous and syncretic, as is typical of cultural contact.

Nevertheless, the power of orientalist discourse is not only that it produces knowledge about the "East" and thereby sets up a relationship of domination, it is also the fact that orientalist discourse creates a limited field of statements through which the "Orient" can be made intelligible. As a result, resistant discourses can potentially be co-opted by the very narrative they seek to subvert. The example of the Ottoman exhibit at the 1893 Chicago World's Fair provides a salient case study through which to examine such counterdiscourses, since it represents an instance in which Ottoman elite sought to create a corrective to orientalist representations, such as belly dancers and reclining odalisques, present at the Fair.

Ottoman self-representation at the Fair itself took a number of forms. The main site of exhibition was the Ottoman Pavilion, which was situated near other national pavilions and designed to simultaneously demonstrate traditional features of Ottoman culture, while displaying evidence of modernization within the waning empire. In addition, the Transportation, Agriculture, Manufacturers, and Mines buildings within the coveted White City itself housed Ottoman displays of technological advancement,[95] which demonstrates a certain amount of standing afforded to the Empire in the international community. Despite its presence in a number of prestigious spaces at the Fair, however, the Ottoman Empire received the bulk of fairgoers' attention at its exhibit on the Midway Plaisance, the Turkish Village. Much like the rest of the "oriental" exhibits on the Midway, the Turkish Village eventually adapted a reproduction of other belly dancing displays in order to attract visitors. Regrettably, this would blur the corrective image of Middle Eastern womanhood Ottoman leaders had worked so hard to construct. In an ironic twist to the carefully constructed counterdiscourse, the power of commodification undermined and usurped the corrective message of the Ottoman Empire.

The incorporation of belly-dancing concessions into the Turkish Village is perhaps evidence enough of the immutability of orientalist discourse. However, I am interested in exploring another attempted intervention on the part of the Ottoman elite, which came in the form of fifty-one photographic albums gifted to the United States by the Sultan Abdul-Hamid II on the occasion of the 1893 Fair. Known as the "Abdul-Hamid II Albums," they were meant to communicate an oppositional set of images of oriental life based on industrialization, modernization, and education rather than exoticized belly dancers and reclining odalisques.[96] These images, arranged largely according to the general categories of educational reform; advanced transportation and industrial technologies; and the modernization of fine arts and architecture, highlighted the theme of modernization as they were created, in the words of Çelik, to "speak back to orientalist discourse."[97] While Çelik argues that the Abdul-Hamid II albums operated as a counterdiscourse, I am interested in exploring the way in which the photographic albums create a narrative that both resists orientalist representations and reifies the underlying binary framework that undergirds the metanarrative of modernity. Rather than proving that "Islam" and the "West" are indeed oppositional, the example of Ottoman self-representation at the 1893 Chicago World's Fair demonstrates the ways in which counterdiscourses often reinforce the binary narratives they seek to deconstruct. In particular, the Ottoman instance elucidates some of the ways in which modernization came to be conflated with westernization.

Though Ottoman rulers had been instituting modernizing reforms since the eighteenth century, including technological innovations, educational reforms, and industrialization, the Abdul-Hamid II Albums seemed keen to reiterate the Ottoman ability to modernize by specifically refuting U.S. and western European stereotypes about the backward, ignorant, irrational, and barbaric Ottoman Empire. Perhaps not surprisingly, then, the largest section in the Albums addresses educational reforms presumably to prove Ottoman enlightenment.[98] A notable similarity between U.S. photographic displays at the Exposition and the Abdul-Hamid II Albums was a focus on demonstrating a commitment to education, yet the differences in these two narratives are striking. In the U.S. display, individual schools, such as the Workingman's School of the Ethical Culture Society in New York City, designed their own displays to represent teaching and learning as active endeavors, as in one scene of a kindergarten group engaged in a lesson. Indeed, the Workingman's Group School display was one of the most admired in the Department of Education exhibit as it successfully highlighted the school's "learning by doing" curriculum[99] and its commitment to providing education for children of the working class.

In contrast, photographs of education in the Abdul-Hamid II Albums focused on the education of girls as a fairly clear rebuttal to the commonly held misconception that girls were not educated in the Middle East.[100] Despite the fact that Turkey had passed legislation advising and then demanding girls' education as early as the 1850s, the Albums concentrate on inundating its U.S. audience with a plethora of images of serious schoolgirls a full forty years later.[101] In fact, it is hardly surprising that the Ottoman Empire would choose the topic of *female* education as one of the primary means of communicating its own "progress" or "advancement." A similar mode of discourse was being deployed concurrently in the British-occupied country of Egypt. British occupation of Egypt in 1882, administered by Lord Cromer, depended upon the rhetoric of the backwardness of Egyptian ways in order to justify English colonial rule. One of the most obvious examples of "traditional" Egyptian society's backwardness, according to the logic of colonial rule, was its failure to educate girls. Regardless of the fact that Cromer had no real interest in supporting education for any segment of the Egyptian population,[102] his line of argument was an effective way of promoting a colonialist agenda by appropriating a feminist stance.[103] The colonialist argument about indigenous backwardness focused in this instance, as in others, around key, sensationalized issues, like girls' education and purportedly barbaric customs, like the veil (to which I will return in chapter 4) and female genital cutting.[104]

However, British occupiers were not the only ones to utilize a feminist logic in the service of another agenda. Indigenous elites sometimes validated the colonialist argument in their own arguments for modernization and reform, wittingly or unwittingly, which is why I am interested here in the Ottoman/Egyptian parallel. Qasim Amin, a famous Egyptian scholar at the turn of the century, is an example of one such elite. Heralded as one of the first Egyptian feminists, he adopted Cromer's discourse about girls' education in order to advance a theory of Islamic modernism that actually capitulated to European colonialist notions. As Leila Ahmed argues in her critique of Amin, his argument for reform conceded Muslim backwardness and advocated a "Western path to success" that focused on the "development" of women.[105] His willingness to denigrate Egyptian womanhood in the service of this argument is evidenced in much of his manifesto, *The Liberation of Women*, but particularly in a passage reminiscent of Buel's description of dancing girls at the 1893 Chicago World's Fair: "Most women are careless about their physical appearance: they do not comb their hair daily, they do not take a bath more than once a week, and they do not know how to use a toothpick."[106] And if these gross generalizations about women's lack of hygiene are not enough, Amin advocates for women's education with the following bold metaphor: "Is it proper to leave our women in a state not much better than that of grazing livestock?"[107] As with Buel's likening of the belly dancers to "stallfed bovines," such colorfully brazen comments operate more as mundane reiterations of tired stereotypes about ignorant, primitive, and lazy natives than to enlighten readers about the conditions of these women's existence. Amin's goal, then, was not actually primarily focused on realizing feminist victories for women, but rather on utilizing women as signifiers to confirm western European perceptions of Egyptian society.

In this respect, Amin's project echoes that of the Ottoman elite at the Chicago World's Fair. Both seek to present evidence of progress in the form of the valuation of girls' education. However, in doing so, each reifies the power of the modernist progressive rhetoric that utilizes the traditional/modern dichotomous paradigm to justify imperialism. Neither succeeds in uncoupling the insidious conflation of modernization and westernization. Although the Ottoman Empire does succeed in formulating an oppositional articulation at the World's Fair, it does not manage to iterate its argument outside of the rigid framework of the metanarrative of modernity. The subversive potential of its message is therefore stabilized within the potent frame of the discourse of progress at the expense of women and girls, whose realities are further flattened into symbolic, categorical forms.

ENCORE

The main focus of this chapter has been an interrogation of the ways that figures of Arab womanhood, imagined and created through U.S. cultural lenses, serve as emblems through which to unpack dominant U.S. narratives about modernity at the turn of the century. As I argued in the introduction to this chapter, I do not see the figure of the belly dancer, or the attending representations of belly dancing, as evidence of the inevitability of the modernity narrative, but rather as a means of problematizing the notion of progress and the disorientations it provokes. Although I am emphatically not discussing the actual conditions of Arab women's lives, it is clear that Arab, Persian, Turkish, and Muslim women's realities are impacted by such orientalist representations, if only to take the example of Mahzar and her colleagues—the women brought to the United States to indulge U.S. fantasies about the exotic and sensual "Orient." While my analysis of the 1893 Fair photographs of dancing girls has focused on the problematic construction of orientalist imagery in the United States, I have not provided any information or analysis of the way in which the belly dancers' experiences affected their own perceptions and images of themselves. The truth is, with the exception of Fahreda Mahzar, there is little record of the women's biographical data, much less their thoughts on their Midway experiences. Furthermore, what little information can be found about Mahzar (pieced together by Carlton in *Looking for Little Egypt* and discussed briefly in Buonaventura's *Serpent of the Nile*) was recorded several years after the Fair (at which time Mahzar had retrospectively claimed the title of Little Egypt) and focuses mostly on the way she adapted herself to her American life and career after the Fair.

The closest inferences that can be made about the belly dancers' own perceptions of the Fair are based on Sol Bloom's autobiography in which he recounts his experiences with the Algerian troop that he brought from France. Needless to say, the information he gives is filtered through numerous layers of translation. There is little reason to believe that the dancers felt unfairly treated or exploited by their sponsors, especially since it is documented that they wrote or traveled back to the Middle East with news of the money there was to be made in dancing for U.S. audiences. Indeed, even Mahzar herself had complaints not about Midway, but about the way in which her dance was interpreted by subsequent belly-dance practitioners. Therefore, I do not see this project as a manifesto against the injustices done to belly-dance performers at the 1893 Chicago World's Fair, but rather as an invitation to explore the complex relationship between representation and reality as well as the ways in which each is constitutive of the other. Because my argument rests so heavily on the premise that representations of Arab women were constructed out of the space where complex social processes, such as imperialism, consumerism, and industrialization merge, I do not believe that I could re-create an accurate picture of the "way things really were" for the dancers even if I had access to their innermost thoughts and feelings. However, by looking at concurrent oppositional discourses, such as the Ottoman presence at the Fair, I believe there is much to be discovered in the interplay between dominant and resistant representations of the "Orient" at the Fair.

Oftentimes these types of resistances can be located in the very same representations that seem to blatantly reflect mainstream attitudes. Reading against the grain of my earlier analysis of the photograph "Three Dancing Girls From Egypt" will enable me to at least honor the critically missing piece of this study—the thoughts and reflections of the belly dancers themselves. Although I was keen to utilize what Barthes calls the "studium" of a photograph to interpret the outside perspective of Arab womanhood, I have not yet considered the other main aspect of a photograph—what Barthes calls its "punctum." Where the studium is idle and bland, the punctum is active and intense. It is that unexpected detail of the photo that can prick its reader and "provoke a tiny shock."[108] Because the punctum is the part of the photograph that is able to reach its viewer at the level of emotion, it is intersubjective in nature. As Barthes explains; "it is an addition: it is what I add to the photograph and *what is nonetheless already there*."[109] It requires an engaged and dedicated reader to bring it out. In the case of "Three Dancing Girls From Egypt," what I add (which is already there) is a critical and intense focus on the distant expressions on the three women's faces. Their gazes act as a punctum for me because they succeed in emerging from the image, which is precisely what the studium ("fastened down" like "butterflies") is unable to do. Their gazes penetrate the boundaries and limitations of the picture album in order to attest to the realities of those women's lives beyond the moment in which the picture was taken. "The *punctum*, then, is a kind of subtle *beyond*" because it "takes the spectator outside its frame."[110] It is this ability to pierce the unwavering resolution of the frame that engages me. Ultimately, I am concerned not just with the women's lives that are sealed behind the frame, but also with the consequences for those lives existing in front of the frame. In other words, my critical investment lies not just with the women pictured in James Buel's photo "Three Dancing Girls From Egypt," but also with the scores of Arab and Arab American women who have since had their realities understood and determined by the flattened image of the "dancing girl." Because categories such as the belly dancer, the harem girl, and the veiled woman can limit one's ability to realize the myriad possibilities of actual Arab, Persian, Turkish, and Muslim women's lives, I highlight the distant gazes on the three Egyptian dancers' faces precisely because they testify to the potential for spectator and subject alike to reach outside the frame of categorical interpretation and toward a more nuanced and complex reading of Arab women's lives.

CHAPTER 3

SELLING LITTLE EGYPT:
THE COMMODIFICATION OF
ARAB WOMANHOOD

Publicity is, in essence, nostalgic. It has to sell the past to the future.

John Berger

The cornucopia of goods that offered themselves up for display and ultimately for consumption at the 1893 Chicago World's Fair left a lasting impact on an increasingly consumerist nation. In years to come, both the themes and the structure of the concessionary exhibits on Midway were replicated in such venues as amusement parks, department stores, and, eventually, in the marketing schemes of the advertising industry. It was in this way that the harem slaves and odalisques of the French orientalist era and the dancing girls of the 1893 World's Fair found their way into advertisements for products such as cigarettes, as exemplified by an ad for *Omar* cigarettes from the second decade of the twentieth century (figure 3.1). In order to sell U.S. consumers on "this Reviving Herb," the advertisers' poetic phrase for tobacco, cigarettes were marketed as products that offered the sensuality and mystery of the Orient in a convenient, packaged form. The orientalist imagery here is unmistakable—recalling the image of the Ottoman sultan, Omar serves as a vague reference to the stereotype of the Terrible Turk, though here he has escaped the political intrigue of the imperial court and seems to represent, instead, only the sexual indulgence and satiety of the harem. His attending

Figure 3.1 Omar Advertisement—"This Reviving Herb"

Source: Warshaw Collection of Business Americana—Tobacco Industry, Archives Center, National Museum of American History, Behring Center, Smithsonian Institution.

harem beauty is clad in the western-style belly-dance outfit popularized in Hollywood films, as she gazes serenely into the gently flowing river. Together, they reinforce the notion that the Orient is always already a feminized and sexualized setting, feminized by the passive rendering of Omar as a romanticized, nonthreatening character, and sexualized by the rendering of his companion as an odalisque, or harem slave. At the same time, though, there is much that is new and distinctive about this orientalist representation, details that reflect particular U.S. engagements with power and progress through the processes of expansionism and consumerism. In this chapter, I will be looking at images of odalisques, exoticized veiled women, dancing girls, and the feminized character of Omar as cultural mythologies through which the contradictions of early-twentieth-century nation-building were negotiated. Although the imperialist process of expansionism invoked the masculinist ideals of rugged individualism and the valorization of conquering "virgin" land, the burgeoning process of consumerism oriented citizens toward the effeteness of leisure and luxury. Remarkably, representations like the *Omar* ad were able to synthesize these seeming contradictions by simultaneously invoking an image of pristine, naturalized space as well as the opulence of material wealth.

Tobacco, especially in the form of cigarettes, provides a particularly salient lens through which to further explore and analyze the gendered notion of civilization as a disciplinary trope. As a luxury product, Turkish blend cigarettes were associated with sophistication and civilization, echoing the ideology of the White City at the 1893 Chicago World's Fair, where civilization gained definition in opposition to the images of backward, primitive others. As demonstrated in the *Omar* ad, this notion of refined civilization also gained clarity in contradistinction to feminized and naturalized orientalist settings. Though early twentieth-century tobacco advertisements come well before the rise of the Marlboro man as popular icon of robust masculinity,[1] cigarette marketing uneasily balanced the contradictory images of the rugged frontier and elite civilization through the well-established mythologies of the veil, the harem, and the belly dancer. They also communicated race, gender, and class ideologies in mainstream society. The cigarette advertisements I analyze in this chapter come from the turn of the century and span the time period from approximately 1900 until just before the United States entered World War I in 1917. During this time period, cigarette smoking comprised less than 7 percent of tobacco consumption in the United States,[2] while chewing tobacco and pipe and cigar smoking were most popular. Though cigarettes would come to be sold as "torches of freedom" for white women[3] after World War I and the achievement of women's suffrage in 1920, cigarette-smoking white women in the early 1900s still faced the stigma of being hypersexualized.[4] This is not to say that cigarette smoking was limited to upper-class white men. In fact, in the late nineteenth century, many consumers associated cigarette smoking with working-class men and women and with immigrants, accounting, in part, for the unpopularity of cigarettes given the xenophobic sentiments of the time. However, *Fatima, Omar,* and *Murad* brands of cigarettes were Turkish blends, and were more expensive,[5] leading them to be marketed mostly to elite, white, male customers. In what they portray as much as what they leave out, advertisements for Turkish blends offer insights into dominant contemporaneous notions of whiteness, civilization, and white femininity. As particularly fraught emblems of masculinity, civilization, and sublimated sexual desire, it is no wonder that cigarettes lent themselves to marketing that utilized orientalist imagery.

Combining all of these interpretive elements, the main trajectory of my argument analyzing *Omar, Fatima,* and *Murad* advertisements is an exploration of the way that an increased orientation toward consumerism, buoyed by new printing and advertising technologies, articulated with both U.S. orientalism and the gender and race ideologies undergirding the product of tobacco. Building on my analysis of the progress narrative at the 1893 Chicago World's Fair, I will be exploring the new permutations of space and time stimulated by the advertising industry and by mass consumerism. Although the commodification of the "Orient" in the United States has roots in world's fairs, which imported and recreated scenes of the exotic East to be consumed by U.S. fairgoers, advertisements combined commodification with printing technologies that enabled orientalist images to reach consumers en masse, thereby significantly collapsing the space between consumer and orientalist image. In the transition from world's fairs as sites of commodity fetish to mass consumerism, traditional notions of distance and time shifted considerably as orientalist images suddenly traveled to spectators, rather than vice versa. Looking at how the 1893 Fair operated, in one sense, as a giant marketplace to be visited and toured, Curtis Hinsley describes it as "an early form of touristic consumption,"[6] thereby highlighting the way that, ironically, shorter distances between fairgoers and replicas of exotic locales enabled them to imaginatively travel great distances. The combination of travel-for-leisure and commercialism in the notion of "touristic consumption" also maps onto early-twentieth-century

Turkish blend advertisements, through which consumers were also meant to experience the indulgences and pleasures of imaginatively traveling to the Orient.

Distance, then, could be compressed into the act of purchase since advertisements such as those for *Omar* cigarettes ostensibly sold a piece of the exotic Orient to the customer. Furthermore, the rise in advertising and printing technologies such as the lithograph and the printing press, which enabled producers to reach mass consumers in a shorter amount of time, compounded the general sense of time and space compression. Just as belly dancers at the 1893 Chicago World's Fair provided a spectacle that organized audience members around the collective act of looking, images of belly dancers in *Omar* advertisements functioned as spectacles that similarly signified the stability of distance and space in the midst of rapidly shifting spatiotemporal realities. Representations of Arab womanhood in early-twentieth-century tobacco advertisements serve as a salient example of the way a complicated structure of feeling, characterized by alienation, nostalgia, and disorientation, inhered in the visual vocabulary of harem girls, belly dancers, and veiled women. Because the rise of consumerism informs this structure of feeling so profoundly, I spend the first part of the chapter both tracing the ways that a consumerist shift in capitalism altered predominant spatial and temporal dimensions and exploring the ways that consumerist institutions, such as world's fairs and the advertising industry, operated as disciplinary and normalizing structures for U.S. citizens. Ultimately, in the second part of the chapter, I argue that *Fatima, Omar,* and *Murad* ads function as cultural mythologies that speak to the disorientations of capitalism, consumerist modernity, and U.S. expansionism.

SELLING DISTANCE

With Frederick Jackson Turner's pronouncement, at the inauguration of the 1893 Chicago World's Fair, that the frontier was gone, the progress narrative became deterritorialized. Though the masculinist project of expansionism continued with the conquest of Hawaii and the Philippines, the general inclination to possess land began to transition into a desire to possess things as consumption metamorphosed into the "driving force of progress."[7] In other words, the notion of progress began to be refigured through the process of consumerism.

The transformation of the notion of material progress into consumerist progress paralleled a significant shift in capitalist stages. As David Harvey argues, it is precisely the moments of transition in stages of capitalism that offer the greatest insights into the way capitalism impacts broader social forces. Because "capitalism is growth-oriented," he explains,[8] it must also be "technologically and organizationally dynamic." In other words, it shifts from one stage to another because it has outgrown the limitations of the former and is dynamic enough to shift itself into the latter. Within a capitalist framework, growth is measured not only in terms of increased production but also in terms of expanded markets. The technologies that contributed to a budding era of consumerism were those that enabled the goods for sale to rapidly and sometimes simultaneously (as with advertising) reach a mass audience or market, thereby drastically reducing the distance between product and consumer. At the same time, because the dynamic nature of capitalism is more transparent during this moment of transition, its unsettling nature once again rises to the surface; according to Harvey, in these moments it is experienced as a "radical, total, and violent rupture with the past."[9] The past, in this case, is one in which the laborers, or "direct producers" had not yet been "violently separated"[10] from the means of their production. Precisely because the moment of transition creates a feeling of rupture, then, it enables an idealization of the time before industrialization, which is symbolized in the United States by the agrarian tradition. As a reminder of this final rupture or separation from the past, the emergent consumerist sensibility manifests intense nostalgia for a lost or timeless past in marketing campaigns.

The notion of progress, then, which had served as an organizing mechanism for the Chicago World's Fair, mutated in the early 1900s both in response to the rise of consumerism and in response to shifts in U.S. imperialist formations. Although the notion of progress constructed at the World's Fair as demonstrated by grand advancements in technological prowess continued to shape U.S. sensibilities of capitalist modernity, the disorientations of such progress began to emerge as well. In particular, the completion of the transcontinental railroad and the invention of printing technologies had the effect of shifting the very dimensions of space and time. While the railroad standardized units of time across the expanse of the U.S. by instituting standard time zones in 1883,[11] the printing industry seemed to collapse the space between the senders and receivers of advertising messages by increasing the speed and volume at which those messages could be produced and disseminated. Indeed, the transcontinental railroad did not only revolutionize the concept of time for Americans, it altered the very boundaries according to which space and time seemed to be divided. According to Alan Trachtenberg, as passenger and cargo trains hurtled through the continental United States and across the boundaries of standard time zones, arriving at destinations according to the schedule of time rather than place, they had the effect of "annihilating space or distance by reconceiving it as time."[12] As the resolute confines of time and space collapsed with the rapidly moving force of progress, a concomitant desire to reinstate the boundaries of distance increased. In the midst of a new social reality in which both spatial and temporal distances seemed to be disappearing altogether, the process of consumerism introduced ways of being that addressed fresh anxieties about the changing nature of time and space. Within such a cultural milieu, images of the exotic and timeless Orient functioned in marketing schemes to sell a sense of distance back to the consumer, which was particularly salient in the midst of such large spatiotemporal shifts. In this respect, images of harem girls in tobacco advertisements continue the orientalist legacy of the photographs from the 1893 Chicago World's Fair. The orientalist representations that were recreated in world's fairs exhibits, amusement park displays, and advertising images all served the paradoxical purpose of enabling U.S. consumers to experience the mystery and sensuality of the Orient up close while simultaneously reifying the boundaries of space that defined the Arab and Muslim worlds as distant and exotic lands. Serving as the receptacles for U.S. consumers' displaced nostalgia for a lost agrarian tradition, representations of the Orient also cast the familiar characters of the harem girl and the belly dancer into a liminal zone of timelessness, which could not be effaced by the progress narrative.

THE COMMODITY COMPLEX

The popularity of belly dancing exhibits at the 1893 Chicago World's Fair not only inspired similar displays at amusement parks and venues in the years after the Fair, it also signaled a larger shift in U.S. society. Therefore, Little Egypt's seemingly effortless transition from the Midway fairgrounds to the various sites of the up-and-coming amusement industry (places such as Luna Park and Coney Island that had roller-coaster rides and exhibits or shows) had as much to do with her utterly marketable shimmy as with the uncertain undulations of U.S. society as it wriggled its way into the early 1900s consumerist era. The set up of the World's Fair as a "display of goods" and likened in that way to the lavish department store displays[13] of subsequent decades actually served as a structural forerunner to the types of institutions that would dominate in an increasingly consumerist society.[14]

Institutions such as world's fairs, amusement parks, department stores, and the advertising industry formed the basis of what I am calling the "commodity complex;" these were cross-referential structures that signaled a shift from colonialist to neocolonialist forms of power and possession, prefiguring the neoliberal imperialism characteristic of the contemporary context. If the United States cultivated a national identity based on its agrarian roots, the project of imperialist expansion by which it had acquired those roots continually troubled the founding mythology of the United States as an anticolonialist nation built on the revolutionary idea of a struggle for independence. The colonization of indigenous American land notwithstanding, formal colonial rule runs contrary to the origin myth of U.S. nationhood. Through an investigation of institutions in the commodity complex, then, I am interested in the ways that consumerism helped inculcate new forms of power and new ways of being increasingly determined by economic relationships.

As precursors to institutions such as department stores and the advertising industry that predominated in a consumerist era, both the amusement industry and the world expositions were structural models for those that followed; they helped cultivate a new paradigm of consumer spectacle that would inform the advertising industry. Indeed, as Kasson argues, the construction of amusement parks according to the convention of spectacle as a means of increasing profits informed the way in which shopping malls would be designed and organized.[15] If, as Walter Benjamin claims, "world exhibitions are the sites of pilgrimages to the commodity fetish,"[16] then examples of the emerging amusement industry—such as Coney Island and Luna Park in New York—can be considered as extensions of these pilgrimage sites. These new amusement fairs and carnivals imitated world's fairs in the way that they similarly packaged and presented a "collection of goods." Furthermore, the network of relationships among commodities at these sites served to mask the deteriorating network of communal or societal relationships in a world characterized by increasing social detachment and isolation. As Guy Debord argues, the "society of the spectacle"[17] mediates human relationships through image and representation; the commodity spectacle, then, alienates consumers while animating commodities and their advertisements.

As the foundations of the commodity complex, the world's exhibitions set a structural precedent for the way that commodity spectacle would intersect with the projects of nation-building and imperialism. If world's fairs were sites of commodity fetish, they were also organized according to a logic of surveillance. Like other modern institutions, such as the military, the hospital, the school, and, of course, the prison,[18] they were highly ordered and regulated around the act of looking. As I have discussed, fairgoers observed the material progress of the nation in terms of technological and structural advancements, but, more importantly, they were also set apart as objective observers of subjugated others who were literally displayed in ethnographic villages and in the Midway concessions. In this way, world's fairs produced and codified imperialist power relationships around the act of surveillance.

These examples of the way imperialism and expansionism manifested in world's fairs demonstrate the emergence of a particular structure of feeling in the context of twentieth-century capitalist modernity. Both the commodity spectacle and the extension of imperialist expansion led to collective feelings of isolation, detachment, and separation from both agrarian and mythical origins. Through "manufacturing the experience of the real"[19] in ethnographic displays, then, world's fairs offered up fabrications of authenticity that were meant to quell fairgoers' anxieties by presenting the progress narrative as the natural order of things.

The ultimate manifestation of one such fabrication of authenticity is the fact that the 1904 World's Fair in St. Louis boasted a replica of Ottoman Jerusalem built almost to scale[20] as one of its central and most prominent exhibits. Building on the success of amusement parks such as the Lakeside at Chautauqua's Holy Land (1874), the replica of Jerusalem at the 1904 Fair tapped into a long-standing U.S. fascination with images of the Holy Land. Like its predecessors, this replication held little similarity to the contemporaneous Ottoman Palestine, but instead attempted to "manufacture the experience of the real," to recall Timothy Mitchell's formulation, where Ottoman Palestine was considered to be the "real" site of Puritan Christian origins. Given the fact that the 1904 Fair was also named the Louisiana Purchase Exposition in commemoration of one of the greatest land acquisitions in U.S. expansionist history, the inclusion of Jerusalem as a site of faux pilgrimage is significant. It operated as an important counterpoint to the dominant narrative of progress through expansion, which emerged as a central theme of the Fair since U.S. expansion to the Philippines and beyond extended the ideology of Manifest Destiny through the logic of economic domination. When understood within the larger context of the St. Louis Exposition narrative, it becomes clear that the Jerusalem exhibit served to buttress a U.S. notion of progress by serving as the symbolic site of origin for that progress, thereby invoking the notion of the Holy Land as the genesis of western (Christian) civilization. As Burke Long argues: "The Fair offered staged but nevertheless reassuring images of a vigorous United States enthroned as the vanguard of civilization, democratic liberty, and cultural progress. And she was heir to God's blessings bestowed on the world through ancient Jerusalem."[21] Through the modality of civilization that understands the Middle East to represent the timeless origins of western civilization, the architects of U.S. nation-building could invest in the notion of progress, while simultaneously projecting the image of a pristine and mythical past. The presence of the Holy Land, in replica form, at the 1904 Fair therefore served the purpose of reifying the mythology of a universal origin while also highlighting the proliferating progress of a growing U.S. nation.[22]

"BILL IT LIKE A CIRCUS:" THE RISE OF THE ADVERTISING INDUSTRY

As a result of popular notions of the Middle East as timeless and pure (as in the Jerusalem replica at the 1904 Fair), orientalist representations lent themselves to fabricating authenticity through advertising as well. In an increasingly manufactured society, shows and displays that focused on a primordial world—innocent of technology—held great appeal for their audiences. The Orient provided one such imagined space in which the innocence of origins could be reclaimed. Indeed, Leach suggests that "Orientalism...symbolized a feeling of something missing from Western culture itself."[23] The "something missing" from western culture was not simply the opulent and exotic oriental goods that were widely coveted in the late 1800s. What was missing was rather something that was felt to have been lost in the process of industrial and technological expansion. The appeal of the Orient was actually a nostalgic desire for a constantly receding natural and innocent past. Furthermore, orientalist objects were portrayed as authentic by virtue of their relationship to this distant past, no matter how fabricated or how "modern" the representation or performance of that "ancient" time and place was. In fact, Phineas Taylor Barnum, father of the freak show, built a "fabulous Oriental villa," called Iranistan, as a "gigantic advertisement for his work" in 1846.[24] Advertising, especially in the mid to late nineteenth century, was thenceforth associated with the outrageous flare of the circus[25] as advertisers' inclination to "bill it like a circus"[26] solidified the link between advertising and other institutions in the commodity complex, such as amusement parks and world's fairs. If sideshows, such as the dancing girls, provided identifiably different bodies that functioned to normalize and discipline mass audiences, orientalist advertisements manufactured notions of the "real," which could speak to the collective experience of alienation and isolation.

Though advertisements paralleled the way in which goods took on magical, animated characteristics at expositions (sites of the "commodity fetish"), the advertising industry was also increasingly invested in presenting and promoting a more sober conception of the way in which technology informed and influenced the progress of a turn-of-the-century United States. What was really magical, according to the emerging industry, was the ability of new technological advancements to increase production and manufacturing capabilities of companies. A 1901 advertisement, for the Chicago Pneumatic Tool Co., reveals this ideological bias toward the magic of industrialization by juxtaposing "Two Magicians:" One is the "oriental" Aladdin (depicted with East Asian features and sitting next to a "palace" that actually looks like a Chinese pagoda). The other is the "occidental" character of the "modern mechanic" who is able to build great monuments and structures such as the Eiffel Tower.[27] The patronizing representation of "oriental" magic, which conflates Middle and Far Eastern cultures, indicates that these ancient civilizations are not able to compete with the new advanced "magic" of modernization. Two modalities of civilization are therefore simultaneously deployed—the notion of the East as romantic and fantastical as well as the notion of the East as an antiquated precursor to western civilization. Both serve the purpose of rationalizing progress.

The advertising industry's own relationship to technological progress can be measured largely in terms of the rise of printing as one of the largest industries in the United States.[28] Not only did printing machinery revolutionize the types of images that advertisers were able to project, but more importantly it also drastically increased the volume of people that the advertisements were able to reach. While world's fairs, amusement parks, and department stores relied on their own mass appeal to bring a large audience to the site of the attraction, the development of printing technologies that enabled mass production succeeded in delivering advertising images to the masses. In this way, the process of consumerism changed the dimensions of spectacle by collapsing the space between the consumer and the product. Like the Midway Plaisance or the Coney Island sideshow, advertising is able to unify the disparate set of onlookers, but it does so by organizing a diffused collective around one normalizing force. Furthermore, it fundamentally alters collective notions of space and distance. In other words, the ability of the advertising message to meet the consumer "halfway" by bringing the spectacle to her or him reinforces the "desire of contemporary masses to bring things 'closer' spatially and humanly,"[29] and emphasizes the disorienting nature of spatiotemporal shifts.

Ultimately, the seemingly paradoxical tension inherent in the simultaneous desire to bring things closer and hold them apart is one that is influenced by the moment of transition in predominant modes of production. The overwhelming shift toward consumerism stimulates a conflicted feeling between a simpler past and a progressive future. Raymond Williams understands this tension in terms of the seemingly oppositional terms of "country" and "city" and the myriad connotations of each:

> On the country has gathered the idea of a natural way of life: of peace, innocence, and simple virtue. On the city has gathered the idea of an achieved centre: of learning, communication, light. Powerful hostile associations have also developed: on the city as a place of noise, worldliness and ambition; on the country as a place of backwardness, ignorance, limitation.[30]

The conflicts and tensions present in the concepts of the country and the city mirror the ambivalent relationship that turn-of-the-century U.S. citizens had toward the notion of progress. On one hand, a nationalist theory and masculinist ideal of western expansion promoted an American identity rooted in the ideals of rugged individualism. On the other hand, the development of technology and machinery worked to alleviate the harsh nature of a frontier sort of life. Ironically, the advancement of technology and increased urbanization had succeeded in progressively "civilizing" the nation away from its rugged roots. This was a tension inherent to the concept of progress, which inevitably moved away from the agrarian ideals of individualism so important to dominant notions of American identity. Although orientalist images of Arab womanhood could not resolve this tension, they ultimately functioned as placeholders to both mark the tension and deflect it. As feminized (male and female) figures of laziness and decadence, they served as foils for an articulation of U.S. masculinist rugged individualism. As emblems of the primitive and backward East, they served to highlight the advancement of U.S. civilization.

If progress brought greater luxury, this opulence threatened to dull the rugged edge of U.S. individualism. The loss of space associated with the myths of the "frontier" and the "Wild West" similarly threatened to soften the image of that U.S. masculinist hero, the cowboy. At the same time, mechanical and technological progress seemed to be crucial to the development of the United States as a world power. The cultural mythologies of veils, harems, and belly dancers in early-twentieth-century tobacco advertisements reflected these conflicting desires through the multi-edged prism of agricultural and manufactured abundance.[31] By framing and manipulating images of the fertile soil, of the efficient machine, and of the luxury of material abundance, advertisers were able to capitalize on the anxieties of a nation nestled uneasily in the matrix of turbulent social processes such as modernization, expansionism, and consumerism. Although images of the rich and fertile land addressed newfound concerns with what these processes seemed to be annihilating, images of technological advances and of increased prosperity reinforced the great promise of the progress narrative. The tobacco industry, as both the producer of a luxury product and as an increasingly influential and burgeoning business in the United States, stood at the matrix of popular notions of progress and abundance and was therefore poised, for many reasons, to co-opt and commodify the readily available imagery of orientalist themes.

SMOKING TO THE SETTING SUN: ADVERTISING TOBACCO

In a promotional booklet published by the American Tobacco Company, entitled *The American Tobacco Story*,[32] the story of tobacco is woven into the origin myth of the Americas by way of its link to the fabled hero-discoverer, Christopher Columbus. Though the booklet was published in 1964, its framing of tobacco as an integral aspect of founding U.S. mythologies parallels the tropes that U.S. advertisers utilized in turn-of-the-century advertisements. As Ella Shohat and Robert Stam have noted, "the Columbus story is crucial to Eurocentrism";[33] it establishes a narrative whereby white European explorers and newcomers act as "Adams in the virgin land"[34] of the Americas, thereby colonizing the land through the logic of colonization as a civilizing mission. In the rhetoric of the Americas as a virgin land, white European settlers are cast as the agential, masculinist penetrators of a feminized, passive, and vacant land. The construction of the Columbus tobacco story in *The American Tobacco Story* bears these claims out. The booklet explains that, "Christopher Columbus was offered tobacco leaves by Caribbean Indians who, perhaps, thought him a god."[35] The suggestion that indigenous peoples of the Americas would have attributed godlike status to Columbus simultaneously inscribes a narrative of Eurocentrism and emphasizes the implied naïveté of indigenous peoples of the Americas. A similar construction of American Indians as noble savages persists in the fable of the first Thanksgiving. Tobacco served as a "sign of peace," the narrative goes, when indigenous Americans taught the settler-colonialists how to survive in the New World and, presumably, as a signal of trusting innocence and nobility, offered them a "peace pipe." In some of the primary founding symbols of U.S. nationhood,[36] the practice of justifying domination and colonization through feminizing territories of conquest, through rendering indigenous people into objectified and naturalized aspects of the landscape, and through deploying the logic of the civilizing mission parallels the orientalist production of knowledge about the Arab and Muslim worlds. It is no wonder, then, that orientalist imagery provides the visual vocabulary through which tobacco advertisers sought to articulate the tropes of superior U.S. progress and civilization in the midst of the turmoil of expansionism and consumerism. Again, as the promotional pamphlet proclaims:

> Cigarettes and civilization—the two seem to go together. Primitive Americans discovered tobacco, and chewed it. When they learned how to cultivate the soil, they raised tobacco and invented pipes for smoking it. Some who reached a higher degree of civilization developed cigarettes.[37]

Here, the American Tobacco Company makes it clear that the white settlers developed the more sophisticated practice of smoking cigarettes as a more advanced form of consuming tobacco than smoking a "peace" pipe or chewing tobacco. Although tobacco is threaded throughout founding U.S. myths, cigarettes in particular play a complex role in the articulation of U.S. nationhood vis-à-vis the notion of civilization. Cigarettes are gendered, raced, classed, and sexualized, and, as such, they are rich symbols for manipulation. At the turn of the century, during the period in which the advertisements I analyze here were produced, Turkish blend cigarettes were cultivated as signifiers of decadence, sophistication, and superiority. Perhaps because of the way in which they draw attention to the mouth, coupled with their phallic shape, they were also quite sexualized; women smoking cigarettes were likely to be labeled as sexually deviant (either seen as masculinized lesbians or as lascivious, eroticized women).[38] Cigarettes emerge, then, as potent markers of elite status, eroticism, masculinity, and whiteness. As such, they serve as multivalent symbols through which to investigate larger notions of civilization, progress, and expansionism as they cohered in images of Arab womanhood.

Selling Cigarettes

In the early twentieth century, one of the biggest challenges tobacco companies faced in selling the product of tobacco was the fact that it was considered to be a leisure or luxury product. Not only did companies have to convince consumers of each particular brand's superiority, but each manufacturer also had to sell the public on the product of tobacco to begin with. In order to do so, advertisers of tobacco products relied on the potent imagery of abundance vis-à-vis American progress and employed a strategy that reflected an intricate interplay of tropes, sometimes focusing on the fertility and fecundity of the earth, sometimes on increased technological prowess and efficient machinery, and sometimes on the notion of plentiful opulence. Given the orientalist association of the Middle East and the Ottoman Empire with decadence, orientalist images of Arab womanhood easily translated into tobacco ads emphasizing cigarettes as a luxury product. In a particularly American iteration of orientalist themes, however, representations of Arab womanhood also served, by way of opposition, to highlight the tropes of the frontier and of rugged individualism.

The set of advertisements that I analyze, all of which incorporate representations of Arab womanhood, hail from the early twentieth century, during which time Turkish tobacco changed both the composition and the marketing of American cigarettes. A blend of different types of tobacco leaf—Bright, Barley, and Turkish or Oriental—comprise most cigarettes. These types have distinctive flavors depending not only on the leaf itself, but also on the type of soil in which they are grown and their method of curing (heat dried, air dried, or sun dried, respectively). While Bright and Barley (domestic) types of tobacco dominated the market in the mid to late nineteenth century, straight Turkish cigarettes began to flood the American market in the 1880s and, by 1902, they had captured 20 percent of sales.[39] During the 1910s, the top-selling cigarette brands were Turkish blends, such as *Fatima* produced by Liggett & Myers.[40] The incorporation of Turkish tobacco leaf into popular cigarette brands suggests an explanation of why the market was flooded with a host of new products that utilized orientalist themes and imagery. However, the relationship between Turkish tobacco leaf and the orientalist imagery associated with the new brands flooding the market was more than a simple metonymic correlation. Though the Turkish blends typically consisted of about 60 percent domestic tobacco and only 40 percent Turkish tobacco,[41] according to *The Tobacco Merchants Association of Cigarette Brand Names 1913– 1977*, there were thirty-five brands of cigarettes between the years of 1892 and 1933 that referenced the "Orient." Moreover, fifteen of those had Egypt, rather than Turkey, in their title. As the majority of brand names did not actually name the geographical region from which the tobacco hailed, the orientalist imagery in the marketing of Turkish blends cigarettes clearly indicates the metaphoric importance of images of veiled women, belly dancers, and reclining odalisques in the marketing and selling of tobacco in the United States. In the following pages, I elaborate on the ways in which *Fatima*, *Murad*, and *Omar* cigarettes utilized representations of Arab womanhood to manipulate notions of luxury and fecundity for U.S. audiences.

The Luxury of Tobacco

Again, tobacco advertisers sought to position Turkish blend cigarettes as luxury products and they were therefore interested in associating it with images of opulence. The European understanding of the Ottoman Empire as excessive, both in terms of its decadence and in terms of its patriarchal machinations here translates into U.S. advertising images that revisit and reinterpret representations of harem girls found in the typical poses of reclining odalisque and belly dancer for their sultan masters.[42] One of the most popular early Turkish blends was *Fatima*, a brand that is represented by a transparently veiled woman (figure 3.2). She wears a regal and jewel-studded headdress and gazes benignly, if not invitingly, out to her audience. She is meant to seem aloof and mysterious, yet approachable and attainable; consumers should buy *Fatima*, the ad suggests, if they would like a taste of the exotic. Like representations of European female nudes in French orientalist paintings, the image of Fatima here seems to replicate U.S. and western European ideals of beauty, while signifying exoticism through the incorporation of orientalist props, such as the elaborate headdress and transparent veil. The transparency of the veil further eroticizes the scene by highlighting the transgression of an implied barrier. In contradistinction to contemporary images of women rendered as hidden behind opaque veils, these early twentieth-century ads concentrate on the symbol of the veil as a sign of exoticism rather than a sign of oppression or potential threat. The metamorphosis of meanings associated with the veil parallels the changing relationship

Figure 3.2   Fatima Advertisement—Black and White Logo

Source: Warshaw Collection of Business Americana—Tobacco Industry, Archives Center, National Museum of American History, Behring Center, Smithsonian Institution.

between the United States and the Middle East. In the early 1900s, as I mentioned earlier, the Middle East primarily invoked associations with the Holy Land, as demonstrated in most *Fatima* ads with the inclusion of the religious symbols of the Maltese cross (as a symbol of Christian origins) and a crescent and star (symbol of Islam).[43] The incorporation of these two symbols in simultaneity also demonstrates

the way in which orientalist imagery is sometimes cast as both familiar and irreducibly different, thereby paralleling the figure of the belly
dancer in 1893 Chicago World's Fair photographs.

Like the eroticized nudes of French orientalist paintings and belly
dancing displays at the 1893 Fair and beyond, though, perhaps the
most salient feature of the *Fatima* advertisement is its (literally) veiled
representation of female sexuality and white aesthetic ideals under the
guise of orientalism. Advertising text from the period of 1913–1915
reads "Have *you* had the pleasure?"[44] and invites the customer to
imagine himself[45] singularly selected to avail himself of the pleasures
Fatima has to offer, where "pleasure" is laden with the fairly overt connotations of sexual pleasure. Mimicking the way that French orientalist
paintings depicted idealized figures of white femininity in European
female nudes who carried or wore orientalist props, the *Fatima* ad
also presents an eroticized image of white femininity, rationalizing its
lascivious content through the incorporation of orientalist elements.
Though the suggestive overtures of sexual pleasure may not have been
acceptable to the "polite" society Liggett & Myers sought to reach, by
casting prurience onto an orientalized setting, the advertisers deployed
the trope of civilization and the lure of erotic fantasy simultaneously.

The advertisers of *Fatima* were careful to round out such messages
of luxury, opulence, and subtle sexuality with advertisements implying that U.S. consumers could afford this exotic indulgence because
of the superiority of the United States, as pinnacle of progress and
civilization. *Fatima* links itself to a refined and cultivated society with
an ad that announces its award-winning status at the 1915 Panama-
Pacific International Exposition in San Francisco and copy that reads:
"Fatima: 'A Sensible Cigarette,'" a message that appeals to the presumed sophistication of its astute and discerning (civilized) customer.
Indeed, here the marketers of *Fatima* use a logic reminiscent of the
Midway Plaisance at the Chicago World's Fair, which was organized
according to the philosophy of scientific racism; the ethnographic
exhibits not only presented people from different parts of the world
as objects of study, they also purportedly arranged these peoples from
least to most evolved cultures. Needless to say, from the fair designers'
perspective, the evolutionary scale culminated at the "White City,"
the U.S. created presentation of its own advancements as the apex
of civilization. The Chicago World's Fair was not alone in operating
according to this logic—it echoed previous and subsequent world's
fairs (such as the 1889 Paris Exposition and the 1915 Panama-Pacific
International Exposition) and anthropological studies, as well as the
booming genre of travel writing. The grand, neoclassical architecture

in the dominant image of this advertisement therefore communicates the notion of the advanced U.S. civilization displayed at world's fairs, while deploying the gendered notion of civilization through oppositional identification with naturalized, primitive others.

Turning now to one last *Fatima* image, I will further explore the way the "Orient" serves as an oppositional counterpoint to the notion of civilized, advanced U.S. and western European societies. As was the case for French orientalist painter Eugène Delacroix, who wrote about his envy of the native Moroccans' "closeness to nature," a number of European travel writers sought out what they imagined to be the more pure and unadulterated natural landscape of distant and exotic lands as a welcome relief from the busy turmoil of their urban-industrial, technologically advanced cities. The expression of this type of relief can be seen on the face of the presumed consumer of *Fatima* cigarettes in another advertisement, a white man whose manicured looks and tailored suit indicate that he is a member of elite society (figure 3.3). He is shown here, in relaxed reverie, holding a pamphlet that reads "A Trip to the Orient." His wistful repose seems to suggest that the cigarette and pamphlet alone are enough to imaginatively transport him on his own "trip to the Orient." Thanks to Liggett & Myers, this *Fatima* image suggests, U.S. citizens in the early twentieth century did not even have to leave their homes to experience the natural decadence of the exotic Orient. They could rely on the power of Turkish blend cigarettes to transport them to exotic and distant lands. Moreover, like the suggestive

Figure 3.3   Fatima Advertisement—"Trip to the Orient"

Source: Warshaw Collection of Business Americana—Tobacco Industry, Archives Center, National Museum of American History, Behring Center, Smithsonian Institution.

ad copy inviting consumers to enjoy the "pleasure" of *Fatima*, the "Trip to the Orient" image suggests that *Fatima* also inspires sexual fantasy, adding an eroticized element to the idea of "touristic consumption."

The notion of colonized lands and peoples as more primitive, innocent, and natural, so central to much travel writing at the time, is embedded in the logic of scientific racism, which purports to use science-based reason to prove the superiority of civilized societies, such as France, Britain, and the United States, in opposition to the assumed inferiority of much of the rest of the world. The implicit assumption of *Fatima*'s "trip to the Orient" advertisement builds on the logic of scientific racism by incorporating it into the process of consumerism, thereby creating what Anne McClintock calls "commodity racism."[46] If scientific racism situates white men at the apex of the evolutionary scale, commodity racism democratizes the flow of this message (though not its content), disseminating it to mass audiences (through advertisements for consumer products), thereby extending the ideology beyond the realm of literate, propertied elite.[47]

Murad, a Turkish Blend made first by S. Anargyros before it was incorporated into The American Tobacco Company, further exemplifies this shift from scientific to commodity racism (figure 3.4). The image on this particular ad demonstrates the way in which the Orient is offered up both as the opposite (and therefore balancing) other to U.S. progress and also as something to be possessed by the desirous and worldly customer. The name of the brand, *Murad*, is borrowed from four sultans of the Ottoman Empire (Murads I, II, III, and IV), each of who ruled in different centuries, beginning in the fourteenth century and ending in the seventeenth. It should come as no surprise, then, that the imagery in the ad closely resembles representations found in French orientalist painting, which intimately engages dominant stereotypes of the Ottoman Empire in its representations of harems and Turkish baths. The central woman in this *Murad* ad is the prototypical harem girl found in paintings such as those by Jean Léon Gérôme, who often placed black female servants next to white nude figures in order to accentuate and highlight the licentiousness of the space of the harem in the mind of his audience. She is pictured gazing at her own image, which is literally reflected off of her racialized other, who holds a rounded object in front of himself so that the centralized white woman can see her own reflection. Like in the *Fatima* ad, the *Murad* representation utilizes an orientalist setting in which to locate an image of idealized white womanhood. That she gazes at her own reflection pictorially reinforces predominant notions of domesticity

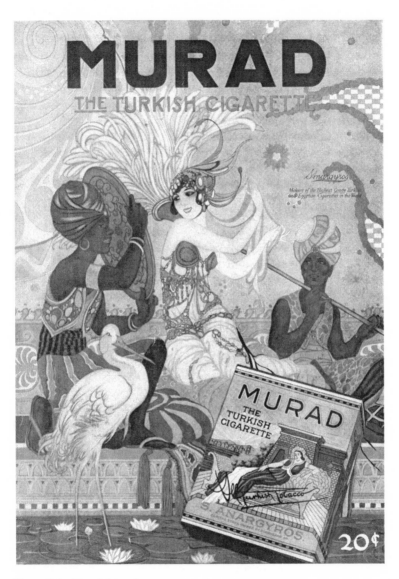

Figure 3.4 Murad Advertisement

Source: Warshaw Collection of Business Americana—Tobacco Industry, Archives Center, National Museum of American History, Behring Center, Smithsonian Institution.

and traditional gender ideologies, according to which idealized figures of elite white femininity attend to the work of self-beautification.
As an "emblem of Enlightenment selfconsciousness,"[48] the mirror
also seems to reiterate the idea that the project of imperialism is a
benevolent, civilizing mission, thereby subtly naturalizing the power
dynamics in the scene, and rendering racial and gender hierarchies as
essentialized aspects of civilization.

The *Murad* advertisement parallels elements of French orientalist painting in that it uses an orientalized setting and set of props
to safely render a sexualized image of white womanhood. Because it
would not be palatable to her audience if she were completely nude,
she wears an erotic costume that looks as if it is an assemblage of
belly dancing outfit styles. Despite the Americanized departure from
French orientalist nudes like *The Grand Odalisque*, the setting of the
Orient still operates as a guise for displaying an image of white female
sexuality. In this sense, it presents a doubly eroticized image both of
an othered sexuality and of the potential transgression of conservative sexual mores for white women. The *Murad* image utilizes the
harem (or bath) trope to eroticize the setting of the scene, but it
relies on another stereotype of the Ottoman Empire—its excessive
indulgence—in order to market its product as an object of opulence
that can be possessed through purchase. What is actually being sold,
therefore, in addition to cigarettes, is the concept of luxury as abundance and the possibility for the consumer to purchase her/his own
piece of it. By depicting the female figure as an odalisque, who is
being fanned by the attending eunuchs and who presumably waits to
attend to the needs of her sultan master, the advertisement communicates a double message of decadence. It sells both the notion of leisure
and opulence in abundance and the notion of sexuality in abundance
to U.S. audiences constrained by the demands of, to paraphrase Max
Weber, the Puritan (work) ethic and the spirit of capitalism.[49]

The Wild East? Harem Girls
in the Virgin Land

Another brand of Turkish Blends, *Omar*, demonstrates the way in
which an agrarian or land-based understanding of abundance min-
gled and merged with the trope of the decadent and opulent Orient.
Like *Murad*, *Omar* parallels some of the images and themes found in
French orientalist painting, but *Omar* ads also manifest a particular
U.S. expansionist adaptation to these themes. Many of the *Omar* ads
from the 1910s deploy the classic orientalist imagery of the harem,

as symbol of both material and sexual availability and abundance.[50] However, in a particularly salient adaptation for the U.S. expansionist context, the *Omar* advertisements combine the imagery of the harem with that of the frontier-as-virgin-land. Omar and his harem beauties are pictured in majestic outdoor scenes, as if to imply that both Arab female sexuality and the American territories are boundlessly available. In fact, the *Omar* scenes construct a space in which the symbolic presence of harem walls and oriental despots does not exist, thereby offering an image of a priori penetration to appeal to the rugged individualist ethos of the early twentieth-century U.S. consumer. In this way, the feminized and sexualized scene signifies passivity, availability, and exotic sexuality to the *Omar* customer. Omar himself represents a peculiarly softened image of the classic powerful sultan. The fact that he is always pictured with women languishing at his feet casts him as sultan master, but his dress and jovial characteristics are reminiscent of what Buel called "the genie of the lamp,"[51] thereby rendering him into a subservient and somewhat trivialized role.

While the representation of oriental masculinity departs here from French orientalist paintings, the depiction of Arab womanhood is, in many ways, consonant with classical orientalist imagery. Omar's attendant harem girls are pictured in ways that deliberately mimic the poses of the figures in French orientalist paintings. In one ad (figure 3.5), the woman reclines in exactly the same fashion as the nude in Ingres's *The Grand Odalisque*. The similarity is so striking, in fact, that one of the most famous and peculiar aspects of Ingres's representation of the woman—the fact that she would need an extra vertebra in order for her back to stretch out at the length that it does—seems to be reproduced in the Omar ad. This similarity is an example of parallel orientalist imagery in the French and U.S. contexts and of the citational nature of orientalism, even while the *Omar* ads also have quite a few elements of departure from a French iteration of orientalism.

In a particularly salient link between the 1893 Chicago World's Fair and early-twentieth-century advertising, many of the *Omar* ads depict him enjoying the entertainment of a dancing girl (figure 3.6). While there are certainly examples of French orientalist paintings that portray belly dancers (such as Gérôme's *Dance of the Almeh*), the inclusion of the belly dancer in the *Omar* ad, and especially her costume, can be more closely linked to the U.S. interest in belly dancing at the turn of the century and in the early 1900s. Belly dancing exhibits had succeeded in drawing crowds to the Midway Plaisance at the Chicago World's Fair and to amusement parks such as Coney Island; in the

Figure 3.5   Omar Advertisement—"Reclining Odalisque"

Source: Warshaw Collection of Business Americana—Tobacco Industry, Archives Center, National Museum of American History, Behring Center, Smithsonian Institution.

Figure 3.6 Omar Advertisement—"Rose-in-Hand"

Source: Warshaw Collection of Business Americana—Tobacco Industry, Archives Center, National Museum of American History, Behring Center, Smithsonian Institution.

world of the consumer spectacle, *Omar* advertisers were counting on its success to draw new customers over to their brand. Again, not only are these figures of Arab womanhood placed on display as examples of the abundant riches of the Orient, they are also meant to signify the availability of the decadence they portray. As opposed to the paintings from the French colonial context, in which the walls and barriers of the harem were intentionally represented (so as to highlight the fact of their penetration), these advertisements recast harem girls not as inaccessible, but as totally available commodities. Buy *Omar* cigarettes and you, too, can enjoy the pleasures and indulgences of a Turkish sultan, they seem to suggest. In this way, they seem to be precursors to the harem imagery in classic Hollywood films, such as *The Thief Goes to Baghdad* (1924), *Ali Baba Goes to Town* (1937), and *Kismet* (1955), where "harem" operated as a transgressive code for the male lead's cadre of beautiful, white women.

Yet there is still another dimension to this *Omar* ad; the jolly Turk does not fit the stereotypical notion of a tyrannical and greedy Ottoman sultan partly because of his relaxed facial expressions and posture, but also because he is pictured reclining outdoors rather than sitting inside his palace surrounded by his attendants. Indeed, this Omar is not merely a figment of a tobacco advertising executive's imagination. Instead, he references a literary figure that much of the early-twentieth-century audience would have recognized: Omar Khayyam. Persian poet Omar Khayyam wrote his quatrains, or *Rubaiyat*, in the eleventh century, but they became popular in Britain and the United States because of the translation work of Edward Fitzgerald, who first rendered Khayyam's poetry into English in 1859. Khayyam's *Rubaiyat*, then, were quickly heralded as a literary feat of the English translator, Fitzgerald, who was said to have woven a poetic tapestry out of its Romantic and timeless themes. In fact, the work was often introduced with praise for Fitzgerald's genius, since he supposedly "took a haphazard collection of isolated bits and made [a] mosaic pattern" and "used Omar's detached thoughts and wove them into a design."[52] In this way, *Rubaiyat* came to be thought of as an English literary work, as Carl Weber makes clear: " 'The abundance of the imagery, the power of the thought, the seduction of the rhetoric, make the poem actually, though not original or English, one of the greatest English poems.' "[53] Moreover, the act of translation had not only transformed a Persian poem into an English masterpiece, it had also converted the Persian poet into a character in his own poetry.

In English, then, Omar Khayyam, though he may have authored an interesting collection of ideas, is portrayed as something of a fool or a dreamer. He is able to express provocative ideas, but he is not able to present them in the organized or coherent (read civilized) manner that Fitzgerald would later bestow upon them. Omar, the character, makes his way into the world of tobacco advertising in the early twentieth century largely due to serendipity. Fitzgerald's original translation of *Rubaiyat*, published in 1859, had made its debut in the U.S. in 1899–1900, when twenty-eight editions were published. However, on the fiftieth anniversary of the original publication, in 1909 and 1910 (just a few years before the bulk of Omar ads), twenty-six more editions were published.[54] In addition, a major motion picture entitled *Omar the Tentmaker: A Persian Love Romance* (1914) had been released just a year before the *Omar* ads proliferated in 1915. Renewed interest in Omar Khayyam's *Rubaiyat* indicates that the representation of Omar in the tobacco ads is at least loosely based on his namesake, the disorganized dreamer.[55] The result is a multifaceted patchwork of orientalist imagery that combines the trope of the harem as a bastion of licentiousness and romanticized notions of the ancient, primitive, or naturalized East with the U.S. expansionist symbol of the frontier.

As I have already indicated, many aspects of the *Omar* advertisements parallel imagery found in French orientalist painting and therefore reference an idea of the Orient as both decadent and indulgent as well as excessively patriarchal and brutal (the two are often conflated in stereotypical representations of the harem as a holding ground for the sultan's sexual fantasies). However, the early-twentieth-century U.S. representation of an Ottoman sultan, represented here as Omar, is a much more benign and less threatening character than the despots who appear in French orientalist paintings (consider, for example, Henri Regnault's *Execution Without Trial*, which displays the image of a swarthy Middle Eastern man who has just cut off his opponent's head—the head lies a few stairs down from the body while blood rushes from the neck). If Omar demonstrates stereotypically masculine qualities, he does so through the implied male privilege of owning and possessing women, both literally and sexually, yet, as in Gérôme's *Dance of the Almeh*, he seems anything but threatening. With eyes half-closed and arms raised to chest, he appears to be a cross between a caricature of a genie riding a "magic carpet" and an (East Asian) orientalist caricature of meditation. One final element rounds out the image as one that cites historical orientalist imagery, while adapting it for a particular U.S. context. Though Omar is portrayed innocuously enough, the feather in his cap serves as a vague reference to his violent Ottoman past. According to E. Cobham Brewer's

Dictionary of Phrase and Fable, published in 1898, a feather in the cap usually alludes to the "general custom in Asia and among the American Indians of adding a new feather to their headgear for every enemy slain." With the image of the violent, brutal despot contained by the feather in Omar's cap, the image both links him to popular imaginings of indigenous American peoples and squarely locates him in an orientalist tradition. As for that which distinguishes him—his jovial nature—it not only references the poet incarnation of Omar Khayyam, it also gestures to the shifting nature of the orientalist construct from the French colonial to the U.S. expansionist contexts. The Ottoman Empire did not hold the same meaning for the U.S. in the 1900s that it did for western Europe in the 1800s. U.S. national identity gained definition in opposition to the tyrannical aristocratic power of Britain—it did not need the example of the brutal and despotic power of the Terrible Turk against which to define itself in the same way that western European powers of the 1800s did.

Therefore, the jolly Omar is an articulation of a particularly American deployment of orientalism at the beginning of the twentieth century—he is an indicator of a Romanticized view of the Orient, which understands it as bounded by questions of nature and origin. It should come as no surprise, then, that he is modeled after the poet-dreamer Omar Khayyam, whose poetry was celebrated in Britain and the United States for its expression of timeless themes. Moreover, he is portrayed engaging with questions about the urgency and meaning of life within the blissful, boundaryless realm of the outdoors. Most *Omar* advertisements include a line from the *Rubaiyat,* as in one ad that includes the latter half of the following quatrain in text (representing the first half of the quatrain—"loaf of bread" and "flask of wine"—pictorially): "Here with a Loaf of Bread beneath the Bough,/ A Flask of Wine, a Book of Verse—and Thou/ Beside me singing in the Wilderness—and Wilderness is Paradise enow"[56] (figure 3.7). The last line of this quatrain, which equates "wilderness" with "paradise," is one that is particularly salient for the United States in the early 1900s, both because of the way it overlaps with the notion of the American Promised Land as an extension of the (original) Holy Land, and because it expresses a structure of feeling that communicates nostalgia for a pastoral past, for innocent (biblical) origins, and for timeless themes all at the same time. In this scene, Omar and his odalisque easily balance the country and the city as they enjoy the paradise of wilderness, while the comforts of progress await them in the distant palatial setting.

Figure 3.7 Omar Advertisement—"Oh Wilderness Were Paradise Enow"

Source: Warshaw Collection of Business Americana—Tobacco Industry, Archives Center, National Museum of American History, Behring Center, Smithsonian Institution.

It follows, then, that *Omar* ads capitalize on images of fecundity and fruitfulness in a unique way. Again, rather than being pictured inside the walls of a harem, the *Omar* scenes all take place outside—in the midst of a majestic natural landscape. Furthermore, the poetic rhyme that accompanies each image (taken from Fitzgerald's translation of *Rubaiyat*) comments on the natural abundance of the environment, thereby creating a metaphoric link to the notion of the virgin land. The stanza immediately preceding the wilderness-as-paradise stanza reads: "With me along the strip of Herbage strown and just divides the desert from the sown." By choosing this line as copy to accompany an image of *Omar* reclining under a tree while a woman dances for him (figure 3.8), the advertisers use the logic of oppositions to emphasize the image of the barren desert, so often associated with the Middle East, in order to highlight the lush beauty of the plentiful oasis where Omar resides, which is presumably where the tobacco is cultivated. Furthermore, the logic of oppositions highlighted by the desert/oasis binary is replicated and solidified in the orientalist oppositions already inherent in the image, such as the erotic sexuality of the female dancer in relation to the implied impotence of the Omar character. While he appears to operate, in one sense, as a symbol of sex and satiety, the benign and banal aspects of his caricature render him sexually nonthreatening. In contradistinction to the increased mechanization and industrialization of the turn-of-the-century U.S. context, in ad after ad, Omar is shown reclining among the natural bounties of gardens, rivers, and streams, thereby combining images of the fecund earth with those of exotic opulence in order to offer a doubly abundant message to the audience of consumers.

The cultivation of land imagery in tobacco advertisements suggests that the Orient functioned as a representative foil for U.S. concerns about industrialization and urbanization—the development of the "city" to the exclusion and loss of the "country." News of the frontier's closing provoked a resurgent nostalgia for the rugged individualism of the Wild West that had helped shape American identity. Tied to the concepts of vacancy and fertility, the loss of the frontier also triggered a sense of loss for a pure and undefiled land. Cigarette advertisements capitalized on the anxiety provoked by this sense of loss by presenting gendered and sexualized scenes of orientalist fantasy, which highlighted the tropes of timeless, natural, and innocent origins. Yet the very notion of timelessness simultaneously invokes an engagement with historicity. Images of the Orient as natural and untouched come to represent a "lost" past in the context of a U.S. focus on progress. If such progress inevitably led to a constantly

Figure 3.8   Omar Advertisement—"With Me Along the Strip of Herbage Strown"

Source: Warshaw Collection of Business Americana—Tobacco Industry, Archives Center, National Museum of American History, Behring Center, Smithsonian Institution.

receding ancient past as well as the penetration of an innocent, virgin space, orientalist advertisements function as one example of an imagined space in which the innocence of origins could be reclaimed. Tobacco customers, then, were to receive the message that all was not lost; evidence of the fertile abundance of the land and the sanctity of the lost past could be purchased for fifteen cents a package.

The nostalgia associated with a pastoral setting usually invoked the image of a majestic and pristine landscape, which was often portrayed as suspended in time, and frozen at the moment of the genesis of Christian civilization. In his analysis of recreated replicas of the Holy Land in the United States, Burke Long suggests that such representations hold meaning because they "purport to speak of things eternal, above the messiness of history."[57] The dizzying momentum of the progress narrative within a consumerist orientation had so altered notions of time and space that history must have seemed quite messy indeed. The desire to reach "above the messiness of history," then, manifested in representations of timelessness, like Frederic Edwin Church's *Jerusalem from the Mount of Olives*, in which the native Arabs that dot the canvas fade into the ancient and naturalized backdrop as elements of frozen time and space. Likewise, in the myth of the U.S. pilgrimage into the desert of its western "Promised Land," the indigenous American peoples resolve into the setting of the so-called "virgin" land.[58] Anne McClintock's notion of "anachronistic space" offers a means of conceptualizing this phenomenon:

> Since indigenous peoples are not supposed to be spatially there—for the lands are "empty"—they are symbolically displaced into what I call *anachronistic space*.... According to this trope, colonized people...do not inhabit history proper but exist in a permanently anterior time within the geographic space of the modern empire as anachronistic humans, atavistic, irrational, bereft of human agency—the living embodiment of the archaic "primitive."[59]

In a further permutation of the notions of time and space, the myth of the frontier as a virgin land constructs a temporally coded and feminized space, as antiquated and passive, in order to rationalize the U.S. project of colonization vis-à-vis the indigenous peoples of the Americas. In this way, the images of indigenous Americans bear a striking resemblance to representations of Arabs as native inhabitants of the original Holy Land. In the parallel construction of the American Promised Land, indigenous Americans occupy the same liminal zone of timelessness and are emasculated in ways that replicate the representation of Omar in the *Omar* ads. Like the feather in Omar's cap, then, Arab and American Indian markers can be combined or conflated within a single representation. Consider, for example, an advertising gimmick developed by *Omar* advertisers, whereby consumers would receive a miniature rug free of charge with every cigarette purchase. Significantly, despite the popularity of oriental rugs in the United States during that time, *Omar* customers received a "Navajo blanket" as their "authentic" prize.[60]

This occasional conflation of Middle Eastern and indigenous American cultures further corroborates my claim that representations of abundance in early-twentieth-century tobacco ads also reflected U.S. anxieties about expansion. One early advertising gimmick utilized by a number of different brands was the practice of including "trade cards." These trade cards were ephemera—they were created as objects that would later be thrown away—but in the meantime they were used as bait to lure consumers to the purchase. As Leach explains, "the cards failed to show the actual goods or services on sale..., but many carried price lists on the back, and—most important—each attempted to associate its business with games, luxury, pleasure, fantasy, or faraway mystery."[61] Each trope (leisure or fantasy, for example) was represented by a thematic series—such as a sports series and a lighthouse series—so that customers could be exhorted to collect the whole set. *Hassan,* another brand of Turkish blends, included two sets of trade cards that particularly addressed concerns about the diminishing frontier; they are the *Cowboy* (Wild West) series and the *Indian Life in the "60's"* (Native American) series. Presumably, these were meant to complement each other, and their exaggerated oppositions serve to further highlight the construction of white American frontier masculinity in contradistinction to that of the innocent noble savage. The *Cowboy* series displays Anglo Americans engaged in lively activities such as "Roping a Steer," "Shooting Up the Town," and "Maverick," who is riding a bull, while the *Indian* series displays ritualistic images, such as "The Rainmaker" and "Smoking to the Setting Sun," or sentimental scenes, such as "Runaway Lovers." These scenes once again reinforce the notion of indigenous Americans as frozen in time and locked into anachronistic space. The caption and image of the natives "smoking to the setting sun," in particular, casts them as some of the last human inhabitants of cyclical—or natural—time; they seem blissfully untouched by the creeping progression of mechanized time. Again, like American landscape paintings of the Holy Land, the trade card depicts them surveying the vast land that stretches out before them and the caption explains that "smoking the ceremonial pipe while watching the sun sink beneath the horizon was a form of devotional worship."[62]

The inclusion of these representations of timelessness in a product utilizing the logic of orientalism for commercial purposes is not a coincidence. It speaks to the overall structure of feeling that determined that creation and the salience of these images. A U.S. nation on the brink of World War I was increasingly, and irreversibly, separated from its agrarian origins. The errand into the wilderness of the American Promised Land was now forsaken for the new promise of the consumerist dream. Orientalist imagery, sometimes conflated with American Indian imagery, of the primordial origins of a developing nation was utilized to navigate this seemingly inevitable break with the past. Feelings of rupture, disorientation, and discontinuity were inevitable by-products of a U.S. negotiation of the project of modernity and the tumultuous processes of expansionism and consumerism. In response to this context of disorientation, images of the timeless East in twentieth-century U.S. tobacco advertisements enabled consumers to hold on to some imaginative vestige of the primordial past. As the century progressed, the United States' relationship to the Middle East would change, and specific elements of these orientalist images would also shift. However, their function as nostalgic, and therefore desirable, remnants of the receding past would remain constant.

In early-twentieth-century tobacco advertisements, figures of Arab womanhood emerge as potent markers of primitivism and nature for a society that was increasingly detached from its agrarian origins. Standing at the nexus of progress and possession, representations of Arab womanhood presented in the guise of harem girls, belly dancers, and reclining odalisques were able to signify the availability of abundance for a nation that had just witnessed its primordial symbol of plenty—the space of the frontier—disappear. In the meantime, the exotic and sensual figures of Arab female sexuality represented in tobacco advertisements of the early 1900s—from *Omar*'s dancing girls and reclining odalisques to the transparently veiled *Fatima* girl—had emerged as reassuring emblems of the endurance and stability of timelessness. As Anne McClintock argues, intense feelings of uncertainty that arise in a nation that is "veering between nostalgia for the past and the impatient, sloughing off of the past...is typically resolved by figuring the contradiction in *time* as a natural division of *gender*."[63] As demonstrated by the characterization of the frontier as "virgin" land, the purity of the pastoral setting, which is frequently idealized by the nostalgic backward glance, is also often cast in gendered terms as a feminine space. Therefore, it is not surprising that the sensual and exotic, yet safely distant, images of belly dancers and odalisques in early-twentieth-century tobacco ads appealed to U.S. consumers. These figures of Arab womanhood were meaningful to a U.S. audience, and therefore profitable to U.S. tobacco companies, because of their ability to articulate the sanctity of temporal certainties and spatial boundaries, and to assure the endurance of primordial pastoral spaces, which seemed to be rapidly disappearing.

CHAPTER 4

VEILED INTENTIONS: THE
CULTURAL MYTHOLOGY OF VEILS,
HAREMS, AND BELLY DANCERS
IN THE SERVICE OF EMPIRE,
SECURITY, AND GLOBALIZATION

In the contemporary context, mythologized figures of Arab womanhood, such as the seemingly ubiquitous image of the veiled woman and the persistent icon of the belly dancer, continue to operate as the visual vocabulary through which collective anxieties about new forms of power and progress manifest. If images of belly dancers and harem girls in twentieth-century tobacco advertisements reflect the disorientations of consumerism and expansionism in the United States at the turn of the twentieth century, contemporary images of Arab womanhood continue to be engaged with consumerism and expansionism in the context of contemporary U.S. neoliberalism and imperialism. In this chapter, I am interested in applying the trajectory of my argument thus far to representations of Arab and Muslim womanhood in what might be called the era of globalization, from the 1970s to the present. Like my analysis of the metanarrative of modernity, I will be investigating mainstream discourses of globalization in terms of their disavowal of the neocolonial and imperialist projects in which they are embedded.

In particular, I am interested in global economic restructuring as an especially salient aspect of globalization, through which I will continue my interrogation of the progress narrative. I have been tracing

the ways in which orientalist images of Arab womanhood have functioned as the "othered" side of the same coin of the notion of progress,
whereby they actually work to shore up the universalizing and positivist
rhetoric of progress. I have also been interested in the appropriation of
orientalist representations of Arab womanhood as nostalgic emblems
that mitigate the disorientations of spatiotemporal shifts in the context of modernization and industrial capitalism. Building on Inderpal
Grewal's suggestion that "global" is a cognate of "universal,"[1] I am
interested here in demonstrating how the rhetoric of globalization
enables a set of assumptions about time-space compression whereby
images of Arab womanhood continue to function as nostalgic foils
for twentieth- and twenty-first-century "progress." In other words,
I will chart the ways in which particular narratives of globalization
have continued the universalizing tendencies of the metanarrative of
modernity vis-à-vis representations of Arab womanhood.

Perhaps the most compelling turn in contemporary orientalist
imagery in the United States, however, occurs along the power axis
of representation. Homogenizing narratives describe globalization
as a process that has facilitated greater interconnectedness worldwide; caused the decreasing salience of the nation-state as a system of
governance; stimulated the increased fluidity of capital, people, and
goods; and therefore encouraged the breakdown of traditional borders. However, the neoliberal policies of free trade, privatization, and
deregulation undergirding the rhetoric of globalization have coincided with greater limitations on the movement of people, as with
the increase in immigration restrictions in the United States in recent
years. The fortification of national borders, then, highlights the ways
in which global economic restructuring has privileged the flow of
capital at the expense of freedoms for people while such barriers are
rationalized under the rubric of national security. As signaled by the
dissolution of the Immigration and Naturalization Service (INS)
and the relocation of immigration and naturalization services from
the Department of Justice to the Department of Homeland Security
in 2003, the surveillance and policing of foreign others is justified
through the rhetoric of security, while the privatization of war and
prisons implies that the rhetoric of national security has privileged
capital and profit over people. In terms of representation on the axis of
power, then, I trace the shifting function of orientalist images of Arab
and Muslim womanhood in relation to the configuration of Arabs
and Muslims as foreign threat and enemy other in the contemporary
context. Because Islamophobia has become an integral aspect of orientalism in the United States since at least the 1970s,[2] I shift here

toward using the phrase "Arab and Muslim womanhood" in order to signal the way in which Arab, Persian, Turkish, Muslim, Afghan, Pakistani, Indian, and sometimes Sikh identities are conflated in the contemporary U.S. imagination as simply Arab and/or Muslim.

In order to ground the trajectory of my argument in a specific example, I will begin the chapter with an analysis of *National Geographic* magazine's representation of the "Afghan girl," Sharbat Gula, which received wide critical attention shortly after the events of September 11, 2001. In my analysis of the *National Geographic* images of Gula, and the attending documentary entitled *In Search of the Afghan Girl*, I will explain the way in which narratives of national security, globalization, and the war on terror manifest in and the mythologies of the veil,[3] the harem, and the belly dancer.

THE AFGHAN GIRL AS CASE STUDY

In March 2002, *National Geographic* magazine made headlines in major newspapers all over the world[4] with its sensationalist story about the "Afghan girl," who had been photographed for the magazine in 1985 and subsequently relocated and photographed again in January 2002. The story presumably received such widespread coverage because of *National Geographic*'s own public relations campaign about the release of its documentary *In Search of the Afghan Girl*, which chronicles photographer Steve McCurry's journey to find the woman (then girl) who had given him recognition when she posed for the 1985 photograph that won numerous awards. However, human interest alone cannot account for the prominent display of the story on such a large number of newspapers internationally. Indeed, as a *Scotsman* article admits, "The crisis of 11 September and the subsequent war against the Taleban rekindled [McCurry's] interest"[5] in finding the woman he had photographed seventeen years earlier, when she was a refugee from Soviet attacks on her village.

Given the fact that the original picture of the Afghan girl (anonymously named because McCurry never bothered to get her name) represented Soviet incursion into Afghanistan and the 2002 "reunion"[6] pictures mark the beginning of the U.S. invasion of the same land, one might expect *National Geographic* coverage to reflect the changing geopolitical dynamics that had impacted this young woman's life.[7] Instead, in its full-length documentary entitled *In Search of the Afghan Girl*, the magazine presents a narrative about the plight of this Afghan woman that reinforces dominant U.S. notions about the passivity and victimization of all Muslim women at the hands of Muslim men while disavowing U.S. culpability for providing the financial support (in the 1980s) that eventually enabled the Taliban's rise to power.[8] In other words, the narrative of Muslim women's oppression both implies that patriarchal oppression is inherent to Islam and effectively erases U.S. patriarchal and militaristic interventions in Afghanistan that brought a particular regime into power, a regime that instituted oppressive policies toward women. Given the history of U.S. support for regimes such as the Taliban in the context of the cold war, the Bush administration's argument that the goal of current military action is to liberate women is suspect at best. Reading past this rhetoric, I am interested in exploring how mythologies of Arab and Muslim womanhood function to legitimate dominant narratives of national security and globalization. For example, as Jasbir Puar and Amit Rai have noted in their article "Monster, Terrorist, Fag,"[9] feminized and sexualized images of Osama bin Laden in U.S. popular culture have served to reinforce the heteronormative and masculinist logic of militarism and national security. Similarly, gendered images of Afghan women as helpless victims reinforce the dominant trope of saving Muslim women through U.S. Military action.[10] Rather than revealing something about Arab and Muslim cultures, however, these images bespeak the peculiarly patriarchal logic of U.S. militarism in the war on terror.

As I have argued, a key characteristic of mythology is its malleability in the service of the dominant narrative while it presents itself as fixed and natural. Because the "Afghan girl" case study spans two decades, it provides a perfect example of the way that mythologies easily shift and adapt to the narratives that appropriate them while consistently maintaining the conceit of truth and innocence. For example, one of the major signifiers upon which the narrative of the Afghan girl rests is that of her eyes, which journalists describe as arresting, glowing, amazing, piercing, bright, striking, and, most of all, haunting. The first photograph, which graced the cover of the June 1985 issue of *National Geographic*, was accompanied by the tagline "Haunted Eyes of an Afghan Refugee's Fears," and the suggestion seems to have stuck as if the photo were dipped in "lyrical fixative," to borrow a phrase used by Catherine Lutz and Jane Collins in their groundbreaking study *Reading National Geographic*.[11] There are, of course, many other ways to read the expression of the girl in this famous photograph; one might describe her eyes, for example, as outraged, incredulous, defiant, or horrified at the tenacity of the foreign white man to simply take a picture in a situation that demands so much more.[12] Such a reading, however, would highlight the need for a political and historical contextualization of the circumstances surrounding Gula's life that made it possible for McCurry to take her photograph in December of 1984, details that would compromise the purported innocence and benevolence of the project. This type of contextualization, in turn, would disenable the abstract mechanism that had allowed Gula's photo to become a symbol for the state of refugee-hood. Instead, according to the media coverage of the famous photograph, her eyes alone have been hailed as universal signifiers of the refugee condition, as one journalist asserts that her "piercing green eyes epitomized the tragic story of dispossessed children everywhere."[13] Her haunting eyes, her childlike innocence, and her girlhood are all characteristics highlighted in the 1985 image in order to implicitly symbolize her victimization at the hands of the U.S. rival global superpower, the U.S.S.R. Similarly, the "search for the Afghan girl" seventeen years later functions to buttress dominant narratives about the brutal oppression of Afghan women at the hands of the Taliban, in order to construct an image of the new enemy to U.S. empire.

Though *National Geographic* photographer Steve McCurry insists that he tried to find the "Afghan girl" repeatedly in his many trips back to Pakistan and Afghanistan in the seventeen years in between their two meetings, his full-fledged search began in 2002, when he was supplied with documentary film crews, financial backing from *National Geographic*, and even forensic help from the FBI, none of which could have taken place without the animating U.S. fascination with Muslim womanhood enhanced by the rhetoric that emerged out of September 11, 2001. The image of the veil had functioned in the United States as shorthand for the oppression of women, and therefore the backwardness of an entire people, since at least the 1979 Iranian Revolution. However, the "war on terror" mobilized the image of the Muslim woman trapped behind the burqa (conflated with the image of the veil) in newly urgent ways,[14] deploying it swiftly as justification for U.S. Military action. The increasing salience of the mythology of the veil here parallels the shifting dimensions of U.S. empire and the concomitant fluctuations in popular images of the enemy—from caricatures of the communist threat to symbolic tropes of the maniacal and irrational terrorist. In short, the sudden and renewed interest in Sharbat Gula's story just a few months after the events of September 11, 2001 is not coincidental. Rather, the plight of the Afghan girl, the quintessential refugee, metamorphosed into the story of Sharbat Gula, tragically oppressed Muslim woman, as her symbolic valence shifted in the urgent context of an increasingly antagonistic U.S. relationship to political Islam. The *National Geographic* documentary reinforces this point by opening with images of the planes flying into the World Trade Center on September 11, 2001, suggesting, again, the ahistorical narrative that casts U.S. involvement in Afghanistan as a purely defensive stance originating in 2001. The cover image of the April 2002 issue of *National Geographic* demonstrates the function of both the 1985 and the 2002 photographs of Gula as cultural mythologies. The 2002 photo that graces the cover of the magazine depicts Gula, wearing a purple burqa, holding the 1985 image of herself as a girl (figure 4.1). In one image, then, the narrative of her tragic victimization at the hands of enemy forces—the Soviet Union and the Taliban—come together visually and rhetorically, while reinforcing the notion of the United States as a civilizing/liberating force.

Contrary to these simplistic narratives, I argue that such powerful imagery, whereby empty signifiers effortlessly communicate a set of assumptions about Arab and Muslim cultures, does not originate from the event known simply as "9/11." The cultural mythology of the veil is compelling because of its citational quality—the U.S. association of the veil with barbaric, backward, regimes and, more recently, Islamic fundamentalism, has been sedimented through media coverage of such events as the Iran hostage crisis, the 1991 Gulf War (where U.S. intervention privileged the sovereignty of Kuwait with no comment on, or criticism of patriarchal laws that enforce veiling for women), and the U.S. invasion of Afghanistan. Because of its importance in the contemporary context, I spend the first third of the chapter fleshing out the mythology of the veil more fully.

That the mythology of the veil, or the "plight" of Arab and Muslim women, has become increasingly salient in the contemporary geopolitical context indicates that such images continue to operate as an integral aspect of the orientalist apparatus in the United States. The "search for the Afghan girl" case study demonstrates key elements of the orientalist apparatus: it participates in producing knowledge about Muslim womanhood while simultaneously referencing, and building on, well-worn orientalist images of oppressed Arab and Muslim women. In framing his mission as a sort of search and rescue operation, McCurry replicates the tired colonialist trope of the "white man's burden" to civilize purportedly primitive natives through the process of colonialism. At the same time, though, the "search" demonstrates the way in which the mythology of the veil, as a contemporary orientalist representation, continues to engage narratives of power and progress through rhetorics of national security and globalization.

Figure 4.1   Sharbat Gula, 2002
Source: © Steve McCurry/Magnum Photos.

However, as the 1985 *National Geographic* image of Gula (as a girl) suggests, the symbol of the veil has not always served as the most salient or appropriate signifier of U.S. concerns with national security. Backing up to the 1970s and 1980s context, I revisit the harem trope in the second section of the chapter in order to explore the intersection of orientalist representations with national security rhetoric. Like representations of the veil, representations of the harem operate as signifiers that engage with popular perceptions of femininity, masculinity, and sexuality in relation to the Arab and Muslim worlds. There is, perhaps, no better instantiation of this than a popular image from the 1977 James Bond film *The Spy Who Loved Me*, which Alev Lytle Croutier has aptly titled "James Bond and His Harem."[15] It is no secret that Bond films are quite engaged with the issue of national security in relation to both the United States and United Kingdom, and with the shifting relationship between the two nations.[16] However, *The Spy Who Loved Me*, like the Afghan girl images, transitions (within the Bond genre) from representing the Soviet Union as the quintessential global enemy to presenting terrorism as a generalized global threat against which superpowers must fight in unison. It allows me, then, to look at the development of the threat of terrorism as a constructed enemy of the United States, and to deconstruct images of the harem and the veil as signifiers that buttress contemporary narratives of national security. Moreover, as a paragon of heteronormativity and masculinity-through-virility, the character of James Bond (and his harem) also enables me to interrogate the gendered and sexualized logic of such rhetoric.

Finally, in the third section of the chapter, I will explore the impact of global economic restructuring on popular images of Arab and Muslim womanhood in the contemporary context. The marketability of the 2002 *National Geographic* narrative of finding, rescuing, and giving voice to Gula (and, by extension, all Afghan women) is a perfect example of the way that national security narratives intersect with the tenets of neoliberalism, a connection that Stephen Hartnett and Laura Stengrim have called "globalization-through-benevolent-empire."[17] In this logic, the notion of U.S. Military action as a project of liberation functions to construct the United States as a benevolent force seeking to spread freedom while obfuscating the ways in which such rhetorics of freedom actually operate in the service of multinational corporations, the true benefactors of U.S. imposed free trade and the privatization of war. In an analysis of a contemporary *Camel* cigarettes advertising campaign for the new product of "exotic blends," I am interested in investigating the ways in which contemporary images of belly dancers and exoticized cigarette girls speak to the latest shift in capitalism, the genesis for which scholar David Harvey locates in 1973—the year of the OPEC (Organization of the Petroleum Exporting Countries) oil embargo. This strand of my argument manifests in the "Afghan girl" case study because it presents itself as an innocuous, apolitical globalized image, while reiterating key facets of neoliberalism, such as the primacy of individual rights and the importance of the marketplace.

The accompanying article to the 2002 photograph also highlights and emphasizes the oppressiveness of the burqa, which the reader is meant to associate with the backward and violent forces (Taliban) from which the U.S. Military supposedly seeks to liberate Afghan women. The dominant narrative, here represented by the *National Geographic* article, consistently simplifies Gula's struggles into a story about patriarchal oppression in her culture and consistently reads her through the traditional/modern binary of the progress narrative, as defined by the confines of patriarchal family life, with no ability to see beyond the boundaries of her individual life. In this sense, it reflects the ideology of neoliberal globalization that inhabits the cultural mythology of the veil. In McCurry's comments on his reunion with Gula, during which he showed her the picture of herself as a young girl and told her that it inspired individuals to aid Afghan refugees, he recounts her reaction thusly: "She is glad her picture was an inspiration. But I don't think the photograph means anything to her. The only thing that matters is her husband and children."[18] Here, he circumscribes her within the limited domain of the family, as if she is so provincial as to have no awareness of broader societal or cultural concerns. His comment contradicts the documentary itself, however, in which Gula expressly requests financial support from *National Geographic*, the U.S. government, and U.S. citizens to enable members of her community to be educated, thereby demonstrating her understanding of who holds responsibility for her current circumstances, an understanding that is more sophisticated and historically informed than the one offered by the *National Geographic* narrative. In fact, the article in the April 2002 *National Geographic* goes so far as to suggest that the patriarchal norms of her culture subdue her very will to exist: "Faced by questions, she retreats into the black shroud wrapped around her face, as if by doing so she might will herself to evaporate."[19] Here, the author describes Gula as complicit in the forces that will her to be invisible and silent, as if she is in desperate need of the benevolent, inquisitive U.S. liberators, represented by the *National Geographic* staff. Crucially, it also foregrounds the framework of individual, rather than structural or collective, rights. It privileges the right of Afghan women to unveil, an act equated with emancipation and liberal-democratic ideals, rather than focusing on meeting women's basic survival needs and addressing the structural violence with which they live as a result of permanent militarism. These narratives consistently ignore systemic forms of violence that impact Afghan women, such as extreme poverty and constant war, that have been exacerbated by U.S. involvement in the region.

Furthermore, any hesitation on her part to speak with McCurry and his colleagues is ascribed to her absolute submission to the patriarchal codes of her culture, rather than to the suspicious project McCurry has taken on to find her, at great cost, and to represent her to the world again. The fact is that in the business of producing images, Gula's 1985 photograph garnered McCurry and the *National Geographic* magazine much fame and money. Throughout the seventeen years in between the two photographs, the 1985 image had become so popular globally, operating within what Arjun Appadurai has called a globalized "mediascape,"[20] that McCurry found a reproduction for sale by a local vendor in Pakistan when he was on his 2002 mission (he began his search by revisiting the refugee camps set up for Afghans in Peshawar, Pakistan). Upon informing the merchant of his ownership of the image, McCurry wryly notes that the merchant offered him a discount on the asking price of the image rather than giving him what he owns free of charge.[21] Embedded in this interaction is a lesson in the ways that neocolonialism intersects with neoliberalism. It demonstrates a neocolonial relationship insofar as it mimics a colonial economic relationship between metropole and colony, where McCurry appropriates raw materials through a complex power relationship, shooting a picture of Gula as a young girl in a refugee camp. He then transforms that image into a product—the lucrative photograph to which he owns rights—and garners wealth from it. The colonialist irony undergirding his interaction with the Pakistani shop owner is the fact that, as McCurry playfully implies, the shop owner owes McCurry money for his use of the image even though McCurry literally took the photograph in the sense of stealing or plundering indigenous "raw" materials. Indeed, Gula herself and her famous image seem to operate as natural resources in the *National Geographic* framework, thereby highlighting the gender dynamics of the imperialist project.

Finally, the greatest irony of the interaction between McCurry and the shop owner is the way in which it reveals neoliberal ideology. In this case, Gula-as-good—the 1985 photo of her as a girl—enjoys more rights and freedoms than does Gula herself. Her image has been globalized in the sense that it has traveled the world, crossing national boundaries and covering great distance with ease, while Gula herself finds her realities circumscribed by limited economic and physical security due to the intervention of global superpowers—the former Soviet Union and the United States—in her homeland. Though these three threads—the mythology of the veil, national security rhetoric, and neoliberal globalization—are intricately intertwined in my overall argument, I separate them out as analytically distinct categories in this chapter, in order to examine each strand more closely. Ultimately, I am arguing that the shifts and changes in contemporary representations of Arab and Muslim womanhood demonstrate a shifting U.S. relationship to empire and capitalism, while the citational quality of the images keeps them tied to the legacy of orientalism and colonialism.

MYTHOLOGY OF THE VEIL

As demonstrated by the 2002 image of Sharbat Gula on the cover of *National Geographic*, contemporary U.S. representations of Arab and Muslim womanhood are often mediated through a fixed image of the veil, which is presented as a signifier of the invisibility and powerlessness of Arab and Muslim women. One need only look as far as the list of books about Arab and Muslim women that have recently saturated the market to notice the way in which the veil is perceived to be an obstacle or barrier behind which Middle Eastern women are forced to hide. The clever titles of these exposés suggest that these books will reveal the realties of Arab and Muslim women hidden "behind the veil."[22] Although the images on the covers of these books reinforce the notion of the veil as a prohibitive barrier, the titles reveal the motivating tension between concealing and revealing Arab and Muslim womanhood in U.S. popular imagination. The clear desire to "unveil" women and to get an "inside" perspective on their lives sublimates a set of concerns that are intimately connected to the political and economic realities determining a U.S. relationship to the Arab and Muslim worlds. Though these images are presented within the rhetorical framework of revealing the truth, or the inside perspective, on Arab and Muslim women's lives, they actually serve as powerful evidence of the way in which representations of Arab and Muslim womanhood serve as receptacles for U.S. centered concerns and anxieties, rather than presenting any of the actual social conditions that determine women's lives in the Middle East and Central

Asia. Contemporary representations of Arab and Muslim woman-hood in U.S. popular culture function, I argue, as visual vocabulary for otherwise ineffable concerns about the shifting power dynamics in a neoliberal imperialist U.S. context.

Theorizing the way in which the symbol of the veil has become a kind of monolithic signifier is not new—it has been discussed and theorized before in myriad sources.[23] Rather than simply reiterating this point, then, I want to ask questions about how and why it has continued to hold meaning for a U.S. audience; to point out how it is connected to other symbols (such as the harem) that have been employed in relation to Arab women; and to explore what it might tell us about the cultures and contexts (in this case, contemporary United States) that continue to invoke and appropriate such symbolic figures. In order to do so, I will first sketch out an anatomy of the veil as cultural mythology, and then apply that framework to the photography of feminist artist Hannah Wilke. I use Hannah Wilke's work for two reasons: first, because I am looking at Wilke's Starification Object Series (S.O.S.), completed in 1974, I am demonstrating the legacy of the mythology of the veil as it extends back over the past few decades. Second, it allows me to gesture to the salience and insidiousness of this particular cultural mythology, which has been uncritically incorporated into work that situates itself as critical of dominant, patriarchal narratives.

One such example of the near ubiquitous nature of the cultural mythology of the veil is in a collection of photographs presented by Annie Leibovitz, with an accompanying essay by Susan Sontag, in the book entitled *Women* (2000). Because the aim of the photo-graphic collection is to defy and challenge predominant stereotypes of "what women are like,"[24] it is particularly interesting to note the way in which Leibovitz interprets and presents the sole image of Arab and Muslim womanhood in the book. The only photo of an Arab American woman is that of Lamis Srour, whose caption indi-cates that she is a teacher in East Dearborn, Michigan. As Dearborn has one of the largest concentrations of Arabs living outside of the Middle East and they are tremendously diverse, especially in terms of dress, there is no doubt that Leibovitz would have had a plethora of examples of Arab womanhood from which to choose for inclusion in the book. Nevertheless, the picture she chose to present matches the seemingly monolithic image of the veiled woman in U.S. society: she covers herself from head to toe in black cloth,[25] leaving a space open only for her eyes, which peek out from behind her enclosure with poignant clarity.[26] Her eyes, because they appear to be her only means of expression, therefore communicate that which a U.S. audience assumes it knows about her: she does not wish to be imprisoned behind the limiting veneer of the veil, but she accepts her fate with quiet and resigned strength. Despite Leibovitz's and Sontag's general claim that the images in *Women* defy stereotypes, the type of knowledge the book presents about Arab and Muslim cultures, as demonstrated in Leila Ahmed's 1982 article, is derived from a long tradition of orientalist thought in European and, later, in U.S. societies.

> Just as Americans "know" that Arabs are backward, they know also with the same flawless certainty that Muslim women are terribly oppressed and degraded. And they know this not because they know that women everywhere in the world are oppressed, but because they believe that, specifically, Islam monstrously oppresses women.[27]

Indeed, it is not only a "flawless certainty" about Arab/Muslim women's oppression that functions in the photo of Lamis Srour, it is also an unquestioned assumption. The photograph would not work within the framing narrative of defying stereotypes unless the function of the veil as signifier of invisibility and silence were so naturalized that it did not even arise as a potential item of contention and/or interpretation.

Given the self-proclaimed goal of Leibovitz's project to subvert predominant stereotypes of women, a generous reading of her inclusion of Srour's photo understands that it is meant as a corrective to predominant stereotypes about women in general, thereby invoking a universalized approach to gender liberation. Sontag echoes the optimism of this approach in her accompanying essay: "Just as photography has done so much to confirm these stereotypes, it can engage in complicating and undermining them."[28] Ostensibly, the image of Srour is meant to defy the stereotype about the particular women she represents (as silent and oppressed) by virtue of the fact that Srour is a teacher. Indeed, Srour's biography in the back of the collection says that she was raised in a Lebanese Muslim family in Dearborn, is a graduate of the University of Michigan, and that she teaches in an elementary school, highlighting her religion, her education, and her profession. Rather than being "terribly oppressed" and utterly silenced by the restrictive customs of her culture, the audience receives the message (only upon reading her bio) that she has overcome these supposed restrictions and succeeded not only in educating herself, but also in becoming an educator of others.

However, despite the optimism of this message as it relates to a decidedly abstract notion of the concept of womanhood, it can only deliver its argument by corroborating problematic assumptions and biases about Arab and Muslim cultures in the United States. In Sontag's essay, which is embedded in the middle of Leibovitz's book, the impact of such biases on representations of Arab/Muslim womanhood become clearer:

> We assume a world with a boundless appetite for images, in which people, women and men, are eager to surrender themselves to the camera. But it is worth recalling that there are parts of the world where to be photographed is something off-limits to women. In a few countries, where men have been mobilized for a veritable war against women, women scarcely *appear* at all. The imperial rights of the camera—to gaze at, to record, to exhibit anyone, anything—are an exemplary feature of modern life, as is the emancipation of women.[29]

When she references countries in which "women scarcely *appear* at all," Sontag is undoubtedly gesturing to those countries in the Arab world from which Srour's ancestry and culture derive. She also could be referring to a country such as Afghanistan, since the Feminist Majority's awareness campaign about the brutal patriarchal regime of the Taliban was already widespread before the time of publication of Leibovitz's book (which was in 2000). Most importantly, however, she is reinforcing a simplistic equation of being uncovered (unveiled), or revealed, with being modern and emancipated. In this way, she makes a distinct connection between the visibility of women's bodies and their subsequent potential for liberation. The overall message articulated by the book *Women* about Arab and Muslim American women seems to be that in spite of their clear oppression, they still manage to occasionally break through the inherent cultural barriers that seek to silence and limit them. Moreover, the boundaries and limitations of the veil are understood to be a direct result of the failure to modernize, as is the inability to celebrate the "imperial rights of the camera." Much like the liberation projects promulgated by French colonialists in Algeria, British colonialists in Egypt, and the Bush adminstration's linking of Afghan liberation with freeing Afghan women from the burqa, this framework of rights demands that indigenous women reveal themselves to the imperial gaze. Perhaps unwittingly, then, Sontag's comments can be situated squarely within a tradition of manipulating the veil as a political symbol for colonialists and patriarchal nationalists alike. In her analysis of the event of May 16, 1958, during which French generals staged the unveiling of Algerian women by French women, Marnia Lazreg notes that in the midst of such manipulations "little has been written about [the veil's] meaning for *women*."[30] Indeed, to recall Sontag's metaphor, the rights of the camera seem to subsume those of the women. Not only does this logic corroborate the ways in which vision is linked to power and possession, it also casts the "covered" woman, in diametrical opposition to the "modern" and "emancipated" woman, as bounded by tradition. Again, to quote Sontag: "In many countries struggling with failed or discredited attempts to modernize, there are more and more *covered* women."[31] In this construction, covered women seem to function as the imaginative foil through which narratives of power and progress are mediated.

To further invoke the stultifying cocoon of traditionalism, Srour herself is not only dressed in all black, but she is pictured against a dark gray background. In this respect, she stands in stark contrast to most of the other images of women in the book, which picture their subjects against a backdrop that reflects either their occupation or the surroundings in which the picture was taken.[32] Consider, for example, the other photograph of a teacher in the Leibovitz collection, Morgan Kelly, who is shot (in color) against the backdrop of the blackboard in her classroom. The location of Srour's photograph, the East Dearborn International Arab-American Festival, would have undoubtedly offered a wide array of colorful backgrounds against which she could have been pictured, such as circles of *debke* dancers, tables of *tabbouleh, hummus, shawarma,* and *kibbeh,* and samples of a wide range of cultural dress and decorative arts. Instead, Leibovitz presents a singular, monolithic interpretation of that culture as one that is trapped within the shadows of an old tradition, especially when it comes to the treatment of women.

Leibovitz's depiction of Arab and Muslim womanhood as synonymous with the image of the oppressive veil is far from unique; it parallels a contemporary U.S. understanding of the veil that understands it as a static marker, remaining unchanged across varied historical and geographic contexts. It participates in the construction of a mythology of the veil, by which a dynamic cultural element transmogrifies into an empty signifier. To be fair, the singular understanding of the veil in the United States can be credited, in part, to linguistic limitations since the English term *veil* has no single correlative term in Arabic. As Fadwa el Guindi points out in her book *Veil: Modesty, Privacy and Resistance,* there are over one hundred terms used for parts of dress in Arabic, many of which refer to the practice of veiling.

Some of these and related Arabic terms are *burqu', 'aabayah, tarhah, burnus, jilbab, jellabah, hayik, milayah, gallabiyyah, dishdasha, gargush, gina', mungub, lithma, yashmik, habarah, izar.*....All this complexity reflected and expressed in the language is referred to by the single convenient Western term "veil," which is indiscriminate, monolithic, and ambiguous.[33]

Therefore, the monolithic understanding of the veil in the United States might be attributed to a problem of translation. However, there are two problems with such an assertion. The first is that it precludes the option of simply using the appropriate Arabic terms (such as *hijab* and *niqab*) as has been done for other forms of dress, such as sari, kilt, and *tarboosh*. The use of the term veil, then, emphasizes the fact that it always enters into a framework of U.S. and British interpretation, with the respective perspectival biases. The second problem is that the English term, "veil" carries the following meaning, according to the fourth entry of the *Oxford English Dictionary's* definition: "to conceal from apprehension, knowledge, or perception; to deal with, treat, etc. so as to disguise or obscure; to hide the real nature or meaning of something, frequently with implication of bad motives."[34] Such a connotation (of deceit and bad motives) cannot be denied in common metaphorical usage in the English language, as I mean to highlight by the title of this chapter, "Veiled Intentions," in which I seek to assign those motives to the creators of the representations, rather than the cultures of the women represented.

Not only does the English term *veil* limit the interpretive scope of a U.S. perspective, it has also evolved into the image of a totalizing shroud, as represented in Srour's photo. Evidence for this lies in the fact that a 2001 advertisement from Reebok International, featuring the image of a veiled woman, is strikingly similar in form and color to the Leibovitz photo (figure 4.2). Reflecting the mainstream U.S. understanding of the veil as that which covers and masks the woman "behind" it, the Reebok image displays a woman who is covered from head to toe in black dress, except for the shockingly white Reebok shoes that peek out from underneath it and a narrow opening that reveals her eyes. Moreover, rather than representing one specific type of dress from a particular region in the Arab and Muslim worlds (such as the ones that el Guindi lists), the actual elements of her clothing are a conglomeration of incongruent markers of Islamic forms of dress. The most glaring example of this incongruency is the fact that she holds a *misbahah*, or a set of prayer beads, in her left hand. If she were really as conservative as her clothing suggests, not only would she be likely to cover her hands, she would also not hold the beads, which, as a mark of piety, are typically reserved for men and older women to carry.

Figure 4.2   Reebok Classic Advertisement

Source: *Honey*, 43 (July 2001).

These details suggest that the image of the veiled woman in U.S. popular culture has been entombed within the logic of its own mythology, whereby the symbol of the veil grows large with the hegemonic narratives of the U.S. cultural context in which it operates, expanding to the point of rigidity. In the process of mythmaking, Barthes explains,

> A conjuring trick has taken place; it has turned reality inside out, it has emptied it of history and filled it with nature...The function of myth is to empty reality: it is, literally, a ceaseless flowing out, a haemorrhage, or perhaps an evaporation, in short, a perceptible absence.[35]

Like representations of odalisques in French orientalist paintings, the Reebok model operates as emptied form, while the realities of veiled women "evaporate," leaving an absence. Indeed, in images such as the Reebok ad, a recovery of the particular realities that might define her experience is impossible due to the ambiguity of the cultural markers that surround her. In this way, she functions as a "perceptible absence:" she is visible as a symbolic form through which mainstream U.S. narratives about globalization and imperialism are mediated, but she is absent from any indication of her own historical and cultural reality.

The appropriation of the image of the veiled woman is particularly illustrative in the example of the advertisement for Reebok Classic shoes. Because of the relationship between image and text in the advertisement, it is clear that the representation of the (covered) woman is meant to pictorially reinforce the text, displayed across the bottom of her body, which reads "Hidden Classic." While the audience is meant to understand that the Hidden Classic being sold is the Classic series of Reebok shoes, the overt meaning of the ad is buttressed by the blatant ways in which the woman herself denotes both the concepts of "hidden" and of "classic."

The image of the veil in the ad functions as a potent signifier of hiddenness since its powerful symbolism serves to elide the presence of the woman and her realities. The representation seems to focus on the garment as covering, rather than on the woman herself, a perspective that depends on an orientalist construction of the practice of veiling, which links the custom metonymically to seclusion, and, it is implied, oppression. In other words, the practice itself is understood as the forced enclosure and restriction of women, rather than a means of ensuring "sacred privacy" and "sanctity," as el Guindi points out.[36] Furthermore, the interpretation of the veil as an absolute boundary for women (and as a barrier to the colonial or imperial gaze) ignores its function in many Muslim societies as a garment that enables (rather than restricts) women's movement between and among a variety of public institutions and contexts. It also completely disavows what Frantz Fanon famously called the "historic dynamism of the veil," in his description of the way in which the veil was strategically employed in the Algerian resistance to a French colonial presence.[37] Finally, static and monolithic images of the veil imply that the garment has only one function and meaning, eliding the fact that there are multiple reasons for veiling, which shift according to political and cultural context. Women who do not wear *hijab* in their homeland may choose to wear it in North America in order to assert and affirm their identity in the context of intense Islamophobia.[38] Further, women may choose to wear *hijab* for reasons unrelated to nationalist or identity politics, donning the garment as a personalized expression of piety and faith.[39]

Even popular images of the veil have been historically dynamic, demonstrating what Faegheh Shirazi has called the "semantic versatility of the veil."[40] As evidenced even by a comparison of the image of the transparently veiled Fatima in early-twentieth-century tobacco advertisements and the 2001 Reebok image of a woman "hidden" behind her veil, the symbol of the veil, and its meaning, shifts according to historical and cultural context. While the representations and meanings of the veil are fluid, however, the impulse to co-opt the veil and transform it into a cultural mythology seems not to be. According to Lazreg, even Fanon himself submits to this impulse as the "mystique of the veil" clouds his analysis of women's participation in Algerian resistance to colonialism, relegating their political action into a "conflict with their bodies."[41] In this construction, Fanon shares the assumption of the French colonizers as well as the Reebok advertisers, it seems, that oppression is written onto Arab and Muslim women's bodies.

In the modern context, the association of oppression or submission with Arab and Muslim women's bodies is so powerful that it even withstands internal contradictions.[42] The Reebok advertisement, for example, does not offer a completely simplistic representation of Arab womanhood as silent and oppressed. Instead, in the act of appropriation of the seemingly fixed image of Arab women as victims of cultural oppression, it adds another dimension of interpretation and meaning. Though the woman in the ad is covered from head to toe, her gaze is not passive but rather confrontational. While she still seems to be hidden behind the veil, she also seems to exude a sense of power. As with photographs of dancing girls from the 1893 Chicago World's Fair, however, I argue that the image maintains coherence precisely because it captures and presents the tension inherent in the cultural mythology. If photographs of belly dancers at the 1893 Fair could be treasured as emblems of distance, the Reebok ad functions by playing on the motivating tension of simultaneously concealing and revealing Arab womanhood. In his article "The Photographic Message," Barthes argues that "signification is only possible to the extent that there is a stock of signs, the beginnings of a code."[43] The Reebok image draws on the "stock of signs," or, in Foucauldian terms, the field of statements available in orientalist discourse about Arab womanhood. The all-encompassing veil is one of these signs; however, other elements of the image, such as her defiant stance and her unwavering gaze, are reminiscent of the figure of the female vamp, popularized by Theda Bara (an anagram for Arab Death) and performances of Salome. When taken in combination, these elements of the Reebok image reference the well-known orientalist stock of signs to appropriate, and play on, the notion of the "Orient" as both exotic and sensual as well as submissive. The ad is sexy, chic, and, most importantly, effective, because it commodifies those qualities of Arab womanhood that make her alluring: she is simultaneously exotic, untouched, and timeless.[44]

In terms of the "Classic" nature of the Reebok image, the veil again serves as a meaningful symbol due to the orientalist construction of it as a traditional custom, or an antiquated remnant of an ancient cultural practice. The opposition of the woman's all-black dress with her crisp, white shoes emphasizes the juxtaposition of the concept of tradition, symbolized by the woman, and the concept of modern progress, associated with the new shoes. While the shoes are presumably meant to be understood as a contemporary reinterpretation of the "Classic" model of Reebok shoes, the figure of Arab womanhood is relegated to the shadows of tradition (reinforced pictorially by the gray backdrop that frames her black dress) and frozen within the confines of this "backward reference," which functions as the benchmark "against which contemporary change can be measured."[45] Williams describes the persistent emergence of such backward references as characteristic of transitional modes of capitalism.[46] Following this assertion, the nostalgic allure of the mythology of the veil lies in its ability to mitigate the anxieties associated with such moments of transition. Representations of veiled women in U.S. popular culture, then, appear to be univocal and fixed because they hold a fixed meaning within the system of representation in which they are produced. They hold meaning for a mainstream U.S. audience not because of their metonymical relationship to the conditions and realities of Arab women's lives, but because of the way in which they can be used to articulate U.S. based concerns about the changing nature of time and space in a postindustrial capitalist society.

CITATIONAL ORIENTALISM:
THE LANGUAGE OF BARRIERS

In terms of the axis of power, the contemporary salience of the veil in an imperialist U.S. context echoes that of the harem in the late-nineteenth-century French colonial context. The notion of the veil as an absolute boundary to Arab women parallels that of the harem in French orientalist paintings. Just as French orientalist renderings of the space of the harem were ultimately focused on its walls and therefore on the colonial ability to gain access to Arab female sexuality by way of the power of representation, the popular U.S. obsession with the veil in the contemporary context is similarly concerned with penetrating the perceived barrier of the seemingly symbolic cloth covering. In this respect, it is no surprise that representations of the veil have proliferated during the past decade simultaneously with increased U.S. Military action in Iraq and Afghanistan, despite the fact that women in Iraq were not forced to don the veil. Again, as with the signifier of the harem in the French colonialist context, the symbol of the veil serves important purposes for the project of U.S. imperialism: it demonstrates the supposed inferiority of the Arab male's excessive patriarchy and therefore functions as an implicit justification for U.S. Military action. Again, this type of appropriation of the veil is a reiteration of instances of French and British orientalisms. For example, in "The Discourse of the Veil,"[47] Ahmed discusses the way in which the veil functioned in early-twentieth-century Egypt in similar ways to the U.S. contemporary context. Lord Cromer, the British consul general in Egypt at the time, advocated for, in essence, "saving" Egyptian women from the veil and ensuring equal education. But, as Ahmed demonstrates, his actions must be put into the larger colonial context. His goals with regard to women actually led to the goal of justifying British occupation of Egypt, which was seen as a backward country and in need of modernization, in part, because of its treatment of women. The fact that Lord Cromer's primary concern was not, in fact, women's rights is evidenced by his leadership in the anti-suffrage organization in Britain—he firmly and publicly denounced women's rights in his native country. Ahmed describes the construction of the veil as symbolic icon thusly:

> Veiling—to *Western* eyes, the most visible marker of the different-ness and inferiority of Islamic societies—became the symbol now of both the oppression of women...and the backwardness of Islam, and it became the open target of colonial attack and the spearhead of the assault on Muslim societies.[48]

The contemporary U.S. mythology of the veil parallels such appro-priation of feminist rhetoric to justify imperialist means. Indeed, dur-ing both the 1991 Gulf War and the 2001 military action against Afghanistan, mainstream U.S. feminist organizations such as the National Organization for Women (NOW) and the Feminist Majority offered arguments about the oppression of Arab/Muslim women that ultimately buttressed the hegemonic project of U.S. imperialism. Saliba describes the way in which NOW acted in cooperation with the military project of the Gulf War by demanding that Arab women in the region align themselves against their "overly oppressive"[49] male relatives in the midst of a crushingly oppressive U.S. Military offen-sive. Similarly, the Feminist Majority rallied behind a U.S. invasion of Afghanistan in the months following the events of September 11, 2001 in the interest of advancing its long-waged "cause" of liberating Afghan women from the brutal oppression of the Taliban (a liberation that was almost always represented pictorially with the lifting of the burqa). As with Lord Cromer's appropriation of a feminist argument to justify colonial rule when he opposed basic feminist demands in his homeland, the Bush administration has appropriated mainstream U.S. feminist organizations' arguments in order to cast military inva-sion and occupation of Afghanistan and Iraq as projects of libera-tion, while it has opposed the basic demands of these organizations (e.g., abortion rights) in the United States. In both the cases of the Gulf War and of Afghanistan, the claim to liberate women from their patriarchal oppressors effectively eclipses the hegemonic project of domination advanced by U.S. Military action in the region. As Saliba suggests:

> In formulating a feminist anti-war agenda, NOW might have more effectively attacked the U.S. military for posing as liberators of Arab women and for their treatment of U.S. military women, rather than targeting Saudi Arabia and Kuwait as the seats of patriarchal oppression.[50]

Likewise, the Feminist Majority might have more effectively worked toward the liberation of women in Afghanistan by developing a critical consciousness about the militaristic role of the United States, which utilized Afghanistan as a (literal) battleground for its own concerns and power struggles, during twenty-five years of devastating conflict and occupation. Instead, in focusing on individual rights as abstracted from the contexts of militarism and imperialism-through-proxy-wars, the Feminist Majority campaign supports a neoliberal appropriation of the mythology of the veil.

Consider, for example, a 2003 advertisement for the United Colors of Benetton, which features a two-page spread of Basmina, a woman living in Kabul (figure 4.3). The left side of the advertisement pictures the bold image of a brilliant, mustard yellow burqa. The right side of the ad reveals Basmina's face (the burqa is literally lifted and rests on top of her head). The ad copy reads "Basmina, 15, is now free to find work in Kabul. Food Aid supports her while she looks for a job." Not only does this image reinforce, again, the idea that the U.S. invasion of Afghanistan has liberated Afghan women, it also sends the message that this symbolic, if incomplete, liberation is indebted to liberal-democratic ideals which are particularly embedded in a capitalist system. Through the logic of neoliberalism, it implies that the

Figure 4.3   "Food for Work #1"—Benetton Advertisement
Source: © 2003 Benetton Group S.p.A. Photo by James Mollison.

market can regulate itself, eventually equalizing wealth and opportunity, even for women in Afghanistan.

These examples demonstrate that the figure of Arab/Muslim womanhood as reflected through the overdetermined signifier of the veil is employed in a U.S. discourse of liberation that has little to do with the realities of Arab and Muslim women's lives; instead, it represents complex processes of imperialism and neoliberalism. The "lifting" of the veil (to use the language of popular book titles), like the French colonial penetration of the harem walls, represents the success of U.S. powers to dominate the region. In this manner, the symbol of the veil becomes a mythology that offers a sanitized narrative of female oppression and Arab and Muslim backwardness to gloss over a U.S. project of neoliberal imperialism.

HANNAH WILKE: A CASE STUDY

The deployment of the cultural mythology of the veil in the service of empire is not unique to the U.S. context. In his famous study of the French colonial postcards produced in Algeria between 1900 and 1930, Malek Alloula writes: "The first thing the foreign eye catches about Algerian women is that they are concealed from sight."[51] Alloula begins his project by looking at postcards that picture groups of veiled Algerian women walking the streets of Algiers, but he quickly shifts his focus to representations of women inside their homes, where a transgression of the harem walls by the colonialist camera is apparent. From a colonial perspective, the harem is a space where women would have been secluded and where the colonizer might observe them unveiled, or revealed. Some of the postcards Alloula analyzes take this symbolic unveiling one step further by representing the women bare-breasted as well as unveiled. The final set of postcards he considers have succeeded in liberating the women represented from both their harems *and* their clothes—the women are now not only bare-breasted, but completely topless in images with thinly disguised captions such as "The Cracked Jug" (in which the jug is clearly not cracked) and "Oh! Is It Ever Hot!" In the ultimate demonstration of colonial power to penetrate the symbolic harem walls and lay bare Algerian womanhood, Alloula argues: "The colonial postcard says this: these women, who were reputedly invisible or hidden, and, until now, beyond sight, are henceforth public; for a few pennies, and at any time, their intimacy can be broken into and violated."[52] The ability to reveal Algerian womanhood, he argues, confers power and authority on the French colonial project.

One might point out, as Rey Chow does,[53] that the women represented are indeed inscribed by a complex struggle for power—one in which Alloula, in a paternalistic move, seems to battle with the legacy of French colonial power over ownership of these women's bodies. Nevertheless, given that his stated intention is to "return this immense postcard to its sender," one wonders what he sought to achieve by surprising his readers with the shock of a final image, surreptitiously placed after the section marked "Notes" at the end of the book and conspicuously left unexamined and unanalyzed. The shock of the image clearly lies in the fact that the woman wears a traditional *yachmak* covering her entire body except for her eyes, yet in this image, the cloth covering her breasts has been removed to render them completely bare save for the strip of cloth that extends down from her face veil in between her breasts and for the folds of cloth extending from her head down over her shoulders, arms, and midriff.[54] The stark contrast between the woman's concealed face and body and her revealed breasts brings together, neatly and intimately in one image, a representation of the powerful tension between concealing and revealing that the mythology of the veil communicates—a tension that belies the imbrications of such representations in gendered and sexualized notions about the power of female sexuality. Contradictions in this image, as in the Reebok image, actually mimic popular stereotypes meant to regulate female sexuality, such as those of the virgin/whore dichotomy.

The appropriation of this rich, and, in some ways, irresistible metaphor can be traced to Hannah Wilke's photographic S.O.S series, which was completed in 1974. Wilke has, no doubt, unknowingly replicated the structure of Alloula's shocking image in one of the prints from the S.O.S. project. The set of prints that comprise S.O.S. depict Wilke sometimes parodying stereotypically feminine poses and sometimes embodying and playing with stereotypically masculine poses. In two of these images, she wears what might be described as a headdress, perhaps familiar to mainstream U.S. audiences through representations of "Lawrence of Arabia." In one of these two, she wears the headdress, wrapping the ends of the cloth around her mouth and covering her shoulders, and leaves her breasts bare.[55] By inhabiting and playing with stereotypically gendered poses, Wilke seeks to subvert the male gaze that fixes the female body, to use Laura Mulvey's phrase, in a "to-be-looked-at-ness."[56] She seeks to both reveal the ways that female sexuality is regulated by a seemingly ever-present male gaze and to simultaneously undermine that gaze by replicating or mimicking it. She undermines the power of the gaze, Amelia

Jones argues, "through a deliberate *reiteration*...[that] can expose the gaze in its insufficiency."[57] In the case of S.O.S., Wilke "perverts the logic" of the female nude by inhabiting the pose and decorating her body with tiny sculptural representations of the vulva. The material she has used to make the sculptures is chewing gum because, as she says: "In this society we use up people the way we use up chewing gum. I chose gum because it's the perfect metaphor for the American woman—chew her up, get what you want out of her, throw her out and pop in a new piece."[58] Wilke clearly advances a feminist argument by unsettling the notion that women are objects. Jones argues that Wilke's body art "performs a woman-as-artist in an empowering way by insistently *unveiling* the artist (who is clearly masculine in her artistic authority) as female."[59] The metaphor of unveiling is significant. Here, it is literally associated with the feminist reclamation of power. However, in attempting to dismantle one form of oppression (patriarchal), Wilke succeeds in reinscribing another by appropriating an orientalist narrative about Arab and Muslim womanhood.

Like the Leibovitz project, the series of stereotypical, and mostly stereotypically feminine poses Wilke adopts are ultimately meant to reveal the wounds that women collect and endure in a patriarchal society, as signified by the chewing gum scars. Her desire to reveal the truth about these patriarchal scars is highlighted by the image that parallels the French colonial postcard, in which she appropriates a widely accepted symbol of oppression to buttress her own claim about the oppression (and objectification) of women. The style Wilke borrows here is not the type of veil one would see a woman wearing; it much more closely resembles male garb, and is called a headdress by several of the scholars who write about her.[60] Even so, at least one critic, Jo Anna Isaak (who writes in the contemporary U.S. context, during the rise of the mythology of the veil as popular signifier), has read it as a veil; she writes: "Each frame figures [Wilke] in some stereotypical pose: a cowgirl, a vamp, a movie star, an Islamic woman wearing a headdress and veil. In this last image, Wilke exposes the irony of another culture's cover-up, which, while seeming to hide and repress female sexuality, has succeeded in creating it in very predetermined and disciplined ways."[61] Notably, Isaak finds the image of the "Islamic women" significant enough to single it out for comment. It seems to exemplify for her the fact that Islam particularly, singularly, and "monstrously" (in Ahmed's words), oppresses women. Despite the inaccuracy of the covering Wilke wears, the image functions as an appropriation of the mythology of the veil. By inhabiting the pose of the female nude while simultaneously representing the "cover-up," or at least the patriarchy, of Muslim culture, she is appropriating the mythology of the veil in order to stake her own claim against patriarchal oppression. In doing so, she replicates the foibles of liberal feminism, which privileges universalized (read white middle class) gender at the expense of a critical understanding of the intersection of patriarchal, racial, and economic oppressions, to name a few. This disruptive feminist move by Wilke, then, actually reveals the veiled function of these types of images: they appropriate potent markers of Arab and Muslim womanhood, through the mythology of the veil, in the service of the logic of their own argument.[62] What is so dangerous and insidious about the mythology of the veil is the ease with which it can be appropriated, often in arguments that do not serve the best interests of the women who are imagined to be represented "behind" the veil.

Both the examples of the Benetton and Reebok advertisements, and the Leibovitz and Wilke photographs, demonstrate the ways in which the symbol of the veil has come to be emptied of any sociohistorical meaning it holds in particular cultural contexts and retooled as a signifier of some of the conditions, such as transnational capitalism and imperialism, that determine the contemporary U.S. context. While it is clear from the Wilke, Leibovitz, Reebok, and Benetton examples that contemporary representations of the veil follow an orientalist logic found in western European representations, a critical analysis reveals that they are clearly shaped by the particular concerns of the U.S. cultural context. Though I have discussed the ways in which U.S. concerns with power and progress are threaded into the logic of the mythology of the veil, in the next section I will look more closely at shifting U.S. narratives of national security in relation to the Middle East in order to trace the impact of these narratives on images of Arab and Muslim womanhood. A preliminary example is a public relations postcard disseminated by a nonprofit organization called "Blue Star PR: The Jewish Ink Tank." The image on the front of this postcard depicts two Israeli women, one who wears a bikini and another who seems to be dressed in traditional-style clothing that covers her entire body. The message on the back of this postcard reads:

> Free to be themselves, free to dress as they please, free to date who they want, free to drive, free to work, free to choose their own mates, free to study, free to travel abroad without the consent of a male relative, free to lead, free to write and publish, free to make reproductive choices. Just like American women, Israeli women have all of these freedoms. Women in the surrounding Muslim countries are still waiting.

Despite the organization's statement that "Blue Star PR does not represent or promote any political ideology,"[63] the power of its message (both visual and written), relies on a notion of freedom that clearly resonates with a set of political and ideological assumptions about the status of Arab, or, here, Muslim women as absolutely and irrevocably unfree. Again, the meaning of the veil is naturalized—it is made to seem like an unquestioned given, as if it is an inherent aspect of the state of being a Muslim woman. In this way, the mythology of the veil encodes a political and ideological message within the symbol of the veil and then fixes it there, giving the impression that it arises innocently from the image itself. Moreover, in this instance, the evocation of freedom as an inherent quality of liberal-democratic, enlightened nations offers a link to the trope of national security and the ways in which the rhetoric of freedom buttresses narratives of security.

FROM SHEIK GIRLS TO CHIC VEILS

Given that the mythology of the veil is firmly embedded in a particular set of sociohistorical conditions, the predominance of the veil as signifier in the contemporary context is clearly historically constructed. In other words, not only have the veil, the harem, and the belly dancer occupied different spaces of meaning throughout U.S. history, the expression of each category of representation has shifted according to the particularities of what I have been calling the power and progress axes. If the veil-as-barrier iteration of the mythology of the veil has functioned in the contemporary U.S. context as a symbol for direct conflict in U.S.-Middle East relations (much as the harem did for the French/Algerian context), a collection of "oil sheik"[64] representations in the 1970s serve as precursors to the mythology of the veil. These oil sheik images emerged in a moment of greatly intensified political conflict between the United States and the Middle East, and they reintroduced the concept of the harem as a prisonlike space for women who were, by nature, at the mercy of brutal or greedy patriarchal figures. Comparing and contrasting 1970s harem images and contemporary veil images, I look here at the ways in which these two sets of images refract the contemporaneous narrative of national security.

It is important to contextualize the caricature of the "oil sheik" within a tradition of orientalist representations of "sheik" characters in Hollywood films, such as *The Sheik, Son of the Sheik, The Thief of Baghdad, Harum Scarum,* and *Lawrence of Arabia.* Notably, like James Bond in *The Spy Who Loved Me,* the title characters in these films are often white (western European or American) men who perform what Sunaina Maira (in another context) has called "Arab face."[65] As Ella Shohat and Robert Stam have argued, sheik narratives often revolve around masculinist and heteronormative desire, and they play into imperialist tropes that Shohat and Stam have labeled the "rape and rescue fantasy" and the "desert odyssey."[66] Within these tropes, the white male character masquerading as "sheik" gains access to an imagined space of orientalist fantasy, where he is afforded the luxury of sexual abandon since the space is assumed to be naturally lascivious. White women in this context serve as the objects to be rescued, so that the symbolic importance of their chaste and virginal sexuality may be preserved, and/or they serve as gracious guardians of the colonialist/imperialist civilizing mission. On the other hand, indigenous women, in the words of Shohat and Stam, "when not merely erotic tokens of their virgin lands—are marginalized, appearing largely as sexually hungry subalterns."[67] In other words, the sexualized native women within the sheik narrative, though marginalized, function to set the eroticized and sexualized scene in the figurative space of the harem. The sheik character, then, necessarily invokes the notion of Arab female sexuality as purportedly naturally licentious, and simultaneously serves as a link to the stereotype of the despotic Ottoman sultan.

One of the latest variations on the theme of the sheik character is that of the oil sheik, predominant in the 1970s and 1980s U.S. context. Like his predecessors, the oil sheik is also depicted within the imaginary space of the harem, yet unlike the sheik characters already mentioned, he embodies the image of the despotic sultan more fully as his ethnicity is Arab. Further, he plays into the trope of the "rape and rescue fantasy" as he is often represented as particularly desirous of white women.[68] For the purpose of my argument, I am particularly interested in the way in which the added layer of oil transmogrifies the sheik image from one that is mostly sexualized to one that is both sexualized and masculinized as a figurehead of brutal, indigenous patriarchy. As I discuss below, particularly in the 1970s and 1980s, access to oil resources became a crucial aspect of financial and national security in the United States. Therefore, the figure of the oil sheik plays a critical role in popular U.S. imagination in terms of the shifting narrative of national security. To flesh these dynamics out, I look in particular at the image of James Bond and his harem from the film *The Spy Who Loved Me* as a transitional figure, which is emblematic of the increased articulation of national security concerns in popular representations of Arab and Muslim womanhood.

Representations of dancing girls from the 1893 Chicago World's Fair and of transparently veiled cigarette girls in early-twentieth-century tobacco advertisements suggest that in those contexts they were metaphorically removed (or liberated) from the confines of protective harem walls characteristic of the French colonial context. Moreover, the figure of the sultan master had been reduced from that of a brutal despot to that of a jovial, nonthreatening fellow as manifested in the image of *Omar*. Therefore, the reemergence of symbolic barriers beginning in the 1970s suggests that such images reflect the complex network of power relations between the neocolonialist U.S. power, the Middle East, and the former colonial powers of France and Britain. In particular, the representation of James Bond and his harem offers a rich articulation of such themes, since James Bond himself signals a shift from British to U.S. primacy in terms of global force (more on this below). As hyperbolic icon of white masculinity, the James Bond character serves as a compelling figure through which to investigate the competing patriarchal and masculinist images that emerge in relation to narratives of national security. Setting the scene for my analysis of the James Bond image, I will first offer some background to explain the national security narrative that undergirds the shift in gendered representations of Arabs during the 1970s and 1980s.

A KINDER AND GENTLER EMPIRE

If French and British powers presented the project of colonialism as liberal and enlightened (i.e., as a civilizing mission) in contradistinction to the brutal and oppressive rule of the Ottoman Empire, post–World War II articulations of U.S. nationhood posit the United States as a still more liberating power for Middle Eastern countries. The construction of U.S. interests in the Middle East in the postwar years as a kind of "benevolent supremacy"[69] served a double purpose of both deflecting critical attention away from the political and economic interests that the United States was developing in the region and of animating, as Melani McAlister notes, "the anti-British and anticolonial rhetoric that formed the heart of American national origin stories."[70] In other words, as U.S. policymakers sought to angle the United States as a leading world power in the decades following World War II, they developed a plan for national security that strategically deployed the narrative of the United States as a nation that had achieved independence from a colonial power and as a nation that would therefore defend all nations' struggles for independence.[71] Such a strategy worked not only because it harnessed the momentum of independence movements of formerly colonized countries in Asia and Africa, it also worked to conceal the far-from-benevolent U.S. militarist goals to achieve military and economic power in the Middle East by way of garnering access to oil resources.

If the official rhetoric of U.S. national security did not acknowledge the increasingly conflicted relationship between the United States and the Middle East, however, popular representations of Arab womanhood in U.S. popular culture did. Contrary to earlier representations of the Arab world in the United States, post-World War II images incorporated elements that belied a shift in global power dynamics. As I argued in chapters 2 and 3, the indigenous Arab patriarchy figured as more of a nuisance than a threat to burgeoning U.S. forces in the late nineteenth and early twentieth centuries. However, in the decades following World War II, and particularly beginning in the 1970s, the barriers metaphorically linked to patriarchy and oppression emerged in popular U.S. images in the form of harem walls and opaque veils.

As the colonization of the Middle East by French and British powers changed shape with an Allied victory following World War II, U.S. policymakers increasingly positioned the United States as an emerging global superpower. Moreover, the development of the United States as an imperialist nation-state, as an extension of its expansionist goals in the late nineteenth and early twentieth centuries, depended greatly on its ability to dominate new territories of material wealth. While Frederick Jackson Turner's proclamation, in 1893, that the frontier was gone certainly marked the fulfillment of U.S. expansion to the west coast of the U.S. "virgin land," it did not foresee the extension of the manifest destiny credo to the Philippines and beyond. As a foil for what was, in actuality, an imperialist project to annex raw materials and resources, the notion of the frontier can easily be applied to the postwar U.S. context, during which the Arab world emerged on the horizon as the new frontier of oil wealth.[72] Similar to early-twentieth-century tobacco advertisements (such as *Omar*) that relied on the metaphor of the frontier, this trope references and reinscribes gendered notions of the feminized Middle East. However, at the same time it set the stage for a competition in masculinity vis-à-vis rhetorics of national security.

The quest for oil and, consequently, for power in the Middle East therefore framed the inevitability of conflict between the United States and the Middle East, as the Arab world increasingly figured in the U.S. narrative of national security.[73] Indeed, the rapidly increasing energy needs in the United States ensured that oil would be unconditionally linked to questions of national security not only after World War II, but also throughout the cold war and beyond. It follows, then, that any barrier posed to U.S. access to oil resources by the Arab and Muslim worlds would be perceived as a serious threat to the sanctity of U.S. imperialist forces.

FROM OMAR THE TENTMAKER TO MOHAMMED THE TERRORIST

Beginning in the 1970s, with the 1973 oil embargo organized by OPEC, and expanding into the contemporary context with increased conflict between the United States and various Arab nations, the benign and jolly image of Omar (in early-twentieth-century tobacco advertisements) gave way to an increasingly sinister, greedy, and threatening image of Arab masculinity.[74] Consequently, the floating image of the belly dancer on display metamorphosed first into a permutation of the French orientalist harem trope (in the 1970s and 1980s) and later into the overdetermined signifier of the veil (in the 1990s and into 2000). This return of symbolic barriers—the walls of the harem and the veil-as-barrier motif—can be linked to the popular perception of increased threat from the Arab and Muslim worlds. This sense of threat, moreover, was emphasized by the intersection of U.S. imperialism and transnational capitalist formations that cohered to make the Arab world seem spatially closer. If representations of the Middle East as Holy Land or of the romanticized caricatures of Omar Khayyam reified the sense of distance between the United States and the Middle East, representations of the harem, the oil sheik, and, eventually, the veil, increasingly signified the notion of Arab and Muslim difference as a threatening presence.[75] While the elevated numbers of Arab immigrants to the United States following the 1965 Immigration Act undoubtedly aided a collective U.S. sense of increased Arab presence in the United States, the shifting perception of Arabs and Arab Americans as "pollutants," to borrow Robert Lee's term,[76] is distinctly tied to media representations of political conflict in the Middle East. The American orientalist construction of Arab difference transformed beginning in the 1970s due to increased media visibility in coverage of events such as the 1973 oil embargo, the Iran hostage crisis, and the ensuing "war against terrorism" declared by presidents Ronald Reagan and George Bush (Sr.) in the 1980s. Images of greedy Arab oil sheiks and extremist terrorists entered into the U.S. collective consciousness by way of extensive media coverage of the hostage crisis and official government warnings for U.S. citizens to lower their thermostats.[77]

What had started out as a political relationship seemingly based in mutuality was clearly entering an era of scripted antagonism. One of the first major threats to U.S. "national security" came with the 1973 oil embargo, especially since the U.S. security policy at the time was so powerfully associated with continued access to oil. As a result, the predominant image of Arab masculinity at the time was the figure of the "oil sheik." As a vague reference to the Ottoman stereotype of the "Terrible Turk," the greedy oil sheik reveled in the decadence of his new riches, and hoarded his resources, which of course included his women, within the confines of his harem. Moreover, his appetite for indulgence was voracious and unquenchable—no amount of gold, oil, or women (no matter what nationality) could satisfy him.[78] Concomitantly, the figure of the belly dancer, which had so determined a mainstream U.S. understanding of Arab womanhood, was increasingly coaxed back into the stewardship of her harem master and into the general context of enclosure.

JAMES BOND AND HIS HAREM

A particularly illustrative example of the way in which the national security narrative manifests in contemporary images of Arab womanhood is in a harem image from the movie poster for the 1977 James Bond film *The Spy Who Loved Me*. The image is particularly noteworthy in that it is a scene that, in fact, never appears in the film itself, but is instead extrapolated from the context of one fleeting scene in which Bond is afforded the sexual pleasures of one of his Egyptian friend's mistresses. Though the heteronormative sexual exploits of the James Bond character are a major structural element of Bond films, the fact that the harem scene is played up on movie posters indicates its salience in a larger mid-1970s U.S. context. In what follows, I first make a case for the importance of Bond films in a U.S. context, I then discuss the significance of *The Spy Who Loved Me* as a transitional film, and I finally analyze the "James Bond and his harem" image as a specific manifestation of the developing national security trope in the context of U.S. popular culture.

The Bond filmic genre originates in the United Kingdom, as it is based upon a set of novels written by Ian Fleming. While the novels were widely popular, and achieved commercial success in the United States as well, the films were largely responsible for inserting the Bond character into U.S. popular imagination. The films, moreover, were a joint project of U.S. and Canadian producers Albert "Cubby" Broccoli and Harry Saltzman (respectively), though, because they split in 1975, *The Spy Who Loved Me* was produced by Broccoli alone.[79] Despite the fact that *The Spy Who Loved Me* opens with the famous British nationalistic scene in which Bond escapes assassination by skiing off of a mountain and deploying a giant Union Jack as a parachute, the film still operates as a U.S. produced and funded narrative about masculinity, sexuality, and national security. Indeed the symbol of the Union Jack serves as a not-so-subtle reminder of the way in which hegemonic articulations of the United States as a global power functioned both by allying the United States with, and by distinguishing the United States from, the waning colonial power of the United Kingdom.

In the majority of James Bond films, the protagonist emerges as a post–World War II hero who is symbolically engaged in the struggle for global power, which audiences are meant to associate with the cold war. Particularly in the Bond films of the 1960s and early 1970s, Bond, the white, western hero of the "free" world is called upon to save the entire world from the supposedly evil threat of the communist bloc. Beginning with *The Spy Who Loved Me* as a transitional film, however, Bond emerges as a hero in the war against terrorism rather than a hero of the cold war per se. Such a shift manifests visually, I argue, in the harem image and is indicative, on a larger level, of popular perceptions of the Middle East as a growing threat to the United States.

The most marked element of change in *The Spy* is the fact that, rather than being pitted against a Russian antagonist, Bond works in collaboration with Russian spy Anya Amasova in what Jeremy Black calls "a new era of Anglo-Soviet co-operation"[80] in Bond films. Indeed, if Bond and Amasova represent an emerging solidarity between what can be loosely (and not quite accurately) termed Western and Eastern powers, they do so in opposition to a newly emerging, generalized global threat, represented in the film by megalomaniacal Karl Stromberg. Stromberg was, in fact, written to embody the general characteristics of a terrorist threat according to western European and U.S. hegemonic perspectives—he represented a new, global and irrational threat to the sovereignty of all state powers. He was based on the organization SPECTRE (Special Executive for Counterintelligence, Terrorism, Revenge, and Extortion), which had a fairly clear link to real-world concerns about the emerging threat of "terrorism." However, because the film rights were granted on the basis that the screenplays did not mimic the novels on which they were based, the right to use Fleming's SPECTRE in Bond films was rejected.[81]

Critics have also noted that *The Spy Who Loved Me* is a transitional Bond film in that it presents a strong female character (Amasova) in response to the contemporaneous narratives of women's liberation and independence.[82] Given this argument, which is compelling in its own right, it is even more interesting to consider the salience of the "James Bond and his harem" image, which, again, occurs nowhere in the film itself. Because Amasova is cast as a central love interest for Bond throughout the film, his sexual escapades in Egypt are actually downplayed. In fact, upon being offered female companionship for his overnight stay with his Egyptian friend (who presumably produces the women from his own harem), Bond initially refuses and only gives in to the logic that it is simply a standard feature of Egyptian hospitality and, therefore, is an offer not to be refused. Here, he replicates the "desert odyssey" trope of empire described by Shohat and Stam, in which "the desert . . . functions narratively as the site of moral liminality."[83] Nevertheless, his eventual acceptance of one mistress notwithstanding, the implication on the movie poster image that he takes four mistresses is worth further consideration.

Egypt provides the setting for a fairly minor portion of the plot narrative. Stromberg, the film villain, has trapped and stolen both British and Soviet nuclear submarines and programmed them to fire nuclear bombs on Moscow and New York respectively. The fact that he chooses New York as the primary target, and not London, speaks both to the importance of the United States as a global superpower and to the notion of a U.S.-UK alliance. Bond and Amasova travel separately to Egypt in search of the "heat-tracking device" Stromberg used to follow and trap the two submarines. Again, given the relatively marginal role of Egypt in the plot narrative, it is curious that the setting should figure in two posters marketing the film. Though the image of James Bond surrounded by four beautiful women is certainly consonant with the popular image of Bond as an irresistible and virile hero, the legibility of the image depends on its deployment of orientalist tropes, which would have had a particularly palpable resonance for U.S. audiences. In many ways, the James Bond image serves as an oppositional precursor to popular representations of terrorists in the contemporary context. As an exaggerated symbol of heteronormativity, he prefigures the way that, as Puar and Rai argue, constructed representations of the deviant sexuality of Osama bin Laden in the contemporary context function to discipline the heteronormative patriotic subject in the United States.[84]

James Bond himself, the central figure in the image, is dressed to invoke a reference to *Lawrence of Arabia*, and is therefore positioned as a benevolent figure to "Arabian" interests. Simultaneously, though, he invokes an association with the U.S. caricature of the oil sheik, which rose to prominence in the mid to late 1970s. The head garb he wears, in combination with the fact that he is surrounded by scantily clad women (in cabaret style belly-dancing costumes) on his sides and at his feet, both implicitly invoke the image of the greedy Arab oil patriarch, who hoards both his natural resources and his women. The implicit reference to the surrounding women as a harem draws on popular perceptions of Arab men as greedy and indulgent; insofar as access to oil is linked to national security in U.S. popular imagination, the implied threat is manifested in this reference to Arab patriarchy as excessive. Particularly in its invocation of the *Lawrence of Arabia* narrative, though, as a figure of heteronormative white manhood, the James Bond harem image articulates with the narrative of benevolent supremacy by implying Bond's own benevolent patriarchy. In doing so, it is able to gesture to the notion of Arab patriarchy as peculiarly oppressive, and therefore to signal the potential of a growing threat. As is the case in the legacy of sheik representations, none of these significations would be possible without the invisible, yet animating, presence of Arab womanhood invoked by the harem scene as bastion of excessive erotic sexuality.

In the years following the release of this image, as the specter of Arab and Muslim threat to U.S. national security loomed larger and larger, predominant images of Arab womanhood also changed. Beginning with the Iran hostage crisis from 1979 to 1981, and continuing throughout the 1980s "war against terrorism" up until the contemporary "war on terror," popular misperceptions of Islam as an oppressive and fundamentally violent religion have impacted representations of Arab and Muslim womanhood by shifting them toward a focus on victimization rather than eroticism.[85] The discourse on terrorism has functioned to construct an image of the enemy as an irrationally violent Muslim male; representations of Arab and Muslim womanhood, then, have largely functioned in the service of such a masculinist and simplistic construction. As I argued in the mythology of the veil section, representations of the veil that cast it as a symbol of oppression serve to position Arab and Muslim women as victims of their culture, and to therefore support the logic of the discourse on terrorism, which operates under the assumption of Arab and Muslim culture as hyper-patriarchal and irrationally violent. In the post–World War II context, representations of harem girls and veiled women operate within the masculinist logic of national security rhetoric. Whether they are nurtured within the benevolent

patriarchy of James Bond and his harem in *The Spy Who Loved Me*
and of Captain Anthony Nelson in *I Dream of Jeannie*,[86] or whether
they are cast as submissive and "hidden" wards of hyper-patriarchal
culture, as in more recent years, they have functioned as cultural
mythologies in the service of U.S. empire-building.

PRIVATIZATION OF EMPIRE

Although representations of the veil have dominated news media
and peppered contemporary popular culture, they are not the only
representations of Arab and Muslim womanhood operating in the
current context. The increased popularity of belly dancing as an
entertainment form in Mediterranean-themed restaurants and as a
chic new form of exercise in the exercise industry demonstrates the
marketability of such images within the contemporary U.S. context.
In this section, then, I shift my focus to what I have been calling the
progress axis of these representations to look at the way in which
neoliberalism, as a contemporary incarnation of the progress narrative, has figured in images of Arab and Muslim womanhood. If U.S.
policy in a post–World War II context positioned the United States
as a benevolent force in the Middle East, it did so, in part, by obscuring national economic interests in the region. In the contemporary
neoliberal context, this sort of elision is enacted once again, though
it now has a slightly different formation. By way of introduction to
my analysis of the way in which neoliberal imperialist formations
manifest in contemporary representations of Arab and Muslim womanhood, I begin here with an admittedly cursory comparison of two
U.S. national security documents, the National Security Council
document 68 (NSC-68, written in 1950) and the National Security
Strategy of the United States (NSSUS, written in 2002). In doing
so, I aim to highlight both the continuities and discontinuities in the
particular ways in which capitalism and imperialism cohered into a
"structure of feeling" reflected in various representations Arab and
Muslim womanhood.

The NSC-68 was crafted in an era in which the United States
sought to construct itself as a "benevolent supremacy," or as a pro-
liberation alternative to colonialist structures of power.[87] As a product
of a historical moment in which the United States began to emerge
as a dominant global power, the NSC-68 positions the U.S. rhetorically as a free, liberal-democratic power in opposition to the slave-
like subjugating power of the Soviet Union. In casting the battle for
supremacy in such moralistic, oppositional terms, it set the stage for a

national security policy that would both garner resources to increase military spending in competition with the Soviet Union and to ensure that the Middle East remained open both politically and economically to U.S. interests. Therefore, during this period the notion of the Middle East shifted in U.S. popular imagination from an impossibly distant, romanticized, or holy space, to a living region of formerly colonized countries filled with valuable resources. Though none of these cultural lenses would fully drop away in popular U.S. perceptions of the Arab world, the strategic and economic importance of the Middle East for U.S. national security would increasingly infiltrate general perceptions of Arabs and Muslims in U.S. popular culture.

By the time the NSSUS was issued to Congress on September 19, 2002 (fifty-two years later), the neoliberal imperialist goals of the Bush administration had necessitated a logic whereby the document implied that the grand, humanist U.S. goal to bring reason and justice to the Middle East had inexplicably resulted in the irrational, backward violence and opposition of terrorism. Therefore, like the NSC-68, the language of the NSSUS positioned the United States as an enlightened benevolent power in opposition to morally bankrupt forces, but those oppositional forces referenced by the document had shifted from the Soviet Union in the cold war era to the Arab and Muslim worlds in the "war on terror" era.[88] The articulation of benevolence, moreover, was now more clearly and overtly couched in a neoliberal framework. The document claims, for instance, that the United States "will actively work to bring the hope of democracy, development, free markets, and free trade to every corner of the world."[89] This type of logic, which conflates liberal-democratic ideals with neoliberal free market ideals, belies the confluence of capitalist and imperialist goals for the United States in relation to the Middle East. The increasingly antagonistic relationship, as I have argued, manifested itself in a set of representations of Arab womanhood that metaphorically enacted the language of barriers.

In addition to the narrative of national security and inevitable conflict, though, contemporary images of Arab and Muslim women also communicate an unarticulated anxiety about the seemingly irreversible spatiotemporal shifts provoked by neoliberal capitalist formations in the context of postmodernity. Just as the increased consumerist orientation in U.S. society manifested in contemporaneous *Omar* tobacco advertisements, which capitalized on pastoral images of open spaces in the midst of the perceived loss of such spaces, contemporary representations of Arab womanhood similarly exploit orientalist nostalgia in the midst of capitalist shifts that seem to shrink space and time. In this final section of the chapter, then, I look at the ways in which dominant narratives of globalization inhere in popular representations of Arab and Muslim womanhood as nostalgic and quaint emblems of the still-receding past.

The sharp economic recession of 1973, which was exacerbated, if not stimulated, by the OPEC oil embargo (begun in the same year), signaled one beginning of a major shift in the structure of capitalism, according to theorists such as Harvey and Jameson, who have described this shift in terms of "the condition of postmodernity" or "the cultural logic of late capitalism" respectively.[90] Both Harvey and Jameson seek to explain the "condition of postmodernity," to use Harvey's phrase, or the characteristics of postmodernism, to use Jameson's formulation, in terms of the relationship of postmodernity to an economic base of late multinational capitalism. Indeed, Jameson even goes so far as to say that "this whole global, yet American, postmodern culture is the internal and superstructural expression of a whole new wave of American military and economic domination throughout the world."[91] The implication here, that U.S. Military and economic power has determined the process of globalization all over the world, has been critiqued as an overly simplistic formulation and one that promulgates the same western European and U.S. centric secularist bias that animates the metanarrative of modernity.[92] While I agree with the argument that the process of globalization is too complex to be accounted for by a hegemonic, one-sided narrative of western European and U.S. domination of the world, I use Harvey's and Jameson's formulations here precisely because I am not interested in the "real" conditions of postmodernity vis-à-vis contemporary shifts in capitalist formations, but rather in the role that popular images of Arab and Muslim womanhood have played in shoring up dominant narratives of globalization, which situate the United States at the center of the process. I am also building on the basic claims of both Harvey and Jameson that the disorientations provoked by foundational capitalist shifts, such as the contemporary shift into late multinational capitalism, profoundly impact popular perceptions of space and time, which, I argue, manifest in popular representations of Arab and Muslim womanhood. Further, Harvey's claim that the condition of postmodernity introduces a "new round of time-space compression"[93] emphasizes the cyclical, rather than purely linear, nature of this aspect of capitalism, thereby offering a means of conceptualizing the continuities between capitalist formations in relation to early-twentieth-century tobacco advertisements and those in contemporary tobacco advertisements.

According to the Harvey narrative, this latest phase of capitalism emerged in the 1970s when the previous capitalist orientation toward growth, the Fordist paradigm of mass production and mass consumption, eventually expanded beyond its means of production and its available markets. The inevitability of the excesses of perpetual growth resulted in an unusable surplus of goods and a dearth of potential consumer markets. The failures of this Fordist model, then, were addressed by a dynamic shift into a new phase of capitalism that Harvey calls "flexible accumulation," which rests on a foundation of flexibility and mobility of goods and labor (as opposed to the rigidity of the previous framework) and which is "characterized by the emergence of entirely new sectors of production, new ways of providing financial services, new markets, and, above all, greatly intensified rates of commercial, technological, and organizational innovation."[94] In short, this new phase of capitalism has found ways of collapsing and shrinking the horizons of time and the boundaries of geographical distance, which have given way to a "new round" of time-space compression. It transgresses the previous limitations of production and consumption because of its "enhanced capacity to switch capital flows around in ways that seem almost oblivious of the constraints of time and space that normally pin down material activities of production and consumption."[95] Late capitalism, then, measures growth by expanding globally both in terms of labor and consumer markets and it manages its own growth not just by regulating the movement of goods across international markets, but also by manipulating capital itself and by having the ability to respond to fluctuations in global capital instantaneously.

The cumulative result of these types of shifts is ultimately a "change in the experience of space and time in Western capitalism."[96] Like turn-of-the-century and early-twentieth-century "feelings of unreality" that emerged in reaction to permutations in the nature of time and space, another "round" of temporal and spatial shifts in the contemporary context implies a new set of disorientations. Given these connections, it is crucial, then, to understand feelings of fragmentation, usually described as characteristic of the postmodern condition, as continuous with, or at least cyclically related to, the experience of alienation that is characteristic of modernity. Rather than positing the narratives of modernity and postmodernity as fundamentally distinct, I am interested in drawing a parallel between the way that figures of Arab and Muslim womanhood operate simultaneously as nostalgic emblems in both modernist and postmodernist frameworks. Indeed, as Harvey warns, it is important to resist "simple polarizations" between modernity and postmodernity and instead see them on the same continuum as similarly constructed social processes.[97] Understanding modernity and postmodernity in opposition to one another not only elides the similar ways in which they reflect the flexibility of spatiotemporal realities, it also imposes a binary framework that reifies the very notions of progress and tradition undergirding stereotypical representations of Arab womanhood. In other words, it contributes to the construction of the traditional/modern binary, which is central to the progress narrative. In his book *The Country and the City*, Raymond Williams demonstrates the way such progress narratives depend on the continuous reinvention of the past whereby the reality of rapid change in a particular historical moment, often stimulated by a shift in capitalist formations, provokes a nostalgic "backward reference" to a presumably simpler time.[98] As he demonstrates, this simpler time, sometimes invoked in terms of tradition, "keeps appearing [and] reappearing at bewilderingly various dates" and functions therefore as a construct "against which contemporary change can be measured."[99] In other words, the notion of tradition and its attending symbolic figures are not actually historically based, but are instead produced as nostalgic markers of stability and stasis as a reaction to the reality of rapid, disorienting change. Because they are shored up by simple dichotomies, these nostalgic figures contribute to a structure of feeling in which contemporary change can only be understood in terms of a break, or rupture, with the past.

I have been arguing that representations of Arab and Muslim womanhood in U.S. popular culture function as visual markers of this structure of feeling in various historical contexts. Yet, while in both modern and postmodern contexts they have marked similar reactions of disorientation to fragmentation and chaos, they manifest these reactions in different ways. If a modernist orientation responds to "feelings of unreality" and the sense of "rupture with the past" by attempting to solidify and reinstate aspects of the real (e.g., by building a replica of the "real" Jerusalem)—a postmodernist orientation responds by romanticizing the past in fragmentary ways. In fact, Harvey claims that a postmodernist response "does not try to transcend [the fact of change], counteract it, or even to define the 'eternal and immutable' elements that might lie within it. Postmodernism swims, even wallows, in the fragmentary and the chaotic currents of change as if that is all there is."[100] In what follows, I look at contemporary images of Arab womanhood in tobacco advertisements in order to demonstrate the way in which the new elements of representation are consonant with the notion of postmodernism as chaotic and fragmentary, though the images can still be squarely located within an orientalist tradition.

EXOTIC PLEASURES FOR THE TWENTY-FIRST CENTURY

The R.J. Reynolds Company's brand of *Camel* cigarettes provides an interesting case-in-point for further understanding the way in which hegemonic narratives of globalization have manifested in the realm of representation. R.J. Reynolds, which changed the nature of the tobacco industry in 1913 when it launched *Camel* as its primary brand, has ironically spent most of its corporate life distancing itself from overt association with orientalist imagery. Though its name, *Camel*, clearly identifies it with the Middle East, R.J. Reynolds advertising campaigns have consistently underplayed the relationship of *Camel* cigarettes to the Arab and Muslim worlds (this is especially apparent with the "Joe Camel" ads during the late 1980s and early 1990s, which attempted to avoid the uncomfortable reality of the Gulf War). It is of considerable interest, then, that from 2002 to the present, the *Camel* Company has capitalized on an abundant array of orientalist markers to advertise its new line of "Exotic" and "Turkish" Blends.

The teaser ads for this line were part of a promotional scheme entitled "seven pleasures of the exotic," which promised to deliver seven pleasures (feast, *carnivale*, rhythm, masquerade, spa, elixir, and *tabac*) at seven-hundred parties planned in seventy cities across the United States. In terms of representing Arab womanhood, the figure that functions as signifier of the pleasure of "carnivale" is most easily recognizable as borrowing from the legacy of U.S. images of Arab womanhood, since it references orientalist representations by depicting the outline of a belly dancer against a red backdrop.[101] Although she is silhouetted against a radiant red backdrop, and is therefore rendered devoid of any particular features because she appears in black outline, she is still immediately identifiable as a belly dancer. Again, because it is not possible to make out the details of her dress, the audience cannot rely on the often-used markers of the ornate halter-bra and ballooning harem pants to identify her as a dancing girl. Nevertheless, the fact that she clearly fits in to the category of belly dancer based on a few trace elements of the image—the bangles on her wrists and arms and the way her arms are positioned above her head as if she is preparing to break into a shimmy—locates her squarely within a long tradition of representations of Arab womanhood and highlights the repetition and the stamina of these images.[102]

The silhouetted shape of the belly dance figure is meant to signify exoticism, and when coupled with her designation of "carnivale" (a detail that references her historic link to the popularity of belly dancing exhibitions), the representation clearly fits within the rubric of orientalist images of Arab womanhood in the United States. However, the generality of the rendering—the fact that the figure itself is only identifiable in outline form—reflects a particularly postmodernist expression of subjectivity. As Jameson laments in his famous article "Postmodernism, or the Cultural Logic of Late Capitalism," the postmodern era is characterized by the way in which the "alienation of the subject is displaced by the fragmentation of the subject."[103] The *carnivale* figure reflects this notion of fragmentation in that she is composed of discrete elements, which, in turn, make up her identity. She therefore has no coherent or centered being around which her subjectivity may be organized. In this way, she can be said to "swim, even wallow, in the fragmentary and the chaotic currents of change," as Harvey says is characteristic of postmodern representation.[104]

Yet, although this representation of Arab womanhood seems to unproblematically reflect the condition of dramatic and continuous change that defines the historical period in which she is created, that does not mean that she does not also simultaneously articulate the collective anxieties that the fact of change provokes. Just as the forces of modernism underscored the ways in which a progress-bound society was experiencing a distinct and profound separation from the past, so, too, do the forces of postmodernism highlight the collective societal concerns about the irrevocably receding past. Again, if, as Harvey claims, capitalism seems to arise out of a "violent rupture with the past,"[105] it makes sense that the transition into a new phase of multinational capitalism would reify this feeling of rupture and stimulate a resurgence in the obsession with the past. However, if modernist paradigms attempt to reincarnate the object of its nostalgia (in terms of its efforts to re-present and re-create ancient and/or primitive spaces such as the more "natural" culture of the Middle East or the timeless image of the Holy Land), postmodernist paradigms reproduce representations (which are themselves reproductions) of the past. In short, rather than simply operating as emblems of nostalgia, representations of Arab and Muslim womanhood in the contemporary context participate in fetishizing nostalgia.

This point is best illustrated with another facet of the 2001–2002 *Camel* advertising scheme, which is meant to sell a new line of "Exotic Blends" and "Turkish Blends." The Turkish Blends—Turkish Royal,

Turkish Jade, and Turkish Gold—are made completely of Turkish tobacco, as opposed to the Turkish and Domestic blend that basic *Camel* cigarettes have used since the early 1900s. Perhaps because the new line of cigarettes is bringing back an all-Turkish blend, something that was introduced by S. Anargyros at the turn of the century, the *Camel* ads accentuate the rich, indulgent decadence of the brand in the marketing campaign. Paralleling the early-twentieth-century tobacco advertisements that sent a message of abundance by highlighting the luxury and decadence of tobacco, these twenty-first-century *Camel* ads send a similar signal with their "Pleasure to Burn" ad scheme. Not only do the *Camel* advertisers rely on the luxury product of tobacco to indicate an abundance of riches, they also suggest that the new Turkish Blends will lead to an abundance of "pleasure." As a clear reference to the indulgence of having "money to burn," these ads suggest that buying *Camel* cigarettes will provide consumers with pleasure to burn. In order to pictorially signify all of this abundance, the "Turkish Blends" ads capitalize on the recognizable markers of orientalized indulgence, which can also be traced to the stereotype of the "imagined plurality" of the Ottoman Empire. The women in the ads carry lavishly decorated oriental trays or plush silk pillows with golden tassels hanging down on which they display and offer up the new cigarettes. These markers function in much the same way that the oriental "props" in French orientalist paintings do: they serve to locate the figure and the product within the lavish setting of an orientalized Middle East—one that seems to draw on the story of *Arabian Nights* (*One Thousand and One Nights*) for its historical accuracy. At the same time, the "exotic blends" line of *Camel* cigarettes operates according to the logic of liberal multiculturalism, whereby elements of ethnic difference serve to enhance the marketability of the product without disrupting the privileged position of whiteness. Each of the female figures representing "Turkish Royal," "Turkish Jade," and "Turkish Gold" uphold dominant notions of whiteness as the aesthetic ideal while simultaneously incorporating minute variations (e.g., blondish hair for "Turkish Gold" and a shiny, black bob cut for "Turkish Jade") to signify the exotic. Notably, the exotic blends advertisements combine an array of exotic markers from the Mediterranean to the "Middle" and "Far" East, a hybridization that is reminiscent of the incorporation of American Indian imagery in early-twentieth-century tobacco ads for Turkish cigarettes. The new flavors in the series include *Mandalay Lime, Aegean Spice, Mandarin Mint, Samsun, Izmir Stinger*, and finally *Basma*, which is described as "Exotic by birth." This mix of orientalized names is coupled with the image of a retrospective cigarette girl who is mildly exoticized by way of her own mix of orientalized props; she may wear a modest nose piercing or carry an ornately decorated tray. In this way, the *Camel* ads are participating in a commodification of diversity by which potentially threatening elements of difference are sanitized into subtle markers of a vague notion of the exotic, since they have been utterly removed from the particularities of the culture from which they derive. The fact that the stylistic props in the ads and the flavors of the cigarettes combine elements of both the "Middle" and the "Far" East, despite their incommensurability, supports the idea that they ultimately function as adornments or extras to an unchanging mainstream notion of beauty.[106]

Perhaps the most notable element of the Turkish and Exotic Blends advertising campaigns is the fact that they do not seem to draw on any of the typical representations of Arab womanhood as belly dancers, harem girls, or veiled women. Instead, the dress and posture of the female figures is reminiscent of American cigarette girls of the 1930s, 1940s, and 1950s. In this respect, then, the postmodern obsession with the past is represented by what Jameson calls a "pastiche of the stereotypical past," or a blend of generalized markers of the past (even if they are from radically different time periods). In this framework, the past is represented with "the spell and distance of a glossy mirage"[107] where "the past as 'referent' finds itself gradually bracketed, and then effaced altogether, leaving us with nothing but texts."[108] In other words, the inclusion of the cigarette girls does not reference a particular historical context, but rather a generalized concept of the "eternal Thirties" and Forties "beyond real historical time,"[109] which then blends with the suspended and timeless image of oriental decadence as present in stories of the *Arabian Nights* and in stereotypical images of the Ottoman Empire, to represent the distance as a "glossy mirage." By forming a "pastiche of the stereotypical past," the *Camel* ads can simultaneously wax nostalgic about the period in U.S. history, in the decades surrounding World War II, when cigarette smoking reached the pinnacle of its popularity while also incorporating orientalist imagery to signal the authenticity of Turkish tobacco. The danger, from Jameson's perspective, of the commodification of difference with no "real" referent is that it collapses the possibility for achieving the critical distance necessary to intervene, as a nonfragmented subject, in the problematic forces of late capitalism. According to this logic, the dimensions of time and space have gone through another round of compression within the framework of late capitalism, and distance is rendered as a glossy mirage, full of fabrications and reproductions. Though one might argue, as Chela Sandoval does, that such an interpretation of subjectivity within a postmodernist paradigm privileges a Euro-U.S.-centric and western capitalist perspective,[110] it is useful here in that it offers a framework for understanding contemporary representations of Arab womanhood as participating in solidifying hegemonic discourses of globalization, which fixate on the phenomenon of time-space compression.

One of the most striking characteristics of these contemporary representations is the fact that dominant images of Arab womanhood seem to have been distilled down to a few basic elements or props. In other words, the repertoire of orientalist representations of Arab womanhood have become so entrenched that the figures of the harem girl, the veiled woman, and the belly dancer are immediately recognizable by way of floating signifiers, such as a woman wearing bangles on her wrists, or holding her arms in a certain position above her head, or the image of the veil, whether or not a woman is wearing it. As is evident from the silhouetted dancing girl on the recent *Camel* "carnivale" ad and the prevalence of images of Arab and Muslim women who are "hidden" behind the veil (particularly after the 2001 invasion of Afghanistan, a picture of a burqa alone is enough to signify the latter), dominant images of Arab womanhood in the United States have been utterly reduced to trace elements of the cultural mythologies of the veil, the harem, and the belly dancer. Perhaps most insidiously, then, they still masquerade as accurate portrayals of the realities of Arab and Muslim women, while functioning in the contemporary U.S. context as fetishized expressions of nostalgia constituted by the project of neoliberal imperialism.

CONCLUSION

At the time of this writing, four years after the 2003 U.S. invasion of Iraq, the news story about the looted Iraq National Museum has largely faded from collective U.S. consciousness (if it was ever a part of it at all). In its place, daily coverage of sectarian violence (the euphemism most sources seem to have settled on to describe the intense war and militarism that now characterize Iraqi life) dominates the news media, while U.S. presidential hopefuls negotiate their relationship to an increasingly unpopular war. Meanwhile, narratives about the sectarian violence in Iraq renew and redeploy the Eurocentric trope of civilization insofar as Iraq is now described as the chaotic home to several squabbling tribes, namely the Sunni, the Shi'a, and the Kurds, regardless of the way in which such a simplistic characterization obscures the complexities of Iraqi life under U.S. occupation.

In a March 4, 2007 article entitled "Game of Putting Hatred on Middle East Map," journalist Robert Fisk draws critical attention to the maps that now circulate in many media sources dividing Iraq into enclaves of a Shi'a south, a Sunni "triangle" in the center, and a Kurdish minority in the north. He argues that the drawing of such maps and, I would add, the deployment of cultural mythologies like those I have been analyzing, function to contain people within an imperialist rubric that ultimately enacts a figurative, if not literal, violence upon them. Cartography is actually an apt metaphor for exploring the orientalist production of knowledge in the United States as mapmaking is always already embedded in the political perspectives and biases of those who draw the map. One must always ask what premises and assumptions guide the creation of each map, determining which vision of the world will be centered. This is not to say that sectarian divisions are nonexistent among local militias in Iraq but to ask why the "sectarian violence" map has such salience and to ask what the history of this salience is. Why not draw maps that trace the impact of the war on Iraqi civilians by representing the numbers of Iraqi people displaced to the surrounding countries or by representing which neighborhoods have access to basic resources like water and electricity? Why not draw a map that charts the many ways in which Iraqi women's movements and freedoms have been curtailed since direct U.S. involvement in the region in 1991? By privileging the narrative of sectarian division as the absolute, irreconcilable truth about the current state of Iraq, this particular map reifies the Euro-U.S.-centric deployment of civilization as a disciplinary trope. It lends authority to the claim that the U.S. invasion of Iraq is a civilizing/liberating mission, while the people of Iraq are somehow naturally determined by barbaric ethnic and religious divisions. As Fisk puts it:

> I could draw an extremely accurate ethnic map of Washington, complete with front-line streets between 'black' and 'white' communities but *The Washington Post* would never publish such a map.... It would be unforgivable, bad taste, something 'we' don't do in our precious, carefully guarded civilization.[1]

Like the cultural mythologies of veils, harems, and belly dancers in the U.S., these maps are, to recall Benjamin's formulation, documents of civilization, which are at the same time documents of barbarism. They do more to reaffirm the Eurocentric Enlightenment-based concept of civilization, which gains definition in opposition to the backwardness of its ethnic others, than they do to promote a complex and nuanced understanding of the way in which sectarian resistances to U.S. occupation have created barbaric conditions for Iraqi civilians.

Further, as I have been arguing, the deployment of civilization as a disciplinary trope operates in a gendered register. The modality of civilization as ancient or of primordial origin is often rendered as female or feminine, while the construction of primitive and barbaric others as the antithesis of civilization finds expression through masculinist paradigms. In the latter scenario, women are often symbolically appropriated by competing patriarchies in the dialectic of saving women from the evils of the other patriarchy. Here, the narrative of Afghan women "trapped behind the burqa" comes to mind as an example of the way in which women are appropriated as emptied signifiers—what I have been calling cultural mythologies—in literal and figurative wars of civilization. Again, I do not argue that Afghan women live a life free from oppression by any means, but rather that their symbolic appropriation in the semiotic war of civilization necessarily muddies and obscures the interlocking systems of oppression (e.g., rampant militarism, extreme poverty, lack of access to basic resources) that determine their realities. Cultural mythologies are insidious because they are too easily emptied of historical context and applied in incommensurate situations, as evidenced by Matthew

Bogdanos's use of the cultural mythology of the veil to begin his tale about the looting of the Iraq museum.

As fraught documents of civilization, the cultural mythologies of the veil, the harem, and the belly dancer have served as imprecise, Euro-U.S.-centric lenses through which mainstream discourses about the Arab and Muslim worlds are framed. I have been focusing on the impact of such images on mainstream narratives about Iraq and Afghanistan, though I could easily use examples from other parts of the Arab world.[2] The crucial point here is to recognize the ways in which cultural mythologies rob the concepts of the veil, the harem, and the belly dancer of historical context while nonetheless purporting to represent the realities of the Arab and Muslim worlds. If nothing else, the sweeping generalizations that cultural mythologies have enabled (such as the notion that women all over the Muslim world experience oppression in the same way) should prove that the boundaries of the notion of civilization—as it is currently configured and deployed—must be redrawn.

In the conclusion to her analysis of representations of Muslim womanhood in western literature, Mohja Kahf explains that "there should be disarray,"[3] as she has revealed the seemingly homogenous image of the Muslim woman to be quite a prolific and differentiated figure in western literature. My own research has been dedicated to understanding why there has not been more "disarray" in popular U.S. imaginings of Arab and Muslim womanhood. Through the framework of cultural mythologies, I have argued that representations of Arab and Muslim womanhood in U.S. popular culture have maintained structural similarity because they speak to concerns and anxieties about power and progress that have emerged and reemerged in various historical moments of U.S. nation-building. The cultural mythologies of the veil, the harem, and the belly dancer are important and compelling footnotes to the progress narrative, which should be read critically and carefully. They have served to quell the disorientations of the contexts in which they arise. The hard questions that must be asked, though, are these: What do these stories miss? What do they gloss over? What ways of knowing and engaging the world have cultural mythologies necessarily obscured? In his conclusion to *The Country and the City*, Raymond Williams suggests that such stories (in his case, the binary of country and city) obfuscate urgent and pressing questions. He writes: "In what is then a tension, a present experienced as tension, we use the contrast of country and city to ratify an unresolved division and conflict of impulses, which it might be better to face in its own terms."[4] What Williams has called an "unresolved division" and "conflict of impulses" manifests in representations of Arab womanhood, as I have discussed, in the figure of the belly dancer at the 1893 Chicago World's Fair to which fairgoers were both attracted and repulsed, in images of harem girls in *Omar* tobacco ads which were both revered and reviled for their "closeness to nature," and in contemporary representations of the veil, which have been used simultaneously to sell luxury products for Reebok and Benetton as well as to promote a seemingly endless war on terror to U.S. citizens. By carrying the weight of a fraught "conflict of impulses," between pursuing advancement and effacing nature, between modern civilization and ancient origins, and between civilized futures and barbaric pasts, the cultural mythologies of veils, harems, and belly dancers maintain the flawed premise of the progress narrative as linear and unidirectional. They obscure critical inquiry into the foundations on which the concept of civilization are built. They help maintain a logic whereby progress is measured by the numbers of women unveiled, regardless of whether they have access to potable water; where progress means building a theme park in Babylon to modernize Iraq by privatizing antiquities; and where civilization is the handmaiden of endless militarism. Although these cultural mythologies have clearly proven useful in mainstream U.S. discourse, the dangers of ignoring their obscured questions far outweigh the mythologies' usefulness.

I have explored the long trajectory of the cultural mythologies of veils, harems, and belly dancers in the United States from the turn of the twentieth century to the present, and have therefore left some compelling questions unexplored, as they would have led this book down another path. One obvious and important question is to ask how cultural mythologies related to the Arab and Muslim worlds have impacted Arab Americans and Muslim Americans. This question, in turn, leads to another, which is to explore the ways these representations have affected the process of racial formation[5] for Arab and Muslim Americans. For example, images of Arab womanhood in early-twentieth-century tobacco advertisements mimic French orientalist paintings insofar as they depict idealized figures of white femininity exoticized with orientalist props whereas contemporary representations of veiled women tend to be more racialized. I have explained this shift in terms of changing power dynamics between the U.S. and the Middle East, but it would also be fruitful to relate it to the process of racialization for Arab Americans, who have increasingly come to be seen in racial terms in the past few decades.[6] Finally, though I have been particularly interested in cultural mythologies as shaped by, and as contributing to, hegemonic U.S. narratives, that does not mean they operate monolithically. As I indicated in my discussion of belly dancers at the 1893 Chicago World's Fair, the analysis of these images opens up onto questions about the myriad ways in which Arabs, Muslims, and Arab Americans have resisted, appropriated, or otherwise engaged with mainstream U.S. representations of Arab womanhood. I hope *Imagining Arab Womanhood* will lend itself to these and other explorations and expansions.

Above all, I have written this book to be a tool for demythologizing the veil, the harem, and the belly dancer as flattened narratives through which mainstream U.S. audiences have imagined Arab womanhood. I am not calling for the eradication of these categories as they would surely be replaced by new, and equally rigid, structures of representation. Rather, I am calling for their return to historical consciousness.[7] I am calling for the kind of careful, critical reflection and introspection it would take to rehistoricize and recontextualize representations of veils, harems, and belly dancers as U.S. cultural artifacts. For far too long, they have carried the heavy burden of signification for vast and variegated U.S. based concerns about power and progress. As cultural mythologies, figures of veiled women, harem slaves, and belly dancers have served as empty forms that can both hold the displaced nostalgia of the progress narrative and that can faithfully reflect the hegemonic construction of U.S. imperialism as a civilizing mission. Returning these figures to history would mean releasing them from their burden of signification in U.S. discourses and directing them toward the twofold purpose of exploring the U.S. based concerns about power and nostalgia they obscure and of restoring to them their multiple, contextualized histories.

In the ruins of the representational war of civilization, it will not do to mummify cultural mythologies and put them on display. Instead of rushing to recover these visual artifacts and restore them to the museum of Civilization, it might be more useful to sift through the layers of cultural and historical sediment in which they are embedded. Only then will it be possible to see the lives they have touched and to potentially find ways of honoring and preserving that life in spite of, or perhaps because of, the destruction that surrounds it.

NOTES

PREFACE

1. The groundbreaking anthology, *Food for Our Grandmothers*, edited by Joanna Kadi, includes several articles that grapple with stereotypes of Arab women in U.S. popular culture. See, for example, Part IV: "Silent Victims and Belly-Dancers: (Mis)Representations of Arab Women," and especially "The Arab Woman in U.S. Popular Culture" by Marsha J. Hamilton.

INTRODUCTION: EXCAVATING ORIENTALIST IMAGES OF ARAB WOMANHOOD

1. Dojc, "How to Start a Harem," 48.
2. Ahmed, "Western Ethnocentrism"; Shohat and Stam, *Unthinking Eurocentrism.*
3. Croutier, *Harem.*
4. Said, *Orientalism.*
5. Barthes, *Mythologies*, 142.
6. Grosrichard, *The Sultan's Court*, 25.
7. Ahmed, "Western Ethnocentrism"; Shohat and Stam, *Unthinking Eurocentrism*; Hoodfar, "The Veil in Their Minds"; Kahf, *Western Representations*; Mernissi, *Scheherezade Goes West.*
8. Barthes, *Mythologies*, 118.
9. Peirce, *The Imperial Harem.*
10. See Sandoval, *Methodology of the Oppressed*, 106–112, for more discussion about technologies of demythologizing as a strategy for resistance.
11. Williams, *Marxism and Literature*, 129.
12. Gramsci, *The Prison Notebooks.*
13. Williams, *Marxism and Literature*, 133.
14. Ibid., 134.
15. I will employ the category "Middle East" as a descriptive category for the geographical region that might be more usefully designated as South and West Asia and North Africa (SWANA) because of the geopolitical considerations of my project. Because I am concerned with U.S. perceptions and imaginative representations of Arab and Muslim women, and because of the way in which the categories of

Arab ethnic and Muslim religious identities are often conflated in a U.S. context, SWANA seems to be the more appropriate term, especially considering the ways in which U.S. Military intervention in both Afghanistan and Iraq have been paired in mainstream discourse. However, because the term "Middle East" has much more resonance as an interpretive category in an American orientalist context, I will use it when referring to the geopolitical region encompassing Arab, Persian, and Turkish nation-states, including North Africa.

16. Hobsbawm, *The Invention of Tradition*.
17. Said, *Orientalism*.
18. Huntington, "The Clash of Civilizations?"
19. Ibid., 31.
20. Ibid., 24.
21. Ibid., 25.
22. I put "Islamic fundamentalism" in quotes here to signal the way in which it has slipped into popular discourse as a catchall term for Muslims, terrorists, and Islam, thereby perpetuating a gross misunderstanding of Islam in a U.S. context.
23. See Said, "The Clash of Ignorance"; Mamdani, *Good Muslim, Bad Muslim*, 20–23, for a critique of Huntington's thesis.
24. Saliba, *Gender, Politics, and Islam*, 1; Moallem, *Veiled Sister*, 23.
25. Moallem, *Veiled Sister*, 2.
26. Ibid., 163.
27. See Amin's *Liberation of Women* as an example of the former and see Chatterjee, *The Nation and Its Fragments*, for an excellent critique of the latter in the Indian context.
28. Conklin, *A Mission to Civilize*, 14; Schaebler, "Civilizing Others," 8.
29. Williams, *Keywords*, 57–60; Conklin, *A Mission to Civilize*, 15.
30. See Shohat and Stam, *Unthinking Eurocentrism*, for their critique of Eurocentrism vis-à-vis the metanarrative of modernity. See also Deeb's explanation of the way the concept of civilization operates as a register of the modern in Shi'i Lebanon in *An Enchanted Modern*.
31. Abu-Lughod, "Do Muslim Women Really Need Saving?"; Saliba, *Gender, Politics, and Islam*, 1; Hesford and Kozol, *Just Advocacy*, 3.
32. CNN.com, "Transcript of President Bush's Address."
33. See Fernandes, "The Boundaries of Terror," for more analysis of the U.S. discourse about the "war on terror."
34. U.S. Government, "Radio Address of the President."
35. U.S. Government, "Radio Address by Laura Bush."
36. Ibid.
37. First Lady Bush does offer this disclaimer: "The poverty, poor health, and illiteracy that the terrorists and the Taliban have imposed on women in Afghanistan do not conform with the treatment of women in most of the Islamic world, where women make important contributions in their societies." Nevertheless, this disclaimer does not withstand the power of her rhetoric.

38. Farrell and McDermott, "Claiming Afghan Women," 37; Hirschkind and Mahmood, "Politics of Counter-Insurgency."

39. Because of the way in which Arab ethnic identities and Muslim religious identities are conflated in U.S. popular imagination, I address both here. Although Arab women may be Christian or Jewish as well as Muslim, the categories of interpretation by which they are largely understood in the United States—the harem, the veil, and the belly dancer, are either tied to, or associated with, Islam. Conversely, though not all Muslims are Arab, some are interpreted as such in the United States, as is the case with Afghan women who are said to be liberated from their burqas by U.S. Forces. As "Muslim" is a relatively recent identity category used in U.S. vernacular, I will use both "Arab" (in chapters 1–3) and "Arab and Muslim" (in chapter 4) as qualifiers for "womanhood."

40. Benjamin, "Theses on the Philosophy of History," 256.

41. There is much debate as to the precise number of stolen or destroyed artifacts. In fact, two of the main sources I will use in my discussion of the artifacts from the Iraq museum, both published in 2005, are at odds regarding these data. Bogdanos, U.S. Marine *cum* investigator who claims to specialize in the classic world, has written a memoir entitled *Thieves of Baghdad*, in which he argues that media reports misrepresent and exaggerate both the museum's losses and corresponding U.S. culpability. He directly argues against many of the authors whose arguments are collected in the other source I reference, *The Looting of the Iraq Museum, Baghdad: The Lost Legacy of Ancient Mesopotamia*.

42. The devastation brought to the coasts of Louisiana and Mississippi by Hurricane Katrina and the faulty levee system in the summer of 2005 highlighted, again through media representation, the constellation of racialized and pejorative connotations associated with the word looting. Though the term is widely used in media reports and scholarship about the theft of antiquities in Iraq, I have resisted and minimized its use here because of the connotations it carries. As in the Hurricane Katrina context, in which the word looting was used to describe the survival strategies of African Americans while the passive verb form of "to find" was used to describe the survival strategies of white victims of the levee breaches, the use of the word "looters" in the context of Iraqi antiquities can conveniently and too easily elide the conditions and circumstances of survival that undergird the act of "looting."

43. This is not to say that the practice of torture by U.S. Military is a one-time event, as reports out of the detention center at Guantánamo Bay clearly demonstrate, but rather to point to the striking way in which those photos underscore the dehumanization of prisoner and soldier alike.

44. Bahrani notes that U.S. Forces constructed a helipad in the middle of the city, which required the removal of several layers of earth at this

archaeological site, thereby destroying the artifacts and historical evidence contained therein. In addition, she reports that "between May and August 2004, the wall of the Temple of Nabu and the roof of the Temple of Ninmah, both of the sixth century B.C., collapsed as a result of the movement of helicopters." Bahrani, "The Fall of Babylon," 214. See also BBC News, "Army Base 'Has Damaged Babylon'" and Charles, "US Marines Offer Babylon Apology."

45. See also Mirzoeff's discussion in *Watching Babylon*, 5–6.
46. McCarthy and Kennedy "Babylon Wrecked by War."
47. Gettleman, "Magic Back in Babylon."
48. Ibid.
49. Polk and Schuster, *The Looting*, 13.
50. Ibid., 10.
51. Moallem also notes the way in which the notion of civilization (constructed in opposition to that of barbarism) is "essential in the historical construction of colonialist racism." See *Veiled Sister*, 21.
52. See, among others, McClintock *Imperial Leather;* Kaplan, Alarcón, and Moallem, *Between Woman and Nation*.
53. Bogdanos, *Thieves of Baghdad*, 141.
54. Polk and Schuster, *The Looting*, xii.
55. Ibid., 8.
56. Bogdanos, *Thieves of Baghdad*, 139.
57. Hammurabi is the 18th century (BCE) ruler whose famous law code contained the "eye for an eye" form of punishment still perceived to be common in the modern Middle East.
58. Bogdanos, *Thieves of Baghdad*, 150.
59. Both *hijab* and *khimar* can technically be used as general terms to refer to a variety of dress styles covering the head and hair that women might wear as a gesture of modesty within Islam. However, they are mostly used to refer to specific styles of what, in English, might be called a "veil." A *khimar* typically refers to a garment that covers head and hair as well as neck and shoulders, and extends to mid-chest. This more conservative style of dress is not what the director of the museum wears, according to the photos Bogdanos has included in his book. Instead, she wears a simple headscarf (commonly referred to as a *hijab*), which covers her head, but not all of her hair.
60. Bogdanos, *The Thieves of Baghdad*, 6.
61. Ibid., 8.
62. See Chatterjee's *The Nation and Its Fragments* for a compelling discussion of the way in which patriarchal nationalist movements have utilized the category of women as symbols of the purity and authenticity of the nation.
63. Amireh, "Palestinian Women's Disappearing Act," 230, also makes the argument that Arab and Muslim women's oppression serves as a justification for U.S. Military action.

64. Particularly in the past few years, as Afghanistan has continued to be lumped into the category of the Middle East in the United States, the limitations and perspectival biases of the term become even more evident. The qualifier "Middle" refers to the distance of the region from Europe in relation to the "Far" East of Asian countries like Japan, Korea, and China. Iraq, Kuwait, and Afghanistan might more appropriately be referred to as West and Central Asia.

65. Haraway, *Primate Visions*; Lazreg, *The Eloquence of Silence*; McClintock, *Imperial Leather*; Mohanty, *Feminism Without Borders*; Narayan, *Dislocating Cultures*; Ong, "Colonialism and Modernity"; Saliba, Arab Feminism; Shohat, *Talking Visions*.

66. Grewal and Kaplan, *Scattered Hegemonies*; Lorde, "Women Redefining Difference: Age, Race, Class, Sex" in *Sister Outsider*; Shohat, "Area Studies"; Sandoval, *Methodology of the Oppressed*; Kaplan, Alarcón, and Moallem, *Between Woman and Nation*.

67. Eisenstein, *Against Empire*.

68. Hall, "Encoding, Decoding."

69. Said, *Orientalism*.

70. Foucault, *The Archaeology of Knowledge*, 192.

71. Ibid., 193.

72. Ibid., 140.

73. Foucault is careful to steer clear of the very connection I am making here; he states that the archaeology of knowledge does not "relate analysis to geological excavation" (Ibid., 131). However, he denies the connection insofar as geological excavation is embedded in a project of "the search for a beginning," which is not how I am using the metaphor.

74. Ibid., 109.

75. See Nochlin, "The Imaginary Orient"; Yeazell, *Harems of the Mind*; Ahmed, "Western Ethnocentrism."

76. Said, *Beginnings*, 55.

1   TRAVELING ORIENTALISM: U.S. ECHOES OF A FRENCH TRADITION

1. Rydell, *All the World's a Fair*, 2.

2. Ibid., 3.

3. For a start, see Bhabha, "The Other Question" and Lowe, *Critical Terrains*.

4. Lowe, *Critical Terrains*, 8.

5. Grosrichard, *The Sultan's Court*, 125.

6. Graham-Brown, *Images of Women*, 80.

7. Said, *Orientalism*, 177.

8. Said says: "The Orient is the stage on which the whole East is confined," 63.

9. Mitchell, *Landscape and Power*, 38.
10. Trachtenberg, *Reading American Photographs*; Berger, *Ways of Seeing*.
11. Said, *Orientalism*, 177.
12. Çelik, *Displaying the Orient*, 5.
13. Rydell, Findling, and Pelle, *Fair America*, 9.
14. Rydell, "Rediscovering," 35.
15. Grosrichard, *The Sultan's Court*, 178.
16. Goffman, *The Ottoman Empire*, 231.
17. For more information about French and British Orientalist representations, see Yeazell's *Harems of the Mind*, especially Part IV, "Pilgrims and Pilgrimages, British and French" and Said's *Orientalism*.
18. Nochlin, "The Imaginary Orient," 127.
19. Grosrichard, *The Sultan's Court*, 146.
20. Anderson, *Imagined Communities*, 6.
21. *Oxford English Dictionary*, 2nd edition, s.v. "harem."
22. Ibid., s.v. "seraglio."
23. Grewal, *Home and Harem*, 18.
24. Ahmed, "Western Ethnocentrism," 524.
25. Ibid., 529.
26. Peirce, *The Imperial Harem*, 9.
27. Ibid., 7.
28. Nochlin, "The Imaginary Orient," 125.
29. Said, *Orientalism*, 177.
30. Nochlin, "The Imaginary Orient," 122.
31. Ibid., 123.
32. My use of the term "Orient" here is intentional. The term "Middle East," although it would indicate the region's sovereignty from Ottoman forces, does not account for the way in which colonialist representations of the region consistently conflated images of the Turkish Ottoman Empire and images of indigenous Arab cultures.
33. Benjamin, *Orientalism: Delacroix to Klee*, 8.
34. Nochlin, "The Imaginary Orient," 123.
35. Rosenthal, *Orientalism*, 31.
36. Delacroix, *The Journal of Eugène Delacroix*, 122.
37. Rosenthal, *Orientalism*, 44.
38. Quoted in Néret, *Eugène Delacroix*, 57.
39. Delacroix, *The Journal of Eugène Delacroix*, 332.
40. Nochlin, "The Imaginary Orient," 122.
41. Djebar, "Women of Algiers," 340.
42. Ibid., emphasis mine.
43. Grewal, *Home and Harem*, 5.
44. See McClintock's *Imperial Leather* for a discussion about the "cult of domesticity" and the relationship of working class women to conceptions of the idealized Victorian home.
45. Nochlin, "The Imaginary Orient," 122.

46. Ahmed, "Western Ethnocentrism."
47. Montagu, *Letters*, 105.
48. Ibid.
49. Ibid.
50. Benjamin, *Orientalism: Delacroix to Klee*, 15.
51. A number of sources echo and expand on this argument. In *The Orient in Western Art*, Lemaires claims that the *Turkish Bath*, painted at the very end of Ingres's career, can be considered as a catalogue of all the idealized nudes he had worked on throughout his life (202). Both Rosenblum and Yeazell also make similar claims; however, Yeazell further asserts that the nudes in the bath resemble and represent various women in Ingres's life (252).
52. Benjamin, *Orientalism: Delacroix to Klee*, 68, emphasis mine.
53. Gilman, "Black Bodies, White Bodies," 221.
54. Benjamin, *Orientalism: Delacroix to Klee*, 68.
55. The extra vertebra in the odalisque's back reflects a Mannerist characteristic of instability in its figures that leads to exaggerations and distortions, like the extra length in the woman's back. Although the human form may still be represented as sinuous and graceful, the anomaly in her form is reminiscent of a Mannerist style, which makes the human figure appear to be somewhat removed from nature.
56. Benjamin, *Orientalism: Delacroix to Klee*, 68.
57. Lemaires, *The Orient*; Rosenblum, *Ingres*, 86.
58. Zuffi, *Titian*, 37.
59. Nochlin, "The Imaginary Orient," 122.
60. Ibid., 125.
61. Montagu, *Letters*, 105.
62. Quoted in Boime, *The Art of Exclusion*, 2.
63. Benjamin, *Orientalism: Delacroix to Klee*, 100.
64. Boime, *The Art of Exclusion*, 4.
65. Gilman, "Black Bodies, White Bodies," 209.
66. Benjamin, *Orientalism: Delacroix to Klee*, 102.
67. Gilman, *Difference and Pathology*, 20.
68. Ackerman, *The Life and Work*, 45.
69. Nochlin, "The Imaginary Orient," 125.
70. Barthes, "Myth Today," in *Mythologies*, 117.
71. Ibid., 119.
72. Ibid., 124.
73. Ibid., 143.
74. Said, "Traveling Theory," 226–227.
75. Ibid., 227.
76. Carr, "Prejudice and Pride," 78.
77. Ibid., 86.
78. Ibid., 87.
79. Ibid., 100.
80. Ibid., 93.

81. Groseclose, *Nineteenth-Century American Art*, 35.
82. Ibid., 50.
83. Ormond, "Sargent's Art," 23.
84. Kilmurray and Ormond, *John Singer Sargent*, 101.
85. Sargent's commissioned portrait, entitled *Almina, Daughter of Asher Wertheimer*, also references Ingres's work. In the portrait, Almina is wearing "an ivory-white Persian costume and a turban entwined with pearls" and is holding a "*sarod*", a musical instrument from northern India, which was owned by the artist (Ibid., 169). In this respect, she resembles the "slave" in Ingres's *Odalisque with a Slave*.
86. Even so, the painting did not necessarily have as many viewers at the World's Fair as his other submissions since it was hung on the second floor of the Fine Arts building (Carr, "Prejudice and Pride," 96). Its position on the second floor does speak to the strict moral codes of the Victorian Era in the United States. However, the fact that it was displayed *at all* during this time period corroborates my claim that the Egyptian girl's body was not viewed in the same way that an American or European woman's body would be.
87. Berger, *Ways of Seeing*, 60.
88. Said, "Traveling Theory," 227.
89. Greenberg, "America—Holy Land and Religious Studies," 52.
90. Quoted in Truman, *History of the World's Fair*, 123.
91. Davis, *Landscape of Belief*, 15.
92. Ibid., 4.
93. For more on nineteenth-century "Holy Land mania," see Obenzinger, *American Palestine*.
94. See Smith, *Virgin Land* for more on the way the notion of the virgin land operated as a sustaining myth in the formation of U.S. national identity.
95. Boime, *The Magisterial Gaze*. See also Miller, *Empire of the Eye* for an argument about American landscape painting as an expression of U.S. imperialism. Finally see Mitchell's *Landscape and Power* for a broader consideration of the intersection of landscape with power dynamics.
96. Boime, *The Magisterial Gaze*, 84.
97. Vogel, *To See a Promised Land* and Davis, *Landscape of Belief*.
98. Fairbrother, *John Singer Sargent*, 104.
99. Ibid., 29.
100. In fact, one of Sargent's most famous Orientalist paintings is *Fumée D' Amber Gris* (Ambergris Smoke), which helped to launch his career. Noted for its expression of the mystery and sensuality of the Orient, Sargent's representation of this "stately Mohameddan" (quoted in Edwards, *Noble Dreams, Wicked Pleasures*, 135) parallels orientalist themes that capitalize on the luxuriant and opulent eroticism of the Middle East, especially because of the aphrodisiac qualities and monetary value of ambergris (whale blubber) itself.

101. For more on the parallels between indigenous Americans and Palestinians, see Salaita, *The Holy Land in Transit.*
102. Davis, *Landscape of Belief* and McAlister, *Epic Encounters.*
103. "Street in Cairo," 2.
104. Davis, "Frederic Church's," 247.
105. I am referencing P. Miller's *Errand Into the Wilderness,* which itself references Danforth's 1670 jeremiad: "A Brief Recognition of New-Englands [*sic*] Errand Into the Wilderness."
106. Davis, *Landscape of Belief,* 186–187.
107. Ibid., 192.
108. Ibid., 8.
109. Carr, *In Search of the Promised Land,* 87.
110. Said, "Traveling Theory," 227.

2   Dancing the Hootchy Kootchy: The Rhythms and Contortions of American Orientalism

1. See, among others, Berman, *All That is Solid*; Donham, *Marxist Modern*; Knauft, *Critically Modern*; Mitchell, *Questions of Modernity*; Rofel, *Other Modernities.* For a critique of Eurocentrism in particular, see Shohat and Stam, *Unthinking Eurocentrism.*
2. Rubin, "Thinking Sex," 267.
3. Lott, *Love and Theft,* 6.
4. Ibid.
5. Lott is building on Bhabha's work on ambivalence in "The Other Question: Stereotype, Discrimination, and the Discourse of Colonialism"; and "Of Mimicry and Man: The Ambivalence of Colonial Discourse," also in *The Location of Culture,* 121–131.
6. Knauft, *Critically Modern,* 18.
7. Thomson, *Freakery,* 10.
8. Buel, *The Magic City.*
9. Allen, *Horrible Prettiness,* 234.
10. Ibid., 235.
11. Smith, "Within the Midway Plaisance," 66.
12. Buel, *The Magic City.*
13. Smith, "Within the Midway Plaisance," 63.
14. Rydell, *All the World's a Fair,* 67.
15. Kasson, *Amusing the Million,* 18.
16. Ibid., 23.
17. Edwards, *Noble Dreams,* 78.
18. Allen, *Horrible Prettiness,* 227–228.
19. "Street in Cairo," 3–5.
20. Rydell, *All the World's a Fair,* 67.

21. Rydell, Trachtenberg, and Edwards are just some of those who have argued that the displays were arranged in terms of a racial hierarchy. However, this line of argument tends to conflate the strictly anthropological exhibits with the concessionary exhibits on Midway. Hinsley's "The World as Marketplace," helps to distinguish between the two.
22. Hinsley, "The World as Marketplace," 348.
23. Ibid., 348–349.
24. Ibid., 349.
25. Carlton, *Looking for Little Egypt*, 3.
26. The terms for the folk dances from which the belly dance is derived vary from country to country, sometimes taking the general name of *al-raqs al-baladi* (roughly translated as an indigenous dance.) Presumably after colonial contact, the Arabic term for the dance metamorphosed into the outwardly referential term of *al-raqs al-sharqi* (or dance of the East). The French term used at the 1889 Paris Exposition, *danse du ventre*, was clearly based on the particular hip and belly movements of the dance, which were so scintillating for French viewers. This same French phrase was imported to the Chicago World's Fair and used interchangeably (at least in sources) with the English translation, "belly dancing." While the term belly dancing has remained the dance's main title for English speakers, French speakers have abandoned *danse du ventre* and instead refer to the dance as the *danse orientale* (see, e.g., Aradoon, *Origins and Philosophy of Danse Orientale*), which is most likely a translation of *al-raqs al-sharqi*.
27. Carlton, *Looking for Little Egypt*, 24.
28. Eco, *Travels in Hyperreality*, 294.
29. Benjamin, *Reflections*, 152.
30. Ibid.
31. Hinsley, "The World as Marketplace," 345.
32. Edwards, *Noble Dreams*, 37.
33. Ibid., 51.
34. Ibid., 192.
35. Ibid., 81.
36. Hinsley, "The World as Marketplace," 356.
37. *The Vanishing City.*
38. Buel, *The Magic City.*
39. Smith, "Within the Midway Plaisance," 59.
40. Buel, *The Magic City.*
41. Edwards, *Noble Dreams*, 39.
42. Allen, *Horrible Prettiness*, 228.
43. Ibid.
44. For more on the relationship between belly dance and striptease, see Allen, *Horrible Prettiness*.
45. Barthes, "Striptease," in *Mythologies*, 84.

46. Ibid.
47. Stoler, *Race and the Education of Desire*, 3.
48. Ibid., 35.
49. Knauft, *Critically Modern*, 18. See note 5, this chapter.
50. Carlton, *Looking for Little Egypt*, 51.
51. Every source I have read claims that Mahzar is from Syria, but it is important to remember that Syria, or Greater Syria, spanned a much larger portion of the Levant at that time than it does today.
52. Buonaventura, *Serpent of the Nile*, 103.
53. Ibid.
54. Allen, *Horrible Prettiness*, 225.
55. For more on these connections and the impact on the American belly dance movement, see Jarmakani, "Belly Dancing for Liberation."
56. Buonaventura, *Serpent of the Nile*, 103.
57. Quoted in Buonaventura, *Serpent of the Nile*, 102.
58. Carlton, *Looking for Little Egypt*, 56.
59. Allen, *Horrible Prettiness*, 230.
60. The cabaret style, and especially the cabaret costume, has been transplanted into the American context by way of characters such as (*I Dream of*) *Jeannie*. Her characteristic and memorable costume—ballooning "harem" pants and halter-bra, leaving the midriff bare—was borrowed not only from the cabaret style, but was also inspired by the Hollywood image of the female vamp. As precursor to the *femme fatale*, the female vamp image was one of a ravenous and heartless woman born in the "shadow of the pyramids" and who had an appetite for serpent's blood (Buonaventura, *Serpent of the Nile*, 152). Again, the contradistinction between the safe and controlled (literally bottled up) sexuality of *Jeannie* and the dangerous and out-of-control sexuality of the female vamp highlights the types of oppositions that determined the simultaneous feelings of attraction and repulsion, which ultimately kept American spectators trained on images of Arab female sexuality.
61. Dox, "Thinking through Veils," 154.
62. Aradoon, *Origins and Philosophy*, 10.
63. al-Rawi, *Grandmother's Secrets*, 33.
64. Ibid., 35–36.
65. Dox, "Thinking through Veils," 151.
66. Buonaventura, *Serpent of the Nile*, 126–128.
67. Ibid., 127.
68. Shay and Sellers-Young, *Belly Dance*, 7.
69. Ruyter, "La Meri," 208.
70. Buonaventura, *Serpent of the Nile*, 126.
71. Shay and Sellers-Young, *Belly Dance*, 17.
72. Carlton, *Looking for Little Egypt*, 84. See also Shay and Sellers-Young, *Belly Dance*, 7.
73. For more on this, see Dox, "Spirit From the Body."
74. Brown, *Contesting Images*, 116.

75. Ibid.
76. Ibid., 5.
77. Graham-Brown, *Images of Women*, 4.
78. For more on the relationship of photography to power, see Tagg, *The Burden of Representation* and Trachtenberg, *Reading American Photographs*.
79. Benjamin, "Short History," 20.
80. Benjamin, "The Work of Art," 223. See also Benjamin, "Short History," 20.
81. Graham-Brown, *Images of Women*, 40.
82. Buel, *The Magic City*.
83. Barthes, *Camera Lucida*, 57.
84. Buel, *The Magic City*.
85. McClintock, *Imperial Leather*.
86. Rydell, *All the World's a Fair*; Said, *Orientalism*; Haraway, *Primate Visions*; Lutz and Collins, *Reading National Geographic*; Shohat and Stam, *Unthinking Eurocentrism*.
87. Steet, *Veils and Daggers*, 35.
88. Ibid., 17. See also Lutz and Collins, *Reading National Geographic*, 26–27.
89. Quoted in Steet, *Veils and Daggers*, 57.
90. Buonaventura, *Serpent of the Nile*, 129.
91. Thomson, *Freakery*, 10.
92. Ibid., 2.
93. Çelik, *Displaying the Orient*.
94. Ibid., 3.
95. Çelik, "Speaking Back at the World's Columbian Exposition," 77.
96. Ibid., 84.
97. Çelik, "Speaking Back to Orientalist Discourse."
98. Ibid., 28.
99. Brown, *Contesting Images*, 36–37.
100. Çelik, "Speaking Back to Orientalist Discourse," 29.
101. Speaking Back at the World's Columbian Exposition, 89–92.
102. Ahmed, *Women and Gender in Islam*, 153.
103. This is the same logic that has been used, in part, by the U.S. government to justify the 2001 invasion of Afghanistan as well as direct military action in Iraq from 1991 to the present, an overlap to which I will return in chapter 4.
104. See James and Robertson, *Genital Cutting*, for more on the sensationalized treatment of female genital cutting, or "female genital mutilation" as it is frequently called, in western European and U.S. contexts.
105. Ahmed, *Women and Gender in Islam*, 156.
106. Amin, *The Liberation of Women*, 21.
107. Ibid., 30.
108. Barthes, *Camera Lucida*, 49.

109. Ibid., 55.
110. Ibid., 59.

3 SELLING LITTLE EGYPT: THE COMMODIFICATION OF ARAB WOMANHOOD

1. In fact, Marlboro cigarettes were developed and marketed primarily to women until the 1950s. They even had pink-tipped filters, so the cigarettes would not show lipstick stains. See Parker-Pope, *Cigarettes*, 88.
2. Tate, *Cigarette Wars*, 65.
3. The American Tobacco Company initiated the "torch of freedom" campaign to sell Lucky Strike cigarettes in 1928. See Gilman and Xun, *Smoke*, 23. Also see Amos and Haglund, "'Torch of Freedom,'" 3.
4. Amos and Haglund, " 'Torch of Freedom,'" 3; Gilman and Xun, *Smoke*, 22.
5. Tate, *Cigarette Wars*, 18.
6. Hinsley, "The World as Marketplace," 363.
7. Laird, *Advertising Progress*, 5.
8. Harvey, *The Condition of Postmodernity*, 180.
9. Ibid., 104.
10. Ibid., 103.
11. Trachtenberg, *The Incorporation of America*, 60.
12. Ibid., 59.
13. Edwards, *Noble Dreams*, 192; Mitchell, *Colonising Egypt*, 11.
14. The comparison of the 1893 World's Fair to department store displays is particularly poignant for the city of Chicago where, during the depression of 1893 (and in the midst of the Chicago Fair which was concerned with presenting the technological and economic prowess of the United States), many smaller retail stores went bankrupt under the shadow of larger conglomerates like Marshall Field's. See Leach, *Land of Desire*, 27.
15. Kasson, *Amusing the Million*, 106.
16. Benjamin, *Reflections*, 151. It is in the same section of this essay, "Grandville, or the World Exhibitions" that Benjamin also makes reference to the fact that the word "advertising" was coined during this same time period, thereby solidifying the connection between world expositions, advertising, and the amusement industry in the process of commodification.
17. Debord, *Society of the Spectacle*.
18. Foucault, *Discipline and Punish*.
19. Mitchell, *Colonising Egypt*, ix.
20. Long, *Imagining the Holy Land*, 45.
21. Ibid., 48.
22. The beginning of the twentieth century also marked an important moment of transition in terms of U.S. perceptions of the

geographical space of the Holy Land. While early Americans, from the seventeenth through the early nineteenth centuries, thought of the United States itself as a "promised" or "Holy Land," citizens of the United States throughout the nineteenth century shifted toward a consideration of Palestine/Israel as the Holy Land. During the early 1900s and into the twentieth century, there seemed to be a synthesis of the previous two ideas. In other words, as Greenberg has noted, America came to be seen as a continuation of the "universal" (Christian) principles begun in the original Holy Land of Palestine/Israel.

23. Leach, *Land of Desire*, 105.
24. Lears, *Fables of Abundance*, 51.
25. Leach, *Land of Desire*, 42.
26. Laird, *Advertising Progress*, 44.
27. Ibid., 67–8. This advertisement also demonstrates another connection between world's fairs and the advertising industry. Not only does the representation of the Eiffel Tower recall the 1889 Paris Universelle Exposition at which it was debuted, but the contrast of Aladdin's "magic" with industrial progress is reminiscent of Buel's introduction to his photographic album of the 1893 Chicago World's Fair, in which he discusses the outmoded "genie of the lamp."
28. Laird, *Advertising Progress*, 66.
29. Benjamin, "Work of Art," 223.
30. Williams, *The Country and the City*, 1.
31. See Lears's *Fables of Abundance* for a more involved argument about the way in which the concept of abundance functioned in the U.S. advertising industry.
32. "American Tobacco Story."
33. Shohat and Stam, *Unthinking Eurocentrism*, 62.
34. Ibid., 141.
35. "American Tobacco Story," 7.
36. See Smith, *Virgin Land* for more on this image and the myth-image-symbol school of American Studies.
37. "American Tobacco Story," 3.
38. Gilman and Xun, *Smoke*; Tate, *Cigarette Wars*.
39. Petrone, *Tobacco Advertising*, 180.
40. *Fatima* was originally produced under the conglomerate of The American Tobacco Company, but after the American Tobacco Company was forced to dissolve in 1911 (because of its violation of antitrust laws), Liggett & Myers took over production.
41. Robert, *The Story of Tobacco in America*, 231.
42. Not only did the images in the ads attest to this crossover, there was even a brand named *Harem Blends*.
43. The name of the brand, "Fatima," further references Islam since Fatima is the prophet Muhammed's daughter and is an important figure within the religion.

44. Edwards, *Noble Dreams*, 204.
45. I assume the customer to be male for the reasons cited earlier; except for brands specifically made for women, such as Marlboro, generally cigarettes were not marketed to women until the late 1920s.
46. McClintock, *Imperial Leather*, 31.
47. Ibid., 36.
48. Ibid., 32.
49. Weber, *The Protestant Ethic*.
50. For more on the "imaginary of the harem" as a trope of empire, see Shohat and Stam, *Unthinking Eurocentrism*, 161.
51. Omar is representative of a significant change in the stereotype of the sultan from the French orientalist to the U.S. expansionist contexts: the image of a brutal despot drops out, leaving a more benign representation of indulgence and decadence in its place.
52. Untermeyer, *Rubáiyát of Omar Khayyám*, xiv and xv.
53. Weber, *Fitzgerald's Rubáiyát*, 32.
54. Ibid., 120.
55. The *Omar* ads also coincided with the popularity of lithographic prints, of which Maxfield Parrish was one of the most renowned artists. Not only did many product brands of candy, coffee, and tobacco (*Omar* included) offer free lithographs to customers who collected enough brand "stamps," but Maxfield Parrish had re-created a scene out of Khayyám's *Rubáiyát* for a chocolate candy company. See Edwards, *Noble Dreams*, 201–206.
56. Fitzgerald, *Rubáiyát of Omar Khayyám*, 10.
57. Long, *Imagining the Holy Land*, 5.
58. In some U.S. interpretations of America as the new promised land, indigenous Americans were even considered to be a lost Israelite tribe. See Davis, *Landscape of Belief*, 14.
59. McClintock, *Imperial Leather*, 30.
60. Petrone, *Tobacco Advertising*, 167.
61. Leach, *Land of Desire*, 44.
62. Hassan Trade Card. For more on American Indian imagery on trade cards and advertisements, see Steele, "Reduced to Images."
63. McClintock, *Imperial Leather*, 359.

4 VEILED INTENTIONS: THE CULTURAL MYTHOLOGY OF VEILS, HAREMS, AND BELLY DANCERS IN THE SERVICE OF EMPIRE, SECURITY, AND GLOBALIZATION

1. Grewal, *Transnational America*, 23. I would stress here that, like Grewal, I do not see globalization as a homogenous process, but rather I see it as adopting a universalizing conceit that has impacted the construction of orientalist imagery.

2. See Said, *Covering Islam.*
3. I use the term "mythology of the veil" in order to emphasize the flattened and orientalist notion of the "veil" that operates in this particular cultural mythology. I am well aware of the fact that the word "veil" is a problematic translation for the forms of head covering and dress that women wear in different parts of the Arab and Muslim worlds.
4. These include *USA Today, The Seattle Times, The Ottawa Citizen, The Independent* (London), *The Daily Telegraph* (London), *The Scotsman, The Daily Telegraph* (Sydney), and *The Atlanta Journal-Constitution.*
5. Mcginty, "The Saga."
6. Vejnoska, "Return to War-torn Landscape."
7. This is especially true given *National Geographic*'s long-standing mission to present edifying and scholarly material about the world outside the United States to its readers. See Lutz and Collins, *Reading National Geographic*, 24.
8. Hirschkind and Mahmood, "Politics of Counter-Insurgency," 342–346.
9. Puar and Rai, "Monster, Terrorist, Fag."
10. See also Abu-Lughod, "Do Muslim Women Really Need Saving?"
11. Lutz and Collins, *Reading National Geographic*, 76.
12. In his critique of the documentary *In Search of the Afghan Girl*, Chengzhi imaginatively attributes such thoughts to the girl when he suggests that "If they are capable of pressing the shutter with a show of friendliness, they are just as capable of pulling the gun trigger with a show of pleasure." See Chengzhi, "The Eyes," 487.
13. Connor, "The Portrait."
14. The "war on terror" rhetoric deployed by the George W. Bush administration is clearly related to Reagan's "war on terrorism," a connection to which I will return in the national security section of this chapter.
15. Croutier, *Harem*, 201.
16. The 1956 Suez crisis is sometimes referenced as a demonstrative moment in the shifting relationship between the United States and United Kingdom, during which the former emerged as an eminent superpower and United Kingdom recognized its own future dependence on the United States to act as a global power.
17. Hartnett and Stengrim, *Globalization and Empire*, 86.
18. McCurry, "Special Report."
19. Newman, "A Life Revealed."
20. Appadurai, *Modernity at Large*, 33.
21. *In Search of the Afghan Girl*, VHS, directed by Lawrence Cumbo.
22. Caner, *Voices Behind the Veil*; Latifa, *My Forbidden Face*; Logan, *Unveiled*; Parshall and Parshall, *Lifting the Veil*; Sasson, *Princess.*

23. A few of these are Enloe's *Bananas, Beaches, and Bases*, in which she talks about the veil as appropriated by a nationalist movement; Mohanty's "Under Western Eyes," in which she cites the veil as one example of the way in which the category of "third world women" had been conceptualized as a monolithic mass in mainstream feminist scholarship; and, more recently, Abu-Lughod's "Do Muslim Women Really Need Saving?" in which she talks about popular U.S. perceptions of the veil as monolithic signifier. See also Lazreg's, *The Eloquence of Silence*, 14.

24. Leibovitz, *Women*, 20.

25. The photograph only reaches to her shoulders, but the style of covering indicates that it is full-length.

26. These particular elements of the image are, in fact, so common that they have come to be used on the covers of books by or about Arab and/or Arab American women even when the authors of the book critique such images. See, for example, Darraj's article "Personal and Political."

27. Ahmed, "Western Ethnocentrism," 522.

28. Sontag, "A Photograph," 35.

29. Ibid., 23.

30. Lazreg, *The Eloquence of Silence*, 136.

31. Sontag, "A Photograph," 24.

32. There are other women who are photographed against a gray background; however, it is interesting to note that many of them are also women of color.

33. el Guindi, *Veil*, 7.

34. *Oxford English Dictionary*, 2nd edition, s.v. "veil"

35. Barthes, "Myth Today," in *Mythologies*, 142–3.

36. el Guindi, *Veil*, 96.

37. Fanon, *A Dying Colonialism*.

38. See Ahmed, "The Veil Debate – Again" and *Under One Sky*, VHS, directed by Kawaja.

39. See Deeb, *An Enchanted Modern*, and Mahmood, *Politics of Piety*.

40. Shirazi, *The Veil Unveiled*, 7–9.

41. Lazreg, *The Eloquence of Silence*, 127.

42. See the introduction to Kahf's *Western Representations of the Muslim Woman* for her description of the way this association colors her students' reading of powerful or aggressive Muslim women characters in premodern western literature.

43. Barthes, "The Photographic Message," 200.

44. Another reading has been suggested to me, in which her stance and gaze can be read as a replication of the kind of pose that is presented in other athletic ads directed at women in the United States. This reading implies that Reebok advertisers seek to exploit an ambivalent reading, or a simultaneous identification with and distancing from the image on the part of a mainstream U.S. audience. The

notion of ambivalence is certainly applicable to this context, and suggests a link to the kind of analysis Lott employs in *Love and Theft*.

45. Williams, *The Country and the City*, 35.
46. Williams, *The Country and the City*.
47. Ahmed, *Women and Gender in Islam*.
48. Ibid., 152.
49. Saliba, "Military Presences and Absences," 132.
50. Ibid.
51. Alloula, *The Colonial Harem*, 7.
52. Ibid., 118.
53. Chow, "Where Have All the Natives Gone?" 125–151.
54. I have chosen not to reproduce the image here because I believe that representations necessarily enact a kind of violence on the subject they portray and, in the case of this image which is so clearly embedded in colonialist patriarchal violence, I am not willing to reenact the explicit and metaphorical exposure of Algerian womanhood.
55. Wilke's performance art and photography often plays on the theme of female nudity; it is not uncommon for her to have bare breasts in her art. However, I am interested here in the logic of the juxtaposition between covering her head, mouth, and shoulders, and revealing her breasts.
56. Mulvey, "Visual Pleasure."
57. Jones, *Body Art*.
58. Frueh, "Essay," 73.
59. Jones, *Body Art*, 155, emphasis mine.
60. I have not been able to find a statement by Wilke herself about that particular image.
61. Isaak, "In Praise of Primary Narcissism," 56.
62. Another example of this type of appropriation is the cover image of the January 2003 issue of *Oneworld* magazine, which depicts Lil' Kim in a lingerie outfit that covers her face in a style mimicking the popular image of the burqa. The cloth of the lingerie then drops away to reveal her nearly completely exposed and sexualized body. She seems to be playing on the notion of the burqa as a symbol of the oppression of female sexuality to demonstrate, in contrast, her own sexual liberation. In this move, then, she is replicating the logic implied in Sontag's remarks, in which sexual freedom is equated with revealing one's body.
63. Blue Star PR, "Frequently Asked Questions."
64. The correct (and now more widely used) transliteration of this word is *sheikh*, rather than *sheik*. However, I use *sheik* here both to reference its interpretation in the United States, through popular films like *The Sheik*, as a greedy, licentious, or romantic character rather than a spiritual or community leader.
65. Maira, "Arab-Face and Indo-Chic."

66. For more on the history of the "sheik" character in U.S. popular culture, see Caton, "The Sheik."

67. Shohat and Stam, *Unthinking Eurocentrism*, 156–57.

68. See Shaheen's analysis of Cannonball Run II in *Reel Bad Arabs* and Stockton's analysis of an oil sheik cartoon in "Ethnic Archetypes and the Arab Image."

69. I am borrowing from, and building on, McAlister's analysis of the phrase "benevolent supremacy" as a useful summary for U.S. national security strategy in the early 1950s. See McAlister, *Epic Encounters.*

70. McAlister, *Epic Encounters*, 47.

71. One of the most influential national security documents during the postwar era was NSC-68. I will provide a fuller analysis of NSC-68 in the "Benevolent Empire" section, in which I compare it to the more recent document, NSSUS.

72. Indeed, this is confirmed by a U.S. State Department report cited in McAlister, *Epic Encounters*, 134.

73. See Little, *American Orientalism*, 50, for a fuller discussion of the relationship between national security and U.S. access to oil in the Middle East.

74. See Alsultany, "Changing Profile of Race in the United States."

75. I am following Lee's analysis of a similar shift in perceptions of Asian American racial difference from "distant" and "exotic" to "present" and "threatening." Lee, *Orientals*, 28.

76. Lee, *Orientals*, 28.

77. See McAlister, *Epic Encounters*, 135 and 137 for examples.

78. See Stockton, "Ethnic Archetypes and the Arab Image," for examples.

79. Chapman, *License to Thrill*, 178.

80. Black, *The Politics of James Bond*, 137.

81. Ibid., 138.

82. Ibid., 137. See also Bennett and Woollacott, *Bond and Beyond*, 191.

83. Shohat and Stam, *Unthinking Eurocentrism*, 169.

84. Puar and Rai, "Monster, Terrorist, Fag."

85. Said's *Covering Islam*, published two years after the end of the Iran "hostage crisis," traces an American media construction of Islam as a monolithic force that is oppositional to a more "advanced" West.

86. For an analysis of the sitcom *I Dream of Jeannie*, see Abraham, "Hollywood's Harem Housewife."

87. See McAlister, *Epic Encounters*, 47–55 for a fuller discussion of NSC-68.

88. Bush's rhetoric in his "World Freedom Day Proclamation," issued November 9, 2001, replicates this logic: "On World Freedom Day, we also honor those who, at this moment, fight for freedom half a world away. On September 11, freedom was attacked, but liberty and justice will prevail. Like the fall of the Berlin Wall and the defeat of

totalitarianism in Central and Eastern Europe, freedom will triumph in this war against terrorism." (U.S. Government, "World Freedom Day.")

89. Quoted in Hartnett and Stengrim, *Globalization and Empire*, 110. See also U.S. Government, "President's Radio Address from Shanghai": "The terrorists attacked the World Trade Center. They fear trade because they understood [*sic*] that trade brings freedom and hope. We're in Shanghai to advance world trade, because we know that trade can conquer poverty and despair. In this struggle of freedom against fear, the outcome is not in doubt—freedom will win. And it will bring new hope to the lives of millions of people in Asia and throughout the world."

90. Harvey, *The Condition of Postmodernity* and Jameson, "Postmodernism."

91. Jameson, "Postmodernism," 57.

92. See Sandoval, *Methodology of the Oppressed*; Grewal and Kaplan, *Scattered Hegemonies*; Jakobsen, "Can Homosexuals End Western Civilization As We Know It?"; Grewal *Transnational America*.

93. Harvey, *The Condition of Postmodernity*, 147.

94. Ibid.

95. Ibid., 164.

96. Ibid., 29

97. Ibid., 42.

98. Williams, *The Country and the City*, 35.

99. Ibid.

100. Harvey, *The Condition of Postmodernity*, 44.

101. See Kalmar, "The *Houkah* in the Harem," 219, for a pictorial representation. I was not able to secure permission to reproduce the image here, because, as an R.J. Reynolds representative explained in her June 7, 2007 e-mail to me, "our company's products and brand communications are intended only for legal-age smokers, and we go to great lengths to ensure that our brand communications are placed only in appropriate publications. We follow careful guidelines to minimize the exposure of minors to tobacco advertising."

102. The image of the silhouetted belly dancer does not only appear in this promotional advertising scheme—she is also represented in "live" form in a Camel magazine published to promote the "seven pleasures of the exotic" parties. Snapshots from the party feature a belly dancer silhouetted against the backlight of the stage with her arms raised in a series of stoic, sphinx-like gestures. "Seven Pleasures of the Exotic," *CML The City Edition*.

103. Jameson, "Postmodernism," 63.

104. Harvey, *The Condition of Postmodernity*, 44.

105. Ibid., 104.

106. See Ma's "Disney, It's Like Re-Orients" in her book *The Deathly Embrace* for a similar analysis with respect to popular images of Asian American culture.
107. Jameson, "Postmodernism," 68.
108. Ibid., 66.
109. Ibid., 68.
110. Sandoval, *Methodology of the Oppressed*.

CONCLUSION

1. Fisk, "Middle East Map."
2. See, for example, the impact of the categories of the "inadequate Palestinian mother," the "super-oppressed Arab woman," and the "nameless veiled woman" on mainstream discourses about Palestine in Naber, Desouky, and Baroudi, "The Fogotten '-ism'."
3. Kahf, *Western Representations of the Muslim Woman*, 176.
4. Williams, *The Country and the City*, 297.
5. Omi and Winant, *Racial Formation in the United States*.
6. For more on the process of racialization for Arab Americans, see Jamal and Naber, *Race and Arab Americans*; Alsultany, "Changing Profile of Race in the United States."
7. Sandoval describes this as the act of "meta-ideologizing," which can "restore consciousness to history" in *Methodology of the Oppressed*, 110–111.

BIBLIOGRAPHY

Abdulhadi, Rabab, Nadine Naber, and Evelyn Alsultany. "Gender, Nation, and Belonging: Arab and Arab-American Feminist Perspectives." *MIT Electronic Journal of Middle East Studies* 5 (special issue, Spring 2005). www.web.mit.edu/cis/www/mitejmes/ (accessed April 10, 2007).

Abraham, Stephanie. "Hollywood's Harem Housewife: Orientalism in *I Dream of Jeannie*." MA thesis, California State University Los Angeles, 2006.

Abu-Lughod, Lila. "Do Muslim Women Really Need Saving? Anthropological Reflections on Cultural Relativism and Its Others." *American Anthropologist* 104, no. 3 (2002): 783–790.

———. "Feminist Longings and Postcolonial Conditions." In *Remaking Women: Feminism and Modernity in the Middle East*, 3–31. Princeton: Princeton University Press, 1998.

Ackerman, Gerald M. *The Life and Work of Jean-Léon Gérôme: With a Catalogue Raisonné*. London: Sotheby's, 1986.

Afzal-Khan, Fawzia, ed. *Shattering the Stereotypes: Muslim Women Speak Out*. Northampton, MA: Olive Branch Press, 2005.

Ahmed, Leila. "The Veil Debate—Again." In *On Shifting Ground: Muslim Women in the Global Era*, edited by Fereshteh Nouraie-Simone, 153–171. NY: Feminist Press at the City University of New York, 2005.

———. "Western Ethnocentrism and Perceptions of the Harem." *Feminist Studies* 8, no. 3 (1982): 521–534.

———. *Women and Gender in Islam: Historical Roots of a Modern Debate*. New Haven, CT: Yale University Press, 1992.

Allen, Robert C. *Horrible Prettiness: Burlesque and American Culture*. Chapel Hill: University of North Carolina Press, 1991.

Alloula, Malek. *The Colonial Harem*. Translated by Myrna Godzich and Wlad Godzich. Minneapolis, MN: University of Minnesota Press, 1986.

Alsultany, Evelyn. "The Changing Profile of Race in the United States: Racializing and Representing Arab and Muslim Americans Post-9/11." PhD dissertation, Stanford University, 2005.

———. "The Primetime Plight of Arab-Muslim-Americans After 9/11: Configurations of Race and Nation in TV Dramas." In *Race and Arab Americans Before and After 9/11: From Invisible Citizens to Visible Subjects*, edited by Amaney Jamal and Nadine Naber, 204–228. New York: Syracuse University Press, 2007.

Alsultany, Evelyn. "Selling American Diversity and Muslim American Identity through Non-profit Advertising Post-9/11." *American Quarterly* 59, no. 3 (September 2007).

"The American Tobacco Story." In *Tobacco Collection.* Durham, NC: Hartman Center for Sales, Advertising & Marketing History, Duke University.

Amin, Qasim. *The Liberation of Women, The New Woman: Two Documents in the History of Egyptian Feminism.* Translated by Samiha Peterson. Cairo: American University in Cairo Press, 1992 [1899].

Amireh, Amal. "Palestinian Women's Disappearing Act: The Suicide Bomber through Western Feminist Eyes." *MIT Electronic Journal of Middle East Studies* 5 (Spring 2005): 228–242, www. web.mit.edu/cis/www/mitejmes/ (accessed April 10, 2007).

Amos, Amanda and Margaretha Haglund. "From Social Taboo to 'Torch of Freedom': The Marketing of Cigarettes to Women." *Tobacco Control* 9 (Spring 2000): 3–8, www.tc.bmj.com/cgi/content/full/9/1/3 (accessed November 16, 2006).

Anderson, Benedict. *Imagined Communities: Reflections on the Origin and Spread of Nationalism.* New York: Verso, 1991.

Anzaldúa, Gloria. *Borderlands/La Frontera: The New Mestiza.* San Francisco, CA: Aunt Lute, 1987.

Appadurai, Arjun. *Modernity at Large: Cultural Dimensions of Globalization.* Minneapolis: University of Minnesota Press, 1996.

Appignanesi, Lisa. *The Cabaret.* New Haven, CT: Yale University Press, 2004.

Aradoon, Zarifa. *Origins and Philosophy of Danse Orientale.* Stanford, CA: Dream Place Publications, 1979.

Bahrani, Zeinab. "The Fall of Babylon." In *The Looting of the Iraq Museum, Baghdad: The Lost Legacy of Ancient Mesopotamia,* edited by Milby Polk and Angela M. H. Schuster, 214–216. New York: Harry Abrams, 2005.

Barthes, Roland. *Camera Lucida: Reflections on Photography.* Translated by Richard Howard. New York: Hill and Wang, 1981.

———. *Mythologies.* Translated by Richard Miller. New York: Hill and Wang, 1972.

———. "The Photographic Message." In *The Barthes Reader,* edited by Susan Sontag, 194–210. New York: Hill and Wang, 1982.

BBC News. "Army Base 'Has Damaged Babylon.'" January 15, 2005. www.news.bbc.co.uk/2/hi/middle_east/4177577.stm (accessed June 9, 2007).

Benjamin, Roger. *Orientalism: Delacroix to Klee.* New South Wales, Australia: The Art Gallery of New South Wales, 1997.

Benjamin, Walter. *Reflections: Essays, Aphorisms, Autobiographical Writings.* Translated by Edmund Jephcott. New York: Schocken Books, 1978.

———. "A Short History of Photography." *Screen: The Journal of the Society for Education in Film and Television* 13, no. 1 (1972): 5–26.

———. "Theses on the Philosophy of History." In *Illuminations*, edited by Hannah Arendt, 253–264. New York: Schocken Books, 1968.

———. "The Work of Art in the Age of Mechanical Reproduction." In *Illuminations*, edited by Hannah Arendt, 217–252. New York: Schocken Books, 1968.

Bennett, Tony and Janet Woollacott. *Bond and Beyond: The Political Career of a Popular Hero.* New York: Methuen, 1987.

Berger, John. *Ways of Seeing.* London: BBC and Penguin Books, 1972.

Berman, Marshall. *All That Is Solid Melts into Air: The Experience of Modernity.* New York: Penguin, 1988.

Bhabha, Homi K. "The Other Question: Stereotype, Discrimination and the Discourse of Colonialism." In *The Location of Culture*, 94–120. New York: Routledge, 1994.

Black, Jeremy. *The Politics of James Bond: From Fleming's Novels to the Big Screen.* Westport, CT: Praeger, 2001.

Blue Star PR: The Jewish Ink Tank, "Frequently Asked Questions." www.bluestarpr.com/faq.php (accessed November 14, 2007).

Bogdanos, Matthew. *Thieves of Baghdad.* New York: Bloomsbury, 2005.

Boime, Albert. *The Art of Exclusion: Representing Blacks in the Nineteenth Century.* Washington, DC: Smithsonian Institution Press, 1990.

———. *The Magisterial Gaze: Manifest Destiny and American Landscape Paintings, 1830–1865.* Washington, DC: Smithsonian Institution Press, 1991.

Brewer, E. Cobham. "Feather in Your Cap." In *Dictionary of Phrase and Fable.* Philadelphia, PA: Henry Altemus, 1898; Bartelby.com, 2000. www.bartleby.com/81/6294.html (accessed July 4, 2007).

Brown, Julie K. *Contesting Images: Photography and the World's Columbian Exposition.* Tucson: University of Arizona Press, 1994.

Buel, James W. *The Magic City.* St. Louis, MO: Historical Publishing Co., 1894.

Buonaventura, Wendy. *Serpent of the Nile: Women and Dance in the Arab World.* New York: Interlink Books, 1998.

Caner, Ergun Mehmet, ed. *Voices behind the Veil: The World of Islam through the Eyes of Women.* Grand Rapids, MI: Kregel Publications, 2003.

Carlton, Donna. *Looking for Little Egypt.* Bloomington, IN: IDD Books, 1994.

Carr, Carolyn Kinder. "Prejudice and Pride: Presenting American Art at the 1893 World's Columbian Exposition." In *Revisiting the White City: American Art at the 1893 Chicago World's Fair*, by National Museum of American Art, Smithsonian Institution, 63–162. Hanover: University Press of New England, 1993.

Carr, Gerard L. *In Search of the Promised Land: Paintings by Frederic Edwin Church.* New York: Berry-Hill Galleries, 2000.

Caton, Steven C. "The Sheik: Instabilities of Race and Gender in Transatlantic Popular Culture in the 1920s." In *Noble Dreams, Wicked Pleasures: Orientalism in America, 1870–1930*, edited by Holly Edwards, 99–117. Princeton: Princeton University Press, 2000.

Çelik, Zeynep. *Displaying the Orient: Architecture of Islam at Nineteenth-Century World's Fairs.* Berkeley: University of California Press, 1992.
———. "Speaking Back to Orientalist Discourse." In *Orientalism's Interlocutors: Painting, Architecture, Photography,* edited by Jill Beaulieu and Mary Roberts, 19–41. Durham: Duke University Press, 2002.
———. "Speaking Back to Orientalist Discourse at the World's Columbian Exposition." In *Noble Dreams, Wicked Pleasures: Orientalism in America, 1870–1930,* edited by Holly Edwards, 77–97. Princeton: Princeton University Press, 2000.
Çelik, Zeynep and Leila Kinney. "Ethnography and Exhibitionism at the Expositions Universelles." *Assemblage* 13 (1990): 35–60.
Chapman, James. *License to Thrill: A Cultural History of the James Bond Films.* New York: Columbia University Press, 2000.
Charles, Jonathan. "US Marines Offer Babylon Apology." *BBC News,* April 14, 2006. www.news.bbc.co.uk/2/hi/middle_east/4908940.stm (accessed June 9, 2007).
Chatterjee, Partha. *The Nation and Its Fragments: Colonial and Postcolonial Histories.* Princeton: Princeton University Press, 1993.
Chengzhi, Zhang. "The Eyes You Find Will Make You Shiver." *Inter-Asia Cultural Studies* 5, no. 3 (2004): 486–490.
Chow, Rey. "Where Have All the Natives Gone?" In *Displacements: Cultural Identities in Question,* edited by Angelika Bammer, 125–151. Bloomington: Indiana University Press, 1994.
CNN.com. "Transcript of President Bush's Address to a Joint Session of Congress on Thursday Night, September 20, 2001." www.archives.cnn.com/2001/US/09/20/gen.bush.transcript/ (accessed November 12, 2007).
Conklin, Alice L. *A Mission to Civilize: The Republican Idea of Empire in France and West Africa, 1895–1930.* Stanford: Stanford University Press, 1997.
Connor, Steve. "The Portrait of a Life Ravaged by War: For 18 Years, Her Face Was an Iconic Image of Innocence. But Who Was She? Now, At Last, Sharbat Gula Has Been Found." *The Independent,* March 13, 2002. www.lexis-nexis.com/ (accessed July 16, 2006).
Croutier, Alev Lytle. *Harem: The World behind the Veil.* New York: Abbeville Press, 1989.
Danforth, Samuel. "A Brief Recognition of New-Englands [*sic*] Errand into the Wilderness." Election Sermon Delivered in 1670.
Darraj, Susan Muaddi. "Personal and Political: The Dynamics of Arab-American Feminism." *MIT Electronic Journal of Middle East Studies* 5 (Spring 2005): 158–168, www.web.mit.edu/cis/www/mitejmes/ (accessed April 10, 2007).
Davis, Fanny. *The Ottoman Lady: A Social History from 1718–1918.* New York: Greenwood Press, 1986.
Davis, John. "Frederic Church's *Jerusalem from the Mount of Olives*: Progressive Time in Nineteenth-Century America." In *Tempus Fugit: Time*

Flies, edited by Jan Schall, 245–250. Seattle: University of Washington Press, 2000.

———. *The Landscape of Belief: Encountering the Holy Land in Nineteenth-Century American Art and Culture.* Princeton: Princeton University Press, 1996.

Debord, Guy. *Society of the Spectacle.* Detroit, MI: Black and Red, 1983.

Deeb, Lara. *An Enchanted Modern: Gender and Public Piety in Shi'i Lebanon.* Princeton: Princeton University Press, 2006.

Delacroix, Eugène. *The Journal of Eugène Delacroix.* Translated by Walter Pach. New York: Covici, Friede, 1937.

Djebar, Assia. "Women of Algiers in Their Apartment." In *Women and Family in the Middle East: New Voices of Change*, edited by Elizabeth Warnock Fernea, 337–350. Austin: University of Texas Press, 1985.

Dojc, Michael. "How to Start a Harem: When It's Time to Sheik Your Booty and Chase Some Veil." *Maxim*, January 2001.

Donham, Donald. *Marxist Modern: An Ethnographic History of the Ethiopian Revolution.* Berkeley: University of California Press, 1999.

Dox, Donnalee. "Spirit from the Body: Belly Dance as a Spiritual Practice." In *Belly Dance: Orientalism, Transnationalism and Harem Fantasy*, edited by Anthony Shay and Barbara Sellers-Young, 304–340. Costa Mesa, CA: Mazda Publishers, 2005.

———. "Thinking through Veils: Questions of Culture, Criticism and the Body." *Theatre Research International* 22, no. 2 (Summer 1997): 150–161.

Eco, Umberto. *Travels in Hyperreality.* Translated by William Weaver. San Diego, CA: Harcourt Brace Jovanovich, 1986.

Edwards, Holly, ed. *Noble Dreams, Wicked Pleasures: Orientalism in America, 1870–1930.* Princeton: Princeton University Press, 2000.

Eisenstein, Zillah. *Against Empire: Feminisms, Racism, and the West.* New York: Zed Books, 2004.

Enloe, Cynthia. *Bananas, Beaches, and Bases: Making Feminist Sense of International Politics.* Berkeley: University of California Press, 1989.

Fairbrother, Trevor. *John Singer Sargent: The Sensualist.* New Haven, CT: Yale University, 2000.

Fanon, Frantz. *Black Skin, White Masks.* Translated by Charles Lam Markmann. New York: Grove Press, 1967.

———. *A Dying Colonialism.* Translated by Haakon Chevalier. New York: Grove Weidenfield, 1965.

Farrell, Amy and Patrice McDermott. "Claiming Afghan Women: The Challenge of Human Rights Discourse for Transnational Feminism." In *Just Advocacy? Women's Human Rights, Transnational Feminisms, and the Politics of Representation*, edited by Wendy Hesford and Wendy Kozol, 33–55. New Brunswick, NJ: Rutgers University Press, 2005.

Fernandes, Leela. "The Boundaries of Terror: Feminism, Human Rights, and the Politics of Global Crisis." In *Just Advocacy? Women's Human Rights, Transnational Feminisms, and the Politics of Representation*, edited by Wendy Hesford and Wendy Kozol, 56–74. New Brunswick, NJ: Rutgers University Press, 2005.

Fisk, Robert. "Game of Putting Hatred on Middle East Map," *Arab News*, March 4, 2007. www.arabnews.com/ (accessed March 23, 2007).

Fitzgerald, Edward. *Rubáiyát of Omar Khayyám*. Edited by Louis Untermeyer. New York: Random House, 1947.

Forbes, Robert and Terence Mitchell. *American Tobacco Cards*. Richmond, IN: Tuff Stuff Publications, 1999.

Foucault, Michel. *The Archaeology of Knowledge*. Translated by A.M. Sheridan Smith. New York: Pantheon, 1982.

———. *Discipline and Punish: The Birth of the Prison*. Translated by Alan Sheridan. New York: Pantheon, 1977.

———. *The History of Sexuality*. Translated by Robert Hurley. New York: Pantheon Books, 1978.

Fox, Richard Wightman and T.J. Jackson Lears, eds. *The Culture of Consumption: Critical Essays in American History 1880–1980*. New York: Pantheon Books, 1983.

Frueh, Joanna. "Essay." In *Hannah Wilke: A Retrospective*, edited by Thomas H. Kochheiser, 1–166. St. Louis: University of Missouri Press, 1989.

Geller, Katalin. *Nineteenth-Century French Painting*. Budapest, Hungary: Kossuth Printing House, 1985.

Gettleman, Jeffrey. "Unesco Intends to Put the Magic Back in Babylon." *International Herald Tribune*, April 21, 2006. www.iht.com/ articles/2006/04/13/news/babylon.php (accessed June 9, 2007).

Gilman, Sander L. "Black Bodies, White Bodies: Toward an Iconography of Female Sexuality in Late Nineteenth-Century Art, Medicine, and Literature." *Critical Inquiry* 12 (1985): 204–241.

———. *Difference and Pathology: Stereotypes of Sexuality, Race, and Madness*. Ithaca, NY: Cornell University Press, 1985.

Gilman, Sander and Zhou Xun, eds. Introduction to *Smoke: A Global History of Smoking*, edited by Sander Gilman and Zhou Xun, 9–28. London: Reaktion Books, 2004.

Goffman, Daniel. *The Ottoman Empire and Early Modern Europe*. Cambridge: Cambridge University Press, 2002.

Graham-Brown, Sarah. *Images of Women: The Portrayal of Women in Photography of the Middle East, 1860–1950*. London: Quartet, 1988.

Gramsci, Antonio. *The Prison Notebooks*. Translated by Lynne Lawner. New York: Harper and Row, 1975.

Greenberg, Gershon. "America—Holy Land and Religious Studies: On Expressing a Sacred Reality." In *With Eyes Toward Zion III: Western Societies and the Holy Land*, edited by Moshe Davis and Yehoshua Ben-Arieh, 50–62. New York: Praeger, 1991.

Grewal, Inderpal. *Home and Harem: Nation, Gender, Empire, and the Cultures of Travel*. Durham, NC: Duke University Press, 1996.

———. *Transnational America: Feminisms, Diasporas, Neoliberalisms*. Durham, NC: Duke University Press, 2005.

Grewal, Inderpal and Caren Kaplan. "Introduction." In *Scattered Hegemonies: Postmodernity and Transnational Feminist Practices*, edited by Inderpal Grewal and Caren Kaplan, 1–33. Minneapolis: University of Minnesota Press, 1994.

Groseclose, Barbara. *Nineteenth-Century American Art*. Oxford: Oxford University Press, 2000.

Grosrichard, Alain. *The Sultan's Court: European Fantasies of the East*. Translated by Liz Heron. London: Verso, 1998.

el Guindi, Fadwa. *Veil: Modesty, Privacy, and Resistance*. New York: Oxford University Press, 1999.

Hall, Stuart. "Encoding, Decoding." In *The Cultural Studies Reader*, edited by Simon During, 2nd edition, 507–517. NY: Routledge, 1999.

Haraway, Donna. *Primate Visions: Gender, Race, and Nature in the World of Modern Science*. New York: Routledge, 1989.

Hartnett, Stephen John and Laura Ann Stengrim. *Globalization and Empire: The U.S Invasion of Iraq, Free Markets and the Twilight of Democracy*. Tuscaloosa, AL: University of Alabama Press, 2006.

Harvey, David. *The Condition of Postmodernity: An Enquiry into the Origins of Cultural Change*. Cambridge, MA: Blackwell, 1989.

———. *A Short History of Neoliberalism*. New York: Oxford University Press, 2005.

Hassan Trade Card, "Indian Life in the '60s': Smoking to the Setting Sun," *Warshaw Collection of Business Americana*. Archives Center, National Museum of American History, Behring Center, Smithsonian Institution.

Helland, Shawna. "The Belly Dance: Ancient Ritual to Cabaret Performance." In *Moving History, Dancing Cultures: A Dance History Reader*, edited by Ann Dils and Ann Cooper Albright, 128–135. Middletown, CT: Wesleyan University Press, 2001.

Hesford, Wendy S. and Wendy Kozol. Introduction to *Just Advocacy? Women's Human Rights, Transnational Feminisms, and the Politics of Representation*, edited by Wendy Hesford and Wendy Kozol, 1–29. New Brunswick, NJ: Rutgers University Press, 2005.

Hill Collins, Patricia. *Black Feminist Thought: Knowledge, Consciousness, and the Politics of Empowerment*. New York: Routledge, 1991.

Hinsley, Curtis M. "The World as Marketplace: Commodification of the Exotic at the World's Columbian Exposition, Chicago, 1893." In *Exhibiting Cultures: The Poetics and Politics*, edited by Ivan Karp and Steven D. Lavine, 344–365. Washington, DC: Smithsonian Institution Press, 1991.

Hirschkind, Charles and Saba Mahmood. "Feminism, the Taliban, and Politics of Counter-Insurgency." *Anthropological Quarterly* 72, no. 2 (2002): 339–354.

Hobsbawm, Eric. Introduction to *The Invention of Tradition*, edited by Eric Hobsbawm and Terence Ranger, 1–14. Cambridge: Cambridge University Press, 1983.

Honour, Hugh. *The Image of the Black in Western Art IV, Part 2*. Cambridge, MA: Harvard University Press, 1989.

Hoodfar, Homa. "The Veil in Their Minds and on Our Heads: Veiling Practices and Muslim Women." In *The Politics of Culture in the Shadow of Capital*, edited by Lisa Lowe and David Lloyd, 249–279. Durham, NC: Duke University Press, 1997.

Hourani, Albert. *A History of the Arab Peoples*. New York: Warner Books, 1991.

Huntington, Samuel P. "The Clash of Civilizations?" *Foreign Affairs* 72, no. 3 (1993): 22–49.

In Search of the Afghan Girl, narrated by Sigourney Weaver, VHS, directed by Lawrence Cumbo. Los Angeles, CA: National Geographic Television (NGT), 2002.

Isaak, Jo Anna. "In Praise of Primary Narcissism: The Last Laughs of Jo Spence and Hannah Wilke." In *Interfaces: Women, Autobiography, Image, Performance*, edited by Sidonie Smith and Julia Watson, 49–68. Ann Arbor: University of Michigan Press, 2002.

Jakobsen, Janet R. "Can Homosexuals End Western Civilization As We Know It? Family Values in a Global Economy." In *Queer Globalizations: Citizenship and the Afterlife of Colonialism*, edited by Arnaldo Cruz-Malavé and Martin F. Manalansan IV, 49–70. New York: New York University Press, 2002.

Jamal, Amaney and Nadine Naber, eds. *Race and Arab Americans Before and After 9/11: From Invisible Citizens to Visible Subjects*. New York: Syracuse University Press, 2007.

James, Stanlie M. and Claire C. Robertson, eds. *Genital Cutting and Transnational Sisterhood: Disputing U.S. Polemics*. Chicago: University of Illinois Press, 2002.

Jameson, Fredric. "Postmodernism, or the Cultural Logic of Late Capitalism." *New Left Review* 146 (1984): 53–92.

Jarmakani, Amira. "Belly Dancing for Liberation." In *Arabs in the Americas: Interdisciplinary Essays on the Arab Diaspora*, edited by Darcy Zabel, 145–168. New York: Peter Lang Press, 2006.

———. "They Hate Our Freedom, But We Love Their Bellydance: The Spectacle of Belly Dancing in Contemporary U.S. Culture." In *The Cultural Politics of the Middle East in the Americas*, edited by Evelyn Alsultany and Ella Shohat. Ann Arbor: University of Michigan Press, forthcoming.

Jarrasse, Dominique. *Eighteenth Century French Painting*. Translated by Murray Wyllie. Paris: Finest SA/Editions Pierre Terrail, 1998.

Jones, Amelia. *Body Art: Performing the Subject*. Minneapolis: University of Minnesota Press, 1998.

Kadi, Joanna, ed. *Food for Our Grandmothers: Writings by Arab-American and Arab-Canadian Feminists*. Cambridge, MA: South End Press, 1994.

Kahf, Mohja. "Packing 'Huda': Sha'rawi's Memoirs in the United States Reception Environment." In *Going Global: The Transnational Reception of Third World Women Writers*, edited by Amal Amireh and Lisa Suhair Majaj, 148–172. New York: Garland Publishing, Inc., 2000.

———. *Western Representations of the Muslim Woman: From Termagent to Odalisque*. Austin: University of Texas Press, 1999.

Kalmar, Ivan Davidson. "The *Houkah* in the Harem: On Smoking and Orientalist Art." In *Smoke: A Global History of Smoking*, edited by Sander Gilman and Zhou Xun, 218–229. London: Reaktion Books, 2004.

Kaplan, Caren, Norma Alarcón and Minoo Moallem, eds. *Between Woman and Nation: Nationalisms, Transnational Feminisms and the State*. Durham, NC: Duke University Press, 1999.

Kasson, John F. *Amusing the Million: Coney Island at the Turn of the Century*. New York: Hill and Wang, 1978.

Kilmurray, Elaine and Richard Ormond. *John Singer Sargent*. Princeton: Princeton University Press, 1998.

Knauft, Bruce M., ed. *Critically Modern: Alternatives, Alterities, Anthropologies*. Bloomington: Indiana University Press, 2002.

Laird, Pamela Walker. *Advertising Progress: American Business and the Rise of Consumer Marketing*. Baltimore, MD: Johns Hopkins University Press, 1998.

Latifa. *My Forbidden Face: Growing Up under the Taliban, A Young Woman's Story*. New York: Hyperion, 2001.

Lazreg, Marnia. *The Eloquence of Silence: Algerian Women in Question*. New York: Routledge, 1994.

Leach, William. *Land of Desire: Merchants, Power, and the Rise of a New American Culture*. New York: Pantheon Books, 1993.

Lears, T.J. Jackson. *Fables of Abundance: A Cultural History of Advertising in America*. New York: Basic Books, 1994.

———. *No Place of Grace: Antimodernism and the Transformation of American Culture 1880–1920*. New York: Pantheon Books, 1981.

Lee, Robert G. *Orientals: Asian Americans in Popular Culture*. Philadelphia, PA: Temple University Press, 1999.

Leibovitz, Annie. *Women*. New York: Random House, 2000.

Lemaires, Gérard-Georges. *The Orient in Western Art*. Translated by Peter Field Harriet de Blanco, Françoise Jones, and Doris Wolstencroft. Italy: Könemann, 2001.

Lewis, Bernard. *Islam and the West*. New York: Oxford University Press, 1993.

Lewis, Reina. *Gendering Orientalism: Race, Femininity and Representation*. New York: Routledge, 1996.

Little, Douglas. *American Orientalism: The United States and the Middle East since 1945*. Chapel Hill: University of North Carolina Press, 2002.

Logan, Harriet. *Unveiled: Voices of Women in Afghanistan*. New York: Regan Books, 2002.

Long, Burke O. *Imagining the Holy Land: Maps, Models, and Fantasy Travels.* Bloomington: Indiana University Press, 2003.

Lopez, Donald S. *Prisoners of Shangri-La: Tibetan Buddhism and the West.* Chicago: University of Chicago Press, 1998.

Lorde, Audre. *Sister Outsider.* New York: Crossing Press, 1984.

Lott, Eric. *Love and Theft: Blackface Minstrelsy and the American Working Class.* New York: Oxford University Press, 1993.

Lowe, Lisa. *Critical Terrains: French and British Orientalisms.* Ithaca, NY: Cornell University Press, 1991.

———. *Immigrant Acts: On Asian American Cultural Politics.* Durham, NC: Duke University Press, 1996.

Lutz, Catherine and Jane Collins. *Reading National Geographic.* Chicago, IL: University of Chicago Press, 1993.

Ma, Sheng-mei. *The Deathly Embrace: Orientalism and Asian American Identity.* Minneapolis: University of Minnesota Press, 2000.

Mahmood, Saba. *Politics of Piety: The Islamic Revival and the Feminist Subject.* Princeton: Princeton University Press, 2005.

Maira, Sunaina. "Arab-Face and Indo-Chic: Belly Dancing, Orientalist Feminism, and U.S. Empire." In *The Cultural Politics of the Middle East in the Americas,* eds. Evelyn Alsultany and Ella Shohat. Ann Arbor: University of Michigan Press, forthcoming.

Mamdani, Mahmood. *Good Muslim, Bad Muslim: America, the Cold War and the Roots of Terror.* New York: Pantheon Books, 2004.

McAlister, Melani. *Epic Encounters: Culture, Media, and U.S. Interests in the Middle East 1945–2000.* Berkeley: University of California Press, 2001.

McCarthy, Rory and Maev Kennedy. "Babylon Wrecked by War." *The Guardian,* January 15, 2005. www.arts.guardian.co.uk/news/story/0,,1391043,00.html/ (accessed January 28, 2006).

McClintock, Anne. *Imperial Leather: Race, Gender, and Sexuality in the Colonial Context.* New York: Routledge, 1995.

McCurry, Steve. "Special Report." *National Geographic* 201, no. 4 (April 2002).

Mcginty, Stephen. "The Saga behind the Green Eyes." *The Scotsman,* March 16, 2002. www.lexis-nexis.com/ (accessed July 16, 2006).

Mernissi, Fatima. *Scheherazade Goes West: Different Cultures, Different Harems.* New York: Washington Square Press, 2001.

———. *The Veil and the Male Elite: A Feminist Interpretation of Women's Rights in Islam.* Translated by Mary Jo Lakeland. New York: Addison-Wesley Publishing, 1991.

Miller, Angela. *The Empire of the Eye: Landscape Representation and American Cultural Politics, 1825–1875.* Ithaca, NY: Cornell University Press, 1993.

Miller, Perry. *Errand into the Wilderness.* Cambridge, MA: Harvard University Press, 1956.

Mirzoeff, Nicholas. *Watching Babylon: The War in Iraq and Global Visual Culture*. New York: Routledge, 2005.

Mitchell, Dolores. "The 'New Woman' as Prometheus: Women Artists Depict Women Smoking." *Women's Art Journal* 12, no. 1 (Spring/ Summer 1991): 3–9.

Mitchell, Timothy. *Colonising Egypt*. Berkeley: University of California Press, 1991.

———, ed. *Questions of Modernity*. Minneapolis: University of Minnesota Press, 2000.

Mitchell, W.J.T. *Iconology: Image, Text, Ideology*. Chicago: University of Chicago Press, 1987.

———, ed. *Landscape and Power*. 2nd edition. Chicago: University of Chicago Press, 2002.

Moallem, Minoo. *Between Warrior Brother and Veiled Sister: Islamic Fundamentalism and Patriarchy in Iran*. Berkeley: University of California Press, 2005.

Mohanty, Chandra Talpade. "Cartographies of Struggle." In *Third World Women and the Politics of Feminism*, edited by Chandra Talpade Mohanty, Ann Russo, and Lourdes Torres, 1–47. Bloomington: Indiana University Press, 1991.

———. *Feminism Without Borders: Decolonizing Theory, Practicing Solidarity*. Durham, NC: Duke University Press, 2003.

———. "Under Western Eyes: Feminist Scholarship and Colonial Discourses." *Feminist Review* 30 (1988): 61–88.

Montagu, Mary Wortley. *Letters from Lady Mary Wortley Montagu, 1709– 1762*. Introduction by R. Brimley Johnson. Everyman's Library 69. London: J.M. Dent and Sons, 1906.

Moraga, Cherríe and Gloria Anzaldúa, eds. *This Bridge Called My Back: Writings by Radical Women of Color*. New York: Kitchen Table: Women of Color Press, 1981.

Mulvey, Laura. "Visual Pleasure and Narrative Cinema." *Screen* 16, no. 3 (1975): 6–18.

Naber, Nadine, Eman Desouky, and Lina Baroudi. "The Forgotten '-ism': An Arab American Women's Perspective on Zionism, Racism, and Sexism." In *Color of Violence: The INCITE! Anthology*, edited by Incite! Women of Color Against Violence, 97–112. Cambridge, MA: South End Press, 2006.

Narayan, Uma. *Dislocating Cultures: Identities, Traditions, and Third World Feminism*. New York: Routledge, 1997.

Nederveen, Pieterse Jan. *White on Black: Images of Africa and Blacks in Western Popular Culture*. New Haven, CT: Yale University Press, 1992.

Néret, Gilles. *Eugène Delacroix: The Prince of Romanticism*. Translated by Chris Miller. Köln: Taschen, 1999.

Newman, Cathy. "A Life Revealed," *National Geographic* 210, no. 4 (April 2002).

Nochlin, Linda. "The Imaginary Orient." *Art in America* 71, no. 5 (1983): 119–191.

Obenzinger, Hilton. *American Palestine: Melville, Twain, and the Holy Land Mania.* Princeton: Princeton University Press, 1999.

Okihiro, Gary Y. *Common Ground: Reimagining American History.* Princeton: Princeton University Press, 2001.

Omi, Michael and Howard Winant. *Racial Formation in the United States.* 2nd edition. Philadelphia, PA: Temple University Press, 1994.

Ong, Aihwa. "Colonialism and Modernity: Feminist Re-presentations of Women in Non-Western Societies." In *Feminism and "Race"*, edited by Kum-Kum Bhavnani, 108–118. New York: Oxford University Press, 2001.

Ormond, Richard. "Sargent's Art." In *John Singer Sargent*, edited by Elaine Kilmurray and Richard Ormond, 23–43. Princeton: Princeton University Press, 1998.

Oxford English Dictionary. 2nd edition. 20 vols. Oxford: Oxford University Press, 1989.

Parker-Pope, Tara. *Cigarettes: Anatomy of an Industry from Seed to Smoke.* New York: New Press, 2001.

Parshall, Phil and Julie Parshall. *Lifting the Veil: The World of Muslim Women.* Portland, OR: Gabriel Publishing, 2003.

Peirce, Leslie P. *The Imperial Harem: Women and Sovereignty in the Ottoman Empire.* New York: Oxford University Press, 1993.

Petrone, Gerard S. *Tobacco Advertising: The Great Seduction.* Atlgen, PA: Schiffer, 1996.

Polk, Milby and Angela M. H. Schuster, eds. *The Looting of the Iraq Museum, Baghdad: The Legacy of Ancient Mesopotamia.* New York: Harry Abrams, 2005.

Puar, Jasbir and Amit Rai. "Monster, Terrorist, Fag: The War on Terrorism and the Production of Docile Patriots." *Social Text* 20, no. 3 72. (2002): 117–148.

Quataert, Donald. *The Ottoman Empire, 1700–1922.* Cambridge: Cambridge University Press, 2000.

al-Rawi, Rosina-Fawzia. *Grandmother's Secrets: The Ancient Rituals and Healing Power of Belly Dancing.* Translated by Monique Arav. New York: Interlink, 1999.

Robert, Joseph C. *The Story of Tobacco in America.* New York: Knopf, 1949.

Rofel, Lisa. *Other Modernities: Gendered Yearnings in China After Socialism.* Berkeley: University of California Press, 1999.

Rosenblum, Robert. *Ingres.* New York: Harry Abrams, 1990.

Rosenthal, Donald A. *Orientalism: The Near East in French Painting 1800–1880.* New York: Memorial Art Gallery of the University of Rochester, 1982.

Rubin, Gayle. "Thinking Sex: Notes for a Radical Theory of the Politics of Sexuality." In *Pleasure and Danger: Exploring Female Sexuality*, edited by Carole S. Vance, 2nd edition, 267–319. London: Pandora Press, 1992.

Ruyter, Nancy Lee. "La Meri and Middle Eastern Dance." In *Belly Dance: Orientalism, Transnationalism, and Harem Fantasy*, edited by Anthony Shay and Barbara Sellers-Young, 207–220. Costa Mesa, CA: Mazda Publishers, 2005.

Rydell, Robert W. *All the World's a Fair: Visions of Empire at American International Expositions, 1876–1916*. Chicago: University of Chicago Press, 1984.

———. "Rediscovering the 1893 Chicago World's Columbian Exposition." In *Revisiting the White City: American Art at the 1893 World's Fair*, by National Museum of American Art, Smithsonian Institution, 19–61. Hanover: University Press of New England, 1993.

Rydell, Robert W., John E. Findling, and Kimberly D. Pelle. *Fair America: World's Fairs in the United States*. Washington, DC: Smithsonian Institution Press, 2000.

Said, Edward. *Beginnings: Intention and Method*. Baltimore, MD: Johns Hopkins University Press, 1975.

———. "The Clash of Ignorance." *The Nation*, October 22, 2001: 11–13.

———. *Covering Islam: How the Media and the Experts Determine How We See the Rest of the World*. New York: Pantheon, 1981.

———. *Orientalism*. New York: Vintage Books, 1978.

———. "Orientalism Reconsidered." In *Postcolonial Criticism*, edited by Gareth Stanton and Willy Maley Bart Moore-Gilbert, 126–144. London: Longman, 1997.

———. "Traveling Theory." In *The World, the Text and the Critic*, 226–247. Cambridge, MA: Harvard University Press, 1983.

Salaita, Steven. *The Holy Land in Transit: Colonialism and the Quest for Canaan*. New York: Syracuse University Press, 2006.

Saliba, Therese. "Arab Feminism at the Millennium." *Signs: Journal of Women and Culture in Society* 25, no. 4 (2000): 1087–1092.

———. Introduction to *Gender, Politics, and Islam*, edited by Therese Saliba, Carolyn Allen, and Judith A. Howard, 1–13. Chicago: University of Chicago Press, 2002.

———. "Military Presences and Absences." In *Food for Our Grandmothers*, edited by Joanna Kadi, 125–132. Cambridge, MA: South End Press, 1994.

Sandoval, Chela. *Methodology of the Oppressed*. Minneapolis: University of Minnesota Press, 2000.

Sasson, Jean. *Princess: A True Story of Life behind the Veil in Saudi Arabia*. Atlanta, GA: Windsor-Brooke Books, 2001.

Schaebler, Birgit. "Civilizing Others: Global Modernity and the Local Boundaries (French/German, Ottoman, and Arab) of Savagery." In *Globalization and the Muslim World: Culture, Religion, and Modernity*, edited by Birgit Schaebler and Leif Stenberg, 3–29. New York: Syracuse University Press, 2004.

Schueller, Malini Johar. *U.S. Orientalisms: Race, Nation, and Gender in Literature, 1790–1890*. Ann Arbor: University of Michigan Press, 1998.

"Seven Pleasures of the Exotic." *CML The City Edition: Deals, Diversions and Direct Access for Camel's Coveted Customers* (2002): 13–17.

Shaarawi, Huda. *Harem Years: The Memoirs of an Egyptian Feminist.* Translated by Margot Badran. New York: Feminist Press, 1987.

Shaheen, Jack. *Reel Bad Arabs: How Hollywood Villifies a People.* New York: Olive Branch Press, 2001.

Shay, Anthony and Barbara Sellers-Young, eds. *Belly Dance: Orientalism, Transnationalism and Harem Fantasy.* Costa Mesa, CA: Mazda Publishers, 2005.

Shirazi, Faegheh. *The Veil Unveiled: The Hijab in Modern Culture.* Gainesville: University Press of Florida, 2001.

Shohat, Ella. "Area Studies, Transnationalism, and the Feminist Production of Knowledge." *Signs: Journal of Women and Culture in Society* 26, no. 4 (2001): 1269–1272.

———. "Gender and Culture of Empire: Toward a Feminist Ethnography of Cinema." In *Visions of the East: Orientalism in Film,* edited by Matthew Bernstein and Gaylyn Studlar, 19–66. New Brunswick, NJ: Rutgers University Press, 1997.

———. Introduction to *Talking Visions: Multicultural Feminism in a Transnational Age,* edited by Ella Shohat, 1–62. Cambridge, MA: MIT Press, 1998.

———. "Notes on the 'Post-Colonial'." *Social Text* 31/32 (1992): 99–113.

Shohat, Ella and Robert Stam. *Unthinking Eurocentrism: Multiculturalism and the Media.* New York: Routledge, 1994.

Smith, Henry Nash. *Virgin Land: The American West as Symbol and Myth.* Cambridge, MA: Harvard University Press, 1950.

Smith, Joseph. "Within the Midway Plaisance." *Illustrated American, Special Number* (1893): 59–73. In *Warshaw Collection of Business Americana.* Archives Center, National Museum of American History, Behring Center, Smithsonian Institution.

Sontag, Susan. "A Photograph Is Not an Opinion. Or Is It?" In *Women,* by Annie Leibovitz, 18–36. New York: Random House, 1999.

———. *Regarding the Pain of Others.* New York: Farrar, Straus and Giroux, 2003.

Spivak, Gayatri Chakravorty. "Can the Subaltern Speak?" In *Marxism and the Interpretation of Culture,* edited by Cary Nelson and Lawrence Grossberg, 271–313. Basingstoke, UK: Macmillan Education, 1988.

Steele, Jeffrey. "Reduced to Images: American Indians in Nineteenth-Century Advertising." In *The Gender and Consumer Culture Reader,* edited by Jennifer Scanlon, 109–128. New York: New York University Press, 2000.

Steet, Linda. *Veils and Daggers: A Century of National Geographic's Representations of the Arab World.* Philadelphia, PA: Temple University Press, 2000.

"Street in Cairo." In *Warshaw Collection of Business Americana.* Archives Center, National Museum of American History, Behring Center, Smithsonian Institution, 1893.

Stockton, Ronald. "Ethnic Archetypes and the Arab Image." In *The Development of Arab-American Identity*, edited by Ernest McCarus, 119–153. Ann Arbor: University of Michigan Press, 1994.

Stoler, Ann Laura. *Race and the Education of Desire: Foucault's* History of Sexuality *and the Colonial Order of Things*. Durham, NC: Duke University Press, 1995.

Suleiman, Michael W., ed. *Arabs in America: Building a New Future*. Philadelphia, PA: Temple University Press, 1999.

Tagg, John. *The Burden of Representation: Essays on Photographies and Histories*. Minneapolis: University of Minnesota Press, 1993.

Tate, Cassandra. *Cigarette Wars: The Triumph of "the Little White Slaver"*. New York: Oxford University Press, 1999.

Tchen, John Kuo Wei. *New York before Chinatown: Orientalism and the Shaping of American Culture*. Baltimore, MD: Johns Hopkins University Press, 1999.

Thompson, E.P. *Customs in Common: Studies in Traditional Popular Culture*. New York: New Press, 1993.

Thomson, Rosemarie Garland. *Extraordinary Bodies: Figuring Physical Disability in American Culture and Literature*. New York: Columbia University Press, 1997.

———, ed. *Freakery: Cultural Spectacles of the Extraordinary Body*. New York: New York University Press, 1996.

Tobacco Merchants Association of the United States. *The TMA Directory of Cigarette Brand Names 1913–1977*. New York: Tobacco Merchants Assoc., 1978.

Trachtenberg, Alan. *The Incorporation of America: Culture and Society in the Gilded Age*. New York: Hill and Wang, 1982.

———. *Reading American Photographs: Images as History, Mathew Brady to Walker Evans*. New York: Noonday Press, 1990.

Truman, Ben C., ed. *History of the World's Fair: Being a Complete and Authentic Description of the Columbian Exposition from Its Inception*. Philadelphia, PA: Mammoth Publishing Co., 1893.

Under One Sky: Arab Women in North America Talk About the Hijab, VHS, directed by Jennifer Kawaja. Ottawa, Ontario: National Film Board of Canada, 1999.

Untermeyer, Louis. Introduction to *Rubáiyát of Omar Khayyám*, translated by Edward Fitzgerald, vii–xxii. New York: Random House, 1947.

U.S. Government, "President's Radio Address from Shanghai, China," October 20, 2001. www.whitehouse.gov/news/releases/2001/10/print/20011020–4.html (accessed November 12, 2007).

U.S. Government, "Radio Address by Laura Bush to the Nation," November 17, 2001. web.archive.org/web/20021102074651/www.whitehouse.gov/news/releases/2001/11/20011117.html (accessed April 24, 2007).

U.S. Government, "Radio Address of the President to the Nation," October 6, 2001. www.whitehouse.gov/news/releases/2001/10/print/20011006.html (accessed November 12, 2007).

U.S. Government, "World Freedom Day Proclamation," November 9, 2001. www.whitehouse.gov/news/releases/2001/11/20011109–23.html (accessed November 12, 2007).

Vanishing City: A Photographic Encyclopedia of the World's Columbian Exposition. Chicago: Laird & Lee, 1893.

Vejnoska, Jill. "Return to War-torn Landscape Leads Photographer to Reunion." *The Atlanta Journal-Constitution*, March 15, 2002, 3E. www.lexis-nexis.com/ (accessed July 16, 2006).

Vogel, Lester I. *To See a Promised Land: Americans and the Hold Land in the Nineteenth Century.* University Park, PA: Pennsylvania State University Press, 1993.

Weber, Carl J. *Fitzgerald's Rubaiyat, Centennial Edition.* Waterville, ME: Colby College Press, 1959.

Weber, Max. *The Protestant Ethic and the Spirit of Capitalism.* London: Allen & Unwin Press, 1930. Reprinted with Introduction by Anthony Giddens, translated by Talcott Parsons. New York: Routledge, 2001.

Williams, Raymond. *The Country and the City.* New York: Oxford University Press, 1976.

———. *Keywords: A Vocabulary of Culture and Society.* Revised Edition. New York: Oxford University Press, 1983.

———. *Marxism and Literature.* Oxford: Oxford University Press, 1978.

Winnubst, Shannon. *Queering Freedom.* Bloomington: Indiana University Press, 2006.

"World's Columbian Exposition, Chicago, 1893: Department of Ethnology and Archaeology." In *Warshaw Collection of Business Americana.* Archives Center, National Museum of American History, Behring Center, Smithsonian Institution, 1893.

Yeazell, Ruth Bernard. *Harems of the Mind: Passages of Western Art and Literature.* New Haven, CT: Yale University Press, 2000.

Zafran, Eric M. *The Rococo Age.* Atlanta, GA: High Museum of Art, 1983.

Zuffi, Stefano. *Titian.* Translated by Richard Sadleir. Milan: Electa, 1995.

INDEX

Note: Page numbers in **bold** denote figures.

LaVergne, TN USA
23 September 2009
158787LV00001B/84/P